# The Political Influence of Queen Victoria

1861 – 1901

William Nicholson.

# The Political Influence of QUEEN VICTORIA

1861–1901

Frank Hardie

FRANK CASS AND CO LTD

1963

This edition published by Frank Cass & Co. Ltd,
10 Woburn Walk, London W.C. 1, by arrangement
with Oxford University Press

First published 1935
Second edition 1938
New impression 1963

Printed by Thomas Nelson (Printers) Ltd
London and Edinburgh

# CONTENTS



# ABBREVIATIONS

T. = Telegram.

C.T. = Cypher Telegram.

*L.* = *The Letters of Queen Victoria.* The Roman numerals following denote the number of the volume. These nine volumes appeared in three series, but here are numbered consecutively from i to ix.

*To*

MY MOTHER, FATHER
AND BROTHER

'To most Englishmen the extent of the authority actually exercised by the Crown is a matter of conjecture.'

A. V. DICEY, *Law of the Constitution*, 11.

'There cannot be a stronger proof of that genuine freedom which is the boast of this . . . country than the power of discussing with decency and respect the limits of the King's prerogative.'

BLACKSTONE, *Commentaries on the Laws of England*, Book I, Chapter 7.

## PREFACE TO THE SECOND EDITION

I HAVE taken the opportunity of this reprint in the Oxford Bookshelf series to make a number of minor, mainly stylistic, changes. To those who have made suggestions which I have gratefully adopted I must add the names of Mr. A. F. L. Beeston and Mr. Jonathan Griffin.

F. H.

June, 1938.

The London School of Economics and Political Science.

# PREFACE

LET me begin by explaining what I have attempted in this book. I hope later to be able to write another on the history of the monarchy for the whole period from the accession of William IV in 1830 to the death of Edward VII in 1910; I try here to show that the passing of the first Reform Bill in 1832 is the decisive date at which the Crown, ceasing to be powerful, becomes influential, and that therefore there cannot be any effective comparison between the monarchy of Victoria and the monarchy of George III. Meanwhile I have tried to fill the gap which for the reasons given in the first chapter seemed to me most urgently in need of filling. This gap is the period from 1861, the year of the death of the Prince Consort, to 1901, the year of the death of the Queen.

I have said very little about the relations between the Queen and the Prince of Wales, partly because the subject is one which Mr. Hector Bolitho, in an admirable book,[1] has recently made peculiarly his own, and partly, too, because it would more properly belong to a study of the life of King Edward VII than to one of the political influence of Queen Victoria. Also, I have said very little about the relations between the Queen and her cousin, the Duke of Cambridge, as Commander-in-Chief from 1856 to 1895, and of her influence on Army questions generally, because that would have required a knowledge of the technical aspects of military history in the nineteenth century which their obsoleteness deters me from acquiring. What I have done is to concentrate on the Queen's influence in questions of domestic policy generally, because it is in that connexion that most new knowledge has come to light. There is little new to say

[1] *Victoria, The Widow and Her Son* (Cobden-Sanderson, 1934).

about the Queen's influence on foreign policy. There is little new to say about the fine simplicity of her character. Its worth is already widely known and appreciated. What is not widely known and appreciated is the extent and nature of her political influence. It may be objected that what I have discussed in Chapter II and in Chapter III is not so much her political influence as the story of her relations with different Ministers, and of her likes and dislikes among them. But this is not only of interest in itself, but also an indispensable background to any serious estimate of her place in the Constitution.

The biographies of the prominent statesmen of the period, for the most part written either whilst the Queen was still alive or very soon after her death, and adopting towards her a tone of respectful and uncritical loyalty, are full of fascinating hints of possible future additions to our knowledge of this subject. But meanwhile more than enough has already been published not merely to justify, but to demand a serious attempt at a revision of current estimates of the Queen's political influence. Moreover, it seems practically certain that any fresh evidence will only confirm the impression made upon any impartial reader by the rich material already published.

Messrs. William Heinemann and Mr. William Nicholson have kindly given permission for the inclusion of the frontispiece. This famous portrait of Queen Victoria occupies an important place in the historiography of her reign. For example, Graham Wallas wrote: 'Mr. William Nicholson, in the *New Review* of June, 1897, guided by a delicate and kindly sense of Humour, published that charming woodcut of Queen Victoria walking with her Scotch terrier, which began the process, since carried on by Mr. Lytton Strachey, of freeing us from the enormous unrealities of the Jubilees of 1887 and 1897.'[1] Mr. Nicholson's portrait says almost all that there is to be said about the Queen's personality towards the end of her reign. The historian with his many thousands of words must envy the artist who can tell the same story so swiftly and so effectively.

This book is based upon the Essay which I wrote as Gladstone Memorial Exhibitioner of Christ Church for 1932–3. Therefore my thanks are in the first place due to the Gladstone Memorial Trustees; and to the Harmsworth Trustees, Merton College, under whose auspices the book has been completed. Professor Laski has given the stimulus and encouragement which he has led so many students to demand of him as of right. I must also express my thanks to those who have been kind enough to read the typescript and make many valuable suggestions: Mr. E. G. Collieu, of Christ Church; Mr. C. R. M. F. Cruttwell, Principal of Hertford College; Mrs. K. Ellison; Mr. B. Kingsley Martin; Lord Ponsonby of Shulbrede; Mr. K. C. Wheare, Research Lecturer of Christ Church; and Mr. Leonard Woolf. Above all, I should like to take this opportunity of placing on record my debt of gratitude to my three History Tutors at the House: Dr. Keith Feiling, Mr. J. C. Masterman, and Mr. J. N. L. Myres. It would be impertinent of me to praise their scholarship, but I can pay tribute to the inspiration of their teaching, and to their constant readiness 'out of hours' to help and advise, to sympathize and encourage. Of course none of these persons is in any way responsible for any of the opinions I have expressed.

F. H.

OXFORD. *March 1st*, 1935.

[1] *Art of Thought* (cheap edition, Jonathan Cape, 1931), 116; cf. below, p. 27, n. 1.

# I

# INTRODUCTION

IN the spring of 1932 there was published a pamphlet by Professor Harold J. Laski, Professor of Political Science in the University of London, in which, with reference to the change of Government which took place in August, 1931, the author spoke of the new Cabinet as being born of 'a Palace revolution'[1] and of Mr. Ramsay MacDonald as becoming Prime Minister merely through being 'the King's favourite'[2]. This publication was of special interest to students of the British Constitution, but it also aroused the interest of a more general public. It was one of the most direct attacks made on the Monarchy since the Republicanism of the 1870's.

Beside these two remarks of Professor Laski's it is only fair to place the opinion of Sidney Webb (Lord Passfield), a member of the Labour Cabinet which fell from power in August, 1931, that throughout the events of that political crisis the King 'never went outside his constitutional position'[3].

But what here concerns us is not so much the question of whether Professor Laski is wrong in attacking the Monarchy for the part played by it during that political crisis,[4] or Sidney Webb right in defending it, as the fact that Professor Laski's hostility to the Monarchy appears very largely to be founded on a study of the facts re-

[1] H. J. Laski's *The Crisis and the Constitution* (Day to Day Pamphlets No. 9; Hogarth Press), 34.

[2] Ibid. 36.

[3] S. Webb's *What happened in 1931; A Record* (Fabian Tract No. 237), 8.

[4] Possibly the King expected, or was led by Mr. MacDonald to expect, that he would be followed by a large number of Labour M.P.s, so that there would be formed a genuine coalition of the three parties.

vealed by the publication of *The Letters of Queen Victoria.*[1] His general argument on this point is so striking and so forcible that it deserves quotation in full. It runs as follows:

'In the recent crisis, the great unknown factor in the political equation has been the position of the Monarchy. Englishmen rarely ask themselves in what fashion the Crown actually works in the British Constitution. They accept it as a mystery which, on the whole, seems to suit the national genius almost as well as it did when Bagehot, sixty years ago, brought out its activities into the light of that half-amused examination we now know to have been so partial and so incomplete. For the publication of *The Letters of Queen Victoria* has made it clear that the distinction he sought to draw between the "dignified" and the "efficient" parts of the constitution rests upon foundations far less solid than he suspected.

'. . . The influence of the Monarch [continues Professor Laski] is wide and pervasive, and it is felt in a score of different ways. He has the right, at the earliest possible stage, to see all the papers; he must be consulted, and he can express his views. It is clear enough that a monarch who takes his duties seriously is a force to be reckoned with in our system. It is not merely that his place at the very centre of affairs gives him an opportunity of continuous scrutiny and knowledge.[2] It is not only, also, that what comment he may choose to make must be treated with a respect not normally accorded to the opinions of other men.[3] We are still a highly deferential people; and the immense

[1] First Series, 3 vols., 1837–61, edited by A. C. Benson and Viscount Esher (John Murray, Popular Edition, 1911). The references for *L.* i–*L.* iii throughout this book are to this edition. Second Series, 3 vols., 1862–85, edited by G. E. Buckle (John Murray, 1926, 1926, 1928). Third Series, 3 vols., 1886–1901, edited by G. E. Buckle (John Murray, 1930, 1931, 1932).

[2] Cf. Peel: 'A King, after a reign of ten years, ought to know much more of the working of the machine of Government than any other man in the country' (quoted, Low's *Governance of England*, 265).

[3] This means that for most people it is extremely difficult to talk to the monarch as man to man. Thus, to take one example out of many, we find Sir Charles Eastlake recording of an interview with the Prince Consort: 'He soon put me at his ease by his pleasing manner. . . . Two or three times

social prestige of the Monarchy gives to the King's views a weight and an authority it is impossible to ignore. *The Letters of Queen Victoria* make it clear that no Prime Minister can afford not to take these into account. He cannot hope to go on his way regardless of the opinion of the Crown. He must reply to its arguments, weigh its considerations, satisfy its susceptibilities, in a way, and to a degree of which the implication is clearly that if the Crown is a reserve power, it is one of which the possible exercise must never be forgotten. That was made clear in the crisis over the House of Lords in 1909–11; two general elections were necessary to satisfy the scruples of the Monarch. It was made clear again in the conflict over Home Rule, when the Tory party deliberately decided that an appeal to the King over the heads of his Ministers was a possible way of staving off the hour of their defeat. The facts remain obscure; but no one can read what has so far been allowed to appear without the sense that any view of the Crown as merely a dignified relic of a once vital authority is a serious under-estimation of its influence. The Crown is a pervasive and active agent, largely, no doubt, of emollience, which no student of the Constitution can possibly afford to ignore.'[1]

Here is a challenge to Englishmen to-day to inform themselves of the place of the Monarchy in the Constitution, and it is a challenge directly and explicitly based on the facts which have been allowed to appear in the nine published volumes of the Queen's *Letters*. It is a challenge which can only be met by further study of these very remarkable volumes, for they far exceed in importance and interest all the other published material. Cabinet Ministers are in a position to know what is now the nature and extent of the Crown's political influence. The ordinary student of affairs cannot have this knowledge.

I quite forgot who he was, he talked so naturally and argued so fairly . . .' (Martin, i. 123). The point is that to Sir Charles it was unnatural that with him the Prince should be natural. Cf. also below, p. 123: also p. 202 on the relations between the Duke of Wellington and William IV.

[1] Laski, *The Crisis and the Constitution*, 31.

But it is now possible for him to gain a clear understanding of its nature and extent in a period so comparatively recent as the reign of Queen Victoria. So far no attempt to gain such an understanding has been made, nor indeed was the attempt possible until 1932, for it was only in that year that the last volume of the *Letters* was published, a volume which closed with the Queen's death in 1901.

The choice of the year 1861 as the opening date for a study of the political influence of Queen Victoria is justifiable on two grounds.

In the first place the period 1861–1901 is a period which has not been adequately covered by Lytton Strachey's *Queen Victoria.*[1] Whether that book has or has not a claim to be considered a serious contribution to historical knowledge is a matter of controversy, but it certainly has a fascination of style which has assured it a place among the classics of English literature. In consequence, it is from the study of Strachey's biography that the intelligent reading public of to-day is mainly content to form its judgement of Queen Victoria. It is a book, therefore, which has so wide an influence that it cannot be disregarded. Moreover, the author's observations and conclusions on the period from 1837 to 1861 seem on the whole to be both accurate and acute.

But when Strachey published his book in 1921, only the first three volumes of the *Letters* (containing the story of the Queen's reign up to 1861) had been published. He died in 1932 and did not revise his work in the light of the further volumes which were published in his lifetime. Queen Victoria in 1861 was forty-two years old. She lived to be eighty-one. In 1861 she had reigned for twenty-four years. She was to reign for a further thirty-nine. Yet to those first twenty-four years Lytton Strachey

[1] Chatto and Windus, 1921.

devoted 145 pages of his biography: to those last thirty-nine years only 80. The proportion of the *Letters* is more correct: six volumes cover the later and only three the earlier period.

It is probable that one reason for this misproportion of Strachey's book was that he was more interested in the personality of Albert than in that of Victoria, and that in consequence the story-teller lost interest in his story at the moment of the Prince's death. But he also gives as a reason the lack of evidence about the later period:

> 'The first forty-two years of the Queen's life are illuminated by a great and varied quantity of authentic information. With Albert's death a veil descends. Only occasionally, at fitful and disconnected intervals, does it lift for a moment or two; a few main outlines, a few remarkable details may be discerned; the rest is all conjecture and ambiguity. Thus, though the Queen survived her great bereavement for almost as many years as she had lived before it, the chronicle of those years can bear no proportion to the tale of her earlier life. We must be content in our ignorance with a brief and summary relation.'[1]

The authentic information which Strachey lacked is now the possession in overwhelming abundance of any one who turns to the last six volumes of *The Letters of Queen Victoria*.

But apart from the fact that the ground has not so far been covered at all thoroughly, there is another strong reason which justifies the choice of the year 1861 as the opening date for a history of this kind. 'The death of the Prince Consort was the central turning-point in the history of Queen Victoria.'[2] He was no George of Denmark content to live 'reservéd and austere' in 'private gardens, as if his highest plot to plant the bergamot'.

Bagehot, who, as will be seen, was largely ignorant of the real range of the political activities of the Crown at the time when he wrote, was discerning enough of the

[1] Strachey's *Queen Victoria*, 190. [2] Ibid.

Prince's influence to say: 'It is known . . . to every one conversant with the real course of the recent history of England, that Prince Albert really did gain great power. . . . He had the rare gifts of a constitutional monarch. If his life had been prolonged twenty years, his name would have been known to Europe as that of King Leopold is known.' And again: 'Prince Albert did much, but he died ere he could have made his influence felt on a generation of statesmen less experienced than he was, and anxious to learn from him.'[1] The Prince had described himself as 'the husband of the Queen, the tutor of the Royal Children, the private secretary of the sovereign, and her permanent minister'[2]. This was a correct estimate of his own importance. Disraeli in a parliamentary speech in 1862 equally correctly described him as the 'prime councillor of a realm the political constitution of which did not even recognize his political existence'[3].

One of the most fascinating 'ifs' of history is the speculation as to what would have happened if the Prince Consort had not died at the early age of forty-two. The conjecture may be fanciful, but it is possible to imagine a gradual Prussianization of the British Constitution, and, finally, an open conflict between the Crown and the forces of Radicalism, led perhaps by Dilke and by Chamberlain. Disraeli is reported to have remarked of the Prince Consort: 'If he had out-lived some of our "old-stagers" he would have given us, while retaining all constitutional guarantees, the blessings of absolute govern-

[1] *The English Constitution*, by Walter Bagehot, first published in 1867, second edition with additional matter, 1872 (World's Classics edition, Oxford University Press, 1929), 69–70.

[2] Martin, ii. 259–60, Prince Consort to Duke of Wellington (April, 1850).

[3] *Life of Disraeli*, by W. F. Monypenny and G. E. Buckle (new edition in 2 vols., revised by G. E. Buckle, John Murray, 1929), ii. 118.

ment.'[1] Lord Esher went a little farther: 'Had he lived, his tenacity might have hardened into obstinacy, and the relations between him and a Government founded—like ours—on democratic institutions, would have become very strained.'[2] We shall see that even after his death the relations between the Crown and Liberal Governments did in fact become very strained, and it is perhaps justifiable to suppose that a certain tendency to autocratic ways of thought visible in the Queen's mind in the later years of her reign was the fruit of seed implanted in it by the Prince.

But this kind of speculation is, strictly speaking, a digression. What concerns us here is the fact that the Queen had been successively under the influence of Lord Melbourne and of the Prince Consort. Though the process by which the latter established his ascendancy over her mind partook of 'the inevitability of gradualness', the moment at which he took Lord Melbourne's place politically in the Queen's confidence can be fixed almost to a day. We find that at the time of Melbourne's final resignation of office Mr. Anson (the Prince's Secretary) recorded that the Prince had asked him to remind the outgoing Prime Minister 'that his view had always been that from this moment the Prince would take up a new position, and that the Queen, no longer having Lord Melbourne to resort to in case of need, must from this moment consult and advise with the Prince'[3]. Melbourne wrote to this effect to the Queen,[4] and Peel soon began a correspondence with the Prince.

From 1837 to 1841, then, the Queen had been under Lord Melbourne's influence; from 1841 to 1861 under

[1] Monypenny and Buckle, ii. 117 (quoted from Vitzthum, ii, 176).

[2] *Journals and Letters of Reginald Viscount Esher*, edited by Maurice V. Brett (Ivor Nicholson and Watson, 1934), ii. 99 (18.viii.05), Lord Esher to M. V. B.

[3] *L.* i. 304 (30.viii.41), Memorandum by Mr. Anson.

[4] *L.* i. 306.

that of the Prince; only after his death can she be seen acting as a constitutional monarch entirely on her own responsibility. For some few years indeed the shade of Albert ruled the land in the sense that all her actions were dictated by her memories of his preferences. The final argument against any proposal was that the Queen knew that it would have been displeasing to the Prince. But as the years go by this kind of reference to his views and wishes grows less and less frequent in the *Letters*, though that may perhaps be partly due to editorial policy. Situations completely different from those which had prevailed in his life arose in such a way that his recorded and remembered opinions could no longer be considered as relevant criteria. In one all-important instance, at any rate, his marked dislike of one statesman and admiration for another came in time to be completely ignored, and his preference totally reversed, in the Queen's mind.

Not only was it impossible for the Prince's place to be filled, but the Queen had lost or was soon to lose the advisers of her youth. In 1861 Melbourne, Peel, Wellington, and Aberdeen were dead, and Stockmar was living in retirement at Coburg. In Palmerston, Russell, and Derby there survived three 'elder statesmen', but in none of them did she seem to feel any particular confidence. Palmerston died in office in 1865. Russell, though he lived till 1878, retired from public life in 1866. Derby died in 1869. After her bereavement Victoria still turned occasionally for comfort and advice to her uncle, Leopold I, the King of the Belgians, who in her childhood had almost taken for her the place of a Father. But he survived the Prince Consort by two years only, though he lived to stand godfather to a grandson of the Queen, the Duke of Clarence.[1] After 1868, when Derby gave place to Dis-

[1] *King Edward VII: A Biography*, by Sir Sidney Lee (Macmillan, 1925), i. 180.

raeli, there was in fact no prominent statesman to whose opinion the Queen needed to defer on grounds of age or experience. With the exception of the two years of Gladstone's fourth Ministry (1892–4), the country from 1886 to the close of the reign was governed by two Prime Ministers, Lord Salisbury and Lord Rosebery, both of whom were actually younger than herself. Her long experience and accurate memory made her political interventions increasingly decisive as the years passed.

The position was almost the same with regard to the Household. Sir Charles Phipps, who had been Keeper of Her Majesty's Privy Purse since 1849, died in 1866. General the Hon. Charles Grey, who had at one time been Private Secretary to his father, Lord Grey of the Reform Bill, and had been the Prince Consort's Private Secretary since 1849, became the Queen's Private Secretary in 1862. Official scruples as to the formal recognition of the existence of a post which was an institutional innovation delayed his being gazetted as such until 1867. He died in 1870 and was succeeded by General Sir Henry Ponsonby. 'The loss was serious, as Grey had struggled hard against [the Queen's] tendency to make herself a recluse.'[1] Thus, for example, in 1869, 'convinced that there is no other way to save us from great troubles', he urged Ministers to press her to make more public appearances: 'all she says of the "weight of work", "weakened health"—"shattered nerves", &c.—has simply no effect whatever on me'[2]; and eight days later apropos of her being too much at Osborne and Balmoral: '*nothing* will have any effect, but a strong—even a *peremptory* tone.'[3] Grey

[1] *The Queen and Mr. Gladstone*, by Philip Guedalla (Hodder & Stoughton, 1933), i. 58. Cf. below, p. 60.

[2] Guedalla, i. 52 (1.vi.69), Grey to Gladstone.

[3] Ibid. 54 (9.vi.69), Grey to Gladstone.

could dare to be 'very angry with her about the Irish matters'[1].

But this part of Grey's work was not carried on by Ponsonby. She was then too old and too formidable for a newly appointed Secretary to dream of rebuking her. The toning-down of the asperities of her letters seems to have bulked large in his work.[2] This is not to deny that Ponsonby was in a sense the greatest of her Private Secretaries. He created a fine tradition of absolute political impartiality, apparently successfully maintained by Arthur Bigge (Lord Stamfordham), who succeeded him from 1895 to 1901, and was again from 1910 until his death in 1931 Private Secretary to King George V, and by Sir Francis, afterwards Viscount, Knollys, who held the same office under King Edward VII.[3]

The conclusion to be drawn from these facts is that only after 1861 is it possible to trace exactly the political influence of the Queen herself and with complete confidence that what we take for her influence is really her own personal influence. Just as the period from 1694 to 1702 is the reign of William III alone, so the period from 1861 to 1901 is the reign of Queen Victoria alone. It is also the period of her matured wisdom and experience. In 1905 Lord Esher, as joint editor of the first three volumes of *The Letters of Queen Victoria*, gave it as his opinion that—

> 'If ever volumes of the Queen's correspondence subsequent to 1861 are published, it will be seen that the Queen's character underwent a fresh development after that date, and it was from that moment that she began to exhibit qualities of independence

[1] *Later Letters of Lady Augusta Stanley*, 111.

[2] Cf. *Behind the Throne*, by Paul H. Emden (Hodder & Stoughton, 1934), esp. 165–6; cf. also below, pp. 80–1.

[3] Cf. Esher, ii. 106–7 (2.ix.05), Lord Esher to Lord Knollys: 'If I may say so, *your* relations with the Ministers of to-day are those of Sir Henry Ponsonby to their predecessors.'

and self-reliance which before 1861 were wholly foreign to her nature.'[1]

Two other introductory questions remain to be discussed before the main theme is entered upon. The first is as to how far the policy of the editors of *The Letters of Queen Victoria* has been a policy of suppression. The answer is to be found in Mr. Buckle's words: 'Every effort is made to bring out all Queen Victoria's distinctive qualities and opinions; not only those which manifest her greatness, but also those which reveal her limitations.'[2] It is apparent that this has genuinely been the editorial policy, and the Queen's limitations are indeed made manifest. But it is at the same time possible to agree with Arthur Ponsonby in saying: 'Strong as some of the expressions of opinion may be in the letters and memoranda which have now been published, even so we can see that the official blue pencil has sometimes had to operate in order to present an expurgated version of Queen Victoria's opinions for the public consumption even of posterity.'[3]

The second question is as to what was the place of the Sovereign in the Constitution according to the formal constitutional theory of the Queen's contemporaries, and especially of Walter Bagehot, whose *English Constitution* is still rightly considered a classic. Bagehot takes as his text 'the great and general astonishment' caused by the abolition of Army Purchase by an act of prerogative,[4] and goes on in a striking passage to say:

'But this is nothing to what the Queen can by law do without consulting Parliament. Not to mention other things, she could disband the army (by law she cannot engage more than a certain number of men, but she is not obliged to engage any men); she could dismiss all the officers, from the General Com-

[1] Esher, ii. 106 (2.ix.05), Lord Esher to Lord Knollys.
[2] *L.* vii, vi (G. E. Buckle).
[3] Arthur Ponsonby's *Queen Victoria* (Duckworth, 1933), 60.
[4] Cf. below, p. 63.

manding-in-Chief downwards; she could dismiss all the sailors too; she could sell off all our ships of war and all our naval stores; she could make a peace by the sacrifice of Cornwall, and begin a war for the conquest of Brittany. She could make every citizen in the United Kingdom, male or female, a peer; she could make every parish in the United Kingdom a "university"; she could dismiss most of the civil servants; she could pardon all offenders. In a word, the Queen could by prerogative upset all the action of civil government within the government, could disgrace the nation by a bad war or peace, and could, by disbanding our forces, whether land or sea, leave us defenceless against foreign nations.'[1]

All this is, from a legalistic point of view, very interesting; from a practical point of view, utterly fantastic. Bagehot knew, and his readers knew, that the Queen would do none of these things, just as Dicey knew that there were in practice limits to that absolute sovereignty of Parliament which as a legal theory he so strongly upheld.[2] But Bagehot's light-hearted, almost playful estimate of the powers of the Crown is indicative of his failure, and the failure of his contemporaries (except, of course, those Ministers who had good cause to know the truth), to understand how great really was the Queen's political influence. It was an unavoidable failure mainly due to ignorance. Bagehot is heard complaining that 'There is no authentic explicit information as to what the Queen can do, any more than of what she does. In the bare superficial theory of free institutions this is

[1] Bagehot, 283.

[2] Cf. A. V. Dicey's *Law of the Constitution* (8th ed.), 69: 'Every one . . . knows as a matter of common sense that, whatever lawyers may say, the sovereign power of Parliament is not unlimited. . . . There are many enactments, and these are laws not in themselves obviously unwise or tyrannical, which Parliament never would and (to speak plainly) never could pass. If the doctrine of Parliamentary sovereignty involves the attribution of unrestricted power to Parliament, the dogma is no better than a legal fiction. . . .'

undoubtedly a defect'; and again: 'A secret prerogative is an anomaly—perhaps the greatest of anomalies.' But the question was far more than a question of the anomaly of a secret prerogative, or of a defect in bare superficial theory. Only at one point does he show that he has a realization of what was at stake, when he says: '... the courtiers of Queen Victoria are agreed as to the magnitude of the royal influence. It is with [them] an accepted secret doctrine that the Crown does more than it seems.'[1]

Here was a clue, and one which was obviously of first-rate importance since it came from so authoritative a source as the considered opinion of those who were closest to the Crown, that the royal influence was greater in reality than in superficial appearance. Yet it is a clue which Bagehot did not follow up. He is content to emphasize the great extent of the Queen's formal business (especially the signing of commissions in the Army),[2] to compare the English Monarchy to the heroic kings of the Homeric period,[3] to assert dogmatically that 'the nation is divided into parties, but the Crown is of no party'[4], and, although the Schleswig-Holstein War was still recent, to rebuke the childish enthusiasm of the English at treating the marriage of the Prince of Wales as a great political event when it was 'a very small matter of business'[5]. If the English did actually treat the marriage as a great political event, they were less childish than Bagehot thought, though more probably their interest was just the normal human interest in a very human event.

[1] Bagehot, 52–3. Cf. F. W. Maitland's *Constitutional History of England* (Cambridge University Press, 1908), 397: 'I strongly suspect that her influence is rather underrated than overrated by the popular mind.' This book was published in 1908, but is based on lectures delivered in 1887 and 1888.

[2] Bagehot, 54. [3] Ibid. 33. [4] Ibid. 40.

[5] Ibid. 34.

In one passage the distinguished constitutional theorist goes out of his way to be contemptuous:

'The use of the Queen, in a dignified capacity, is incalculable. Without her in England, the present English Government would fail and pass away. Most people when they read that the Queen walked on the slopes at Windsor—that the Prince of Wales went to the Derby—have imagined that too much thought and prominence were given to little things. But they have been in error; and it is nice to trace how the actions of a retired widow and an unemployed youth became of such importance.'[1]

To speak in 1872, which is the year of the second edition of *The English Constitution*, of the Prince of Wales as an unemployed youth was not far wide of the mark, though this was not because he was 'not genuinely seeking work'. His constant wish was for active employment, though only at the very end of the reign was his wish gratified. But to speak of Queen Victoria as 'a retired widow' shows a complete ignorance of her real political influence. It is further extremely interesting to note the disparaging tone of these remarks as one small sign of the wave of republican feeling characteristic of the time when *The English Constitution* was published.[2] The adoption of that kind of tone in discussing the Monarchy at the present day would draw much adverse comment. It is a far cry from Bagehot's 'retired widow' to Kipling's 'Widow at Windsor'.

Bagehot's final conclusion as to the powers of the Monarchy is famous: 'To state the matter shortly, the sovereign has, under a constitutional monarchy such as ours, three rights—the right to be consulted, the right to encourage, the right to warn.'[3]

There is no harm in anticipating one of the conclusions of this study, that Bagehot's view of the Monarchy has

[1] Bagehot, 30.
[2] Cf. below, pp. 207 ff.
[3] Bagehot, 67.

been invalidated by the publication of the *Letters*. Even the anonymous article on 'The Character of Queen Victoria' in *The Quarterly Review*[1] which was the best informed, most discriminating, and least fulsome of the obituaries of the Queen, as early as April, 1901, went so far as to say, mildly enough, that 'the Queen was less ready to yield to ministerial dictation than was commonly supposed'. It is true that the three rights, to be consulted, to encourage, and to warn, are extremely comprehensive. But even this is a summary classification of the Queen's political influence. It was more indefinite, more intangible, more pervasive, and more far-reaching than Bagehot would have us believe. It was felt in every kind of official transaction, alike in the smallest details of business and in the realm of high policy. In short, Professor Laski's main conclusion, which has already been stated, namely, that the Crown is 'a pervasive and active agent' in the Constitution, will only be substantiated by a detailed survey of the whole subject. Especially is this true of the direct executive action of the Crown in the sphere of patronage.[2]

Finally, it is essential in an introductory chapter to say a few words about the Queen's character.

'There was no one element in her mind which would

[1] It is now known that this excellent article was written by Sir Edmund Gosse from information chiefly supplied to him by Lady Ponsonby, Sir Henry's wife. Cf. *Mary Ponsonby: A Memoir*, edited by Magdalen Ponsonby (John Murray, 1927), 207–8 and 233; and also, *The Life and Letters of Sir Edmund Gosse*, by the Hon. Evan Charteris, K.C. (Heinemann, 1931), 269. The article holds an important place in the literature concerning Queen Victoria, for in its method of treating its subject it was in the line of logical descent from William Nicholson's woodcut to Lytton Strachey's biography; its publication caused an immense sensation. '*Queen Victoria as I knew her*, by Sir Theodore Martin . . . was an effort in 1908 to restore the haze of adulation, but it was in vain . . . the lowly adage defining the privilege of a cat in relation to a King had been extended to the consideration of a Queen by a critic, and in the process the way had been thrown open for the historian' (Charteris).

[2] Cf. below, p. 131.

certainly, in other and untoward conditions, have made itself prominently felt.'[1] That undoubtedly is true. Queen Victoria did not achieve greatness: it was thrust upon her. Imagine her for a moment an ordinary member of those upper middle classes to which in a sense she spiritually belonged. She might have been, no doubt, a remarkable matriarchal head of a family, but she would not, especially having regard to the subordinate position of women at the time and her own acceptance of it, have made for herself an outstanding professional career in the manner of Florence Nightingale, Octavia Hill, or Beatrice Webb.

Queen Victoria was an intelligent, but not an intellectual woman. Scott was her favourite reading, and she was partial to Jane Austen. She had no real feeling for poetry, except for her emotional interest in Tennyson's *In Memoriam.* She scarcely ever read modern authors. One doubts whether she ever fully appreciated the great merits of Disraeli's novels. The only studio of an artist she ever visited was that of Leighton. She refused to sit for G. F. Watts. Her favourite musician was Mendelssohn. What she seems to have liked best at the theatre was a good stirring melodrama. Soon after her marriage

'Lord Melbourne said, "The Prince is bored with the sameness of his chess every evening. He would like to bring literary and scientific people about the Court, vary the society, and infuse a more useful tendency into it. The Queen, however, has no fancy to encourage such people. This arises from a feeling on her part that her education has not fitted her to take part in such conversation; she would not like conversation to be going on in which she could not take her fair share, and she is far too open and candid in her nature to pretend to one atom more knowledge than she really possesses on such subjects; and

[1] *Quarterly Review*, April, 1901. This is also the authority for the statements of fact in the next paragraph.

yet, as the world goes, she would, as any girl, have been considered accomplished, for she speaks German well and writes it; understands Italian, speaks French fluently, and writes it with great elegance.'[1]

The Queen had a commanding passion for truth. 'To private letters [wrote Gladstone], unless from very wise people, I attach a moderate value. They are apt to give second-hand knowledge as if it were first-hand, and to treat what is within arm's length distance as if it were representative of the whole country.'[2] 'The Queen commands me to remark [ran Ponsonby's reply] that she has heard much from private letters but that most of her information has been derived from newspapers—not a very trustworthy source. She will therefore be glad of any reports or letters that may tell her the true state of the case. . . .'[3] 'Her acts were sometimes in error [generalizes Mr. Bolitho] but never her motives. This, I think, is the steady light of her greatness.'[4] That is perfectly true.

Her greatest fault was obstinate prejudice. 'In small things as in great, the Queen never believed that she was or could be wrong on a matter of principle.'[5] According to Marlborough's observation it had been much the same with Queen Anne: 'When she thinks herself in the right, she needs no advice to help her to be very firm and positive.'[6] Mary Ponsonby noted of Queen Victoria: 'When she is disagreed with, even slightly, she thinks nothing too bad to say of the culprit.'[7] She was also susceptible to flattery, although she herself boasted that she was not.[8]

[1] *L.* i. 256 (15.i.41), Memorandum—Mr. Anson.
[2] Guedalla, ii. 118 (4.xi.80), Gladstone to Ponsonby.
[3] Ibid. (7.xi.80), Ponsonby to Gladstone.
[4] *The Widow and Her Son*, viii.
[5] *Quarterly Review*, April, 1901.
[6] M. R. Hopkinson's *Anne of England* (Constable, 1934), 246.
[7] *Mary Ponsonby*, 137 (30.viii.77), M. E. P. to H. F. P.
[8] Lee's *Queen Victoria*, 572.

She was 'sometimes a prey to vulgar toadies'[1]. Much is to be learnt from the single incident of her calling 'on Lady Ponsonby at Osborne especially to ask her to tell Sir Henry that when the Queen makes a remark he must not say "it is absurd". She would not tell him herself, but she wanted Lady Ponsonby to tell him kindly.'[2] The kind intention of sparing Sir Henry's feelings is typical of the Queen's character. But equally typical is the drawing of the line beyond which due deference was absolutely insisted upon.

The finest tribute to her character has been paid by Lytton Strachey. Like Balaam he went out to curse and stayed to bless. He analysed, he dissected, he derided, but at the end he could not help admiring. His book does not really detract from, it enhances the Queen's reputation. To the Victorians themselves the tone may have seemed to be that of disrespectful ridicule; to the Georgians it seems only that of critical appraisement.

[1] *Quarterly Review*, April, 1901.
[2] Esher, i. 160 (19.viii.92), Journal.

## II

# THE INFLUENCE OF THE QUEEN ON HOME AFFAIRS; TO GLADSTONE'S LAST MINISTRY

THE story of the Queen's influence on home affairs in the latter half of the nineteenth century is very largely the story of her relations with Gladstone. But the relationship between them can only be fully understood in the light of the relationship between the Queen and Disraeli. Any account of this must begin with an account of his relations with the Prince.

'Of all the English Ministers with whom the Prince was brought in contact, it is known that he preferred the stately and upright Commoner [Peel], who certainly, of all English Ministers, estimated and appreciated the Prince's character most truly and clearly.'[1] It followed that Disraeli as 'Peel's assailant and destroyer was regarded by the Queen and Prince with especial aversion'[2]. Moreover, they were both Free Traders, and Disraeli was a leader of the party of Protection. The first time he enters the pages of the *Letters* is when he is referred to, by implication, under the heading of 'the recklessness of a handful of foolish . . . "Young England" people!'[3] Two years later Peel is told that '. . . the House of Commons ought to be ashamed of having such members as L$^{d}$ G.

[1] *L.* i. 254.

[2] Monypenny and Buckle, ii. 115. Even as late as 1870, in spite of a tendency to make allowances, it could still be the case that 'The Queen quite agrees with what Mr. Martin says about Mr. Disraeli's conduct to Sir R. Peel. It was and is a great blot. . . .' Sir Theodore Martin's *Queen Victoria as I knew her*, 68 (7.vi.70).

[3] *L.* ii. 16 (18.vi.44), Queen to King of the Belgians.

Bentinck and that detestable Mr. D'Israeli.'[1] His name first appears in the *Letters* in 1847 when it is followed—in contrast to those of two other gentlemen—with a mark which can only be taken in its context to express contempt: 'The Queen must mention to Lord John that she was a little shocked at Sir Charles Wood in his speech . . . designating the *future Government*, and selecting Lord George Bentinck, Mr. Disraeli (!), and Mr. Herries as the persons destined to hold *high offices*. . . .'[2] When in 1851 'Lord Stanley said he should have to propose Mr. Disraeli as one of the Secretaries of State', the Prince carefully noted that: 'The Queen interrupted him by saying that she had not a very good opinion of Mr. Disraeli on account of his conduct to poor Sir R. Peel. . . .'[3] The next year the Prince wrote of 'the *laxity of the political consciences*'[4] of Disraeli and Palmerston. The story even goes that the Prince said that Disraeli had not one single element of a gentleman in his composition.

When Disraeli left office in December, 1852, he wrote to Prince Albert: 'I shall ever remember with interest and admiration the princely mind in the princely person.'[5] The language sounds a little extravagant, but perhaps the proper adjective is merely 'Disraelian'; and had he not earlier in the year written to his sister: 'On Sunday I was two hours with the Prince—a very gracious and interesting audience. He has great abilities and wonderful knowledge—I think the best-educated man I ever met; most completely trained, and not over-educated for his intellect, which is energetic and lively.'[6] Again, two years later he

[1] Guedalla, i. 11 (21.vi.46), Queen to Peel.
[2] *L.* ii. 139 (19.xii.47), Queen to Lord John Russell.
[3] Ibid. 303 (25.ii.51), Mem. by Prince Albert.
[4] Monypenny and Buckle, i. 1239 (26.xi.52), Prince Albert to Derby.
[5] *L.* ii. 417 (20.xii.52), Disraeli to Prince Albert.
[6] Monypenny and Buckle, i. 1187 (8.vi.52), Disraeli to Sarah Disraeli.

wrote to a friend: 'The opportunity which office has afforded me of becoming acquainted with the Prince filled me with a sentiment towards him which I may describe without exaggeration as one of affection.'[1] Of a visit to Windsor in 1858 he reports that it 'has been *endless conversation* with the Prince'[2]. By then 'The Prince Consort was obviously beginning to shake off the strong distrust which he had originally entertained of Disraeli. . . .'[3] In 1861 when Mrs. Disraeli paid her first visit to Windsor, he considers it 'very marked on the part of Her Majesty to ask the wife of the leader of the Opposition, when many Cabinet Ministers have been asked there *without* their wives'[4].

But undoubtedly the real foundation of Disraeli's great influence over the Queen was the extent to which he entered into her grief at her husband's death. Her admiration for Albert had been quite unbounded, and Disraeli came forward as one who had always shared that admiration:

'The Prince is the only person, whom Mr. Disraeli has ever known, who realized the Ideal. None with whom he is acquainted have ever approached it. There was in him an union of the manly grace and sublime simplicity, of chivalry with the intellectual splendour of the Attic Academe. The only character in English history, that would, in some respects, draw near to him is Sir Philip Sydney . . .'

This passage Mr. G. E. Buckle confesses to be 'somewhat hyperbolic eulogium'[5]. But it is not surprising that a

[1] Martin, ii. 564.

[2] Monypenny and Buckle, i. 1589 (15.xi.58), Disraeli to Mrs. Disraeli.

[3] Ibid. 1572. Mr. J. A. Farrer, *The Monarchy in Politics* (London, 1917), 304, even goes so far as to speak of 'a certain affinity of spirit between the Prince Consort and Lord Beaconsfield. . . . An anti-Russian policy, vigorous to the point of risk, and a leaning to absolutist government, were the leading ideas of both.'

[4] Monypenny and Buckle, ii. 116 (Jan. 1861), Disraeli to Mrs. Willyams.

[5] Ibid. 128–9 (25.iv.63), Disraeli to Queen.

widow who delighted in hearing men sing the praises of her late husband should say that Disraeli was 'the only person who appreciated the Prince'[1]. She presented Disraeli with a volume of the Prince's Speeches,[2] and at the Prince of Wales's wedding, when all the seats except four had been 'officially appropriated', two were given to the Disraelis.[3]

It is only fair to say that in Disraeli's praise of the Prince there was no doubt a very large element of sincerity, but it is not always easy to disentangle sincerity from insincerity, and at any rate the note rings a little false, especially when we make use of the method of the double column and set beside this letter to the Queen his remark to Matthew Arnold: 'You have heard me called a flatterer and it is true. Everyone likes flattery; and when you come to royalty you should lay it on with a trowel.'[4] Disraeli flattered the Queen, but he was fully aware of the Queen's limitations: 'I had a long letter this morning from the Faery about vivisection which she insists upon my stopping as well as the theft of ladies' jewels. I think she is the most artless person in her style I ever corresponded with.'[5] Yet he informed her that she was 'instinctively appreciative' of the fine arts,[6] and we are told that

[1] Monypenny and Buckle, ii. 119, Memorandum by Disraeli, 1863.

[2] Ibid. 127. Of this gift Disraeli writes to Mrs. Willyams (5.v.63): 'I think you will agree with me that this is the most remarkable inscription which a Sovereign ever placed in a volume graciously presented to a subject!' But it said only: 'To / the Right Honourable Benjamin Disraeli / in recollection of the greatest and best of men / from the beloved Prince's broken-hearted Widow / Victoria. R.'

[3] Ibid. 120. In his account of what he calls 'the only pageant that never disappointed me' Disraeli describes how he 'had never seen the Queen since the catastrophe, and ventured, being near-sighted, to use my glass. I saw H.M. well, and unfortunately caught her glance. . . . I did not venture to use my glass again.'

[4] Ibid. 1335.

[5] *The Letters of Disraeli to Lady Bradford and Lady Chesterfield*, edited by Lord Zetland (Benn, 1929), i. 244 (21.v.75), Disraeli to Lady Bradford.

[6] Monypenny and Buckle, ii. 1340.

'There is no reason to doubt the story which represents him as using more than once, in conversation with Her Majesty on literary subjects, the words: 'We authors, Ma'am.'[1]

But it is true that after the Prince's death the Queen was unutterably lonely, and it was Disraeli who befriended her. Ponsonby was more than justified in speaking to Beaconsfield on his final retirement 'of the service of friendship you have rendered to the Queen personally'[2]. His Mary Anne died in 1872. Perhaps this made it easier for him to understand her sense of the loss of a life's partner. 'I love the Queen [he said]—perhaps the only person in this world left to me that I do love. . . .'[3]

Back in 1852 the Queen informs her uncle: 'Mr. Disraeli (*alias* Dizzy) writes very curious reports to me of the House of Commons proceedings—much in the style of his books. . . .'[4] Later Lady Augusta Stanley was to say that 'Dizzy writes daily letters to the Queen in his best novel style, telling her every scrap of political news dressed up to serve his own purpose, and every scrap of social gossip cooked to amuse her. She declares that she has never had such letters in her life, which is probably true, and that she never before knew everything.'[5] As early as 1852 he had been interested in the Prince's South Kensington schemes,[6] and in 1863 when a proposal to purchase the Exhibition buildings came before the House of Commons he was so keen in its support that he made the mistake, in canvassing his supporters, of 'telling them that he had

[1] Ibid. 389.

[2] P. H. Emden's *Behind the Throne*, 186.

[3] Monypenny and Buckle, ii. 1334 (4.ix.79), Disraeli to the Dowager Lady Ely.

[4] *L.* ii. 386 (30.iii.52), Queen to King of the Belgians.

[5] Maxwell's *Clarendon*, ii. 346.

[6] Monypenny and Buckle, i. 1218–20.

a letter in his pocket from the Queen. This had a disastrous effect, and when he got up the hooting was so terrific that he could not be heard.'[1] 'My marshals even deserted me', reported Disraeli to Grey in a picturesque account of the incident.[2] In 1866 'The Queen thanks Mr. Disraeli for all his interesting reports [as Leader of the House], but she is especially anxious to express to him her great satisfaction at the manner in which he carried the vote for the gun-metal for her dear, great husband's memorial. She knows how truly he appreciated him!'[3] A little later Mr. Disraeli is found to be 'amiable and clever, but is a strange man'[4]. The amiability and cleverness, and indeed the strangeness, were soon to prove completely fascinating. On Derby's resignation in 1868, to send for Disraeli was 'the natural, it was not the inevitable choice'[5]. If the Queen had still in the least disliked him, she could have summoned the Duke of Richmond or Lord Stanley.

When Disraeli for the first time became Prime Minister he informed his Sovereign that it would be 'his delight and duty, to render the transaction of affairs as easy to your Majesty, as possible'[6]. He kept his word. His letters and his reports of proceedings in the House of Commons which, as Leader, he was constitutionally bound to submit to the Queen, continued to be written in a style which was new to her, coming from an official quarter, a style vivid, dramatic, even racy, the style, in short, of a brilliant novelist. Many examples might be given. One must suffice. Mr. Ward Hunt is proposed to

[1] Monypenny and Buckle, ii. 129.
[2] *L.* iv. 96 (3.vii.63), Disraeli to Grey.
[3] Monypenny and Buckle, ii. 184–5 (26.vii.66), Queen to Disraeli.
[4] *L.* iv. 378 (25.xi.66), Journal.
[5] Monypenny and Buckle, ii. 1324.
[6] *L.* iv. 505 (26.ii.68), Disraeli to Queen.

the Queen as a person fit and proper to occupy the office of Chancellor of the Exchequer:

'Mr. Disraeli ought to observe to your Majesty, that Mr. Ward Hunt's appearance is rather remarkable, but anything but displeasing. He is more than six feet four inches in stature, but does not look so tall from his proportionate breadth; like St. Peter's, no one is at first aware of his dimensions. But he has the sagacity of the elephant, as well as the form.'[1]

Disraeli not only treated Victoria as a quite human recipient of gossipy letters, but realized that the Queen of England was also a woman with that personal view of politics which, though there are exceptions, is the rule among women, and his perspicacity had its reward when the Queen recorded of him that 'He certainly shows more consideration for my comfort than any of the preceding Prime Ministers since Sir Robert Peel and Lord Aberdeen'[2], of both of whom she had held a very high opinion. On his resignation as Prime Minister he proposed to continue to lead the Conservative Party, and wrote to the Queen: 'It did not appear after great deliberation that any person could guide this party for your Majesty's comfort and welfare with the same advantage as Mr. Disraeli, as no one could be so intimately acquainted with your Majesty's wishes and objects as himself.'[3]

The rest of the story is fairly well known. In 1874, with regard to the case of Dr. Hayman, who had been dismissed from the headmastership of Rugby, Disraeli went so far as directly to ask the Queen for her advice with the words: 'It may be unconstitutional for a Minister to seek advice from his Sovereign, instead of proffering it; but . . . Your Majesty cannot but be aware how highly

[1] *L.* iv. 507 (26.ii.68), Disraeli to Queen.
[2] Ibid. 539 (28.ix.68), Journal.
[3] Monypenny and Buckle, ii. 438 (23.xi.68), Disraeli to Queen.

Mr. Disraeli appreciates your Majesty's judgment and almost unrivalled experience of public life.'[1] We shall see that nothing that Gladstone said in 1871 could induce the Queen to postpone her departure for Balmoral for two or three days only in order to allay public criticism of the Monarchy. In 1874, when the object was a proper reception for the Tsar, Disraeli succeeded where Gladstone had failed: 'My head is still on my shoulders. The great lady has absolutely postponed her departure! [for two days]. Everybody had failed, even the Prince of Wales . . . Salisbury says I have saved an Afghan War, and Derby compliments me on my unrivalled triumph. . . .[2] But Derby (on whom the full measure of the Queen's wrath was soon to be vented) had also timidly asked a question: 'Nobody can have managed the lady better than you have; but is there not just a risk of encouraging her in too large ideas of her personal power, and too great indifference to what the public expects? I only ask: it is for you to judge.'[3]

The Queen allowed Disraeli as Leader of the House to delegate his duty of writing her each night an account of its proceedings.[4] She gave him her portrait.[5] When she was in town she wrote to him three or four times a day.[6] When he was ill Sir William Jenner had to write a daily report to the Queen,[7] and on one such occasion she even paid him the honour of visiting him in his bedchamber.[8] After the passing of the Public Worship Regulation Act: 'The Faery sent for me the instant I arrived [at Osborne].

[1] *L.* v. 333 (17.iv.74), Disraeli to Queen.
[2] Monypenny and Buckle, ii. 755 (5.v.74), Disraeli to Lady Bradford.
[3] Ibid. 754 (4.v.74), Derby to Disraeli.
[4] Ibid. 1339.
[5] Zetland, ii. 20.
[6] Ibid. i. 150, Disraeli to Lady Bradford (12.ix.74).
[7] Ibid. 251, Disraeli to Lady Chesterfield (1.vi.75).
[8] Ibid. 217, Disraeli to Lady Chesterfield (11.iii.75).

I can only describe my reception by telling you that I really thought she was going to embrace me. She was wreathed with smiles, and, as she talked, glided about the room like a bird.'[1] Years afterwards it was 'still remembered how much more she used to smile in conversation with him than she did with any other of her ministers'[2]. On this occasion she asked him to sit down on account of his gout: 'Only think of that! I remember Lord Derby, after one of his illnesses, had an audience of Her Majesty, and he mentioned it to me as a proof of the Queen's favour, that Her Majesty had remarked to him how sorry she was she could not ask him to be seated, the etiquette was so severe.'[1] Subsequently he records his saying to the Queen: 'When I took my leave at my audience, I would put my golden chair back in its place that the breach of etiquette should be kept a secret. So I told her, and she smiled.'[3] At one moment he expresses a desire, which he can hardly have intended to be taken very seriously, to displace the royal Private Secretary: 'All he can say, and he can say it from the bottom of his heart, is that he wishes he was your Majesty's Secretary: he would willingly relinquish for it his present exalted post.'[4] Using Disraelian language to describe the effect of his influence on her, she now began to open her petals in the rays of a newly risen sun. By 1876, for example, she was beginning again to take an interest in the music which once she had played with her husband: 'After my dreadful misfortune in '61, everything was left untouched, and I could not bear to look at what my darling one and I used to play daily together... only quite lately [have I] re-opened my duet books....'[5]

1 Ibid. 129, Disraeli to Lady Bradford (7.viii.74).
2 *Quarterly Review*, April, 1901.
3 Zetland, i. 258, Disraeli to Lady Bradford (28.vi.75).
4 *L.* v. 608 (11.iii.78), Beaconsfield to Queen.
5 Ibid. 505 (19.xii.76), Journal.

In December, 1877, as a special mark of confidence in her Prime Minister's Near Eastern policy, she visited him at Hughenden.[1] Of all her previous Prime Ministers she had only thus honoured Melbourne and Peel. She gave him the Windsor Uniform, which she had given to Wellington, Melbourne, Aberdeen, and Peel, and gave to no other Prime Minister, except—subsequently—Salisbury.[2] Disraeli as Prime Minister for the second time had the same fascination of mysteriousness for the Queen as had twenty years earlier Napoleon III,[3] though she had realized that the Prince was less enthusiastic about the French Emperor than she was.[4] In short, no other Prime Minister throughout the reign established so complete an ascendancy over the Queen's mind. He was amply justified in saying in May, 1874: 'I must say I feel fortunate in having a female Sovereign. I owe everything to woman....'[5]

As soon as the Queen heard of his defeat at the polls she wrote:

'Dear Lord Beaconsfield / I cannot thank you for your most kind letter, which affected me much, in the 3rd person—it is too formal; and when we correspond—which I hope we shall on many a *private* subject and without any one being astonished or offended, and even more without any one knowing about it—I hope it will be in this more easy form. You can be of such use to me about my family and other things and about great public questions.'[6]

Certainly if no one was to know about the correspondence no one would be astonished or offended. But this was a letter which must have made Stockmar turn in his grave.

[1] Monypenny and Buckle, ii. 1075. [2] Ibid. 1339.
[3] See, for example, Martin's *Queen Victoria*, 83.
[4] *L.* iii. 140 (1.ix.55), Queen to Stockmar.
[5] Zetland, i. 92, Disraeli to Lady Bradford (23.v.74).
[6] Monypenny and Buckle, ii. 1399 (9.iv.80).

He had struggled hard to bring to an end a correspondence with Melbourne after 1841, which fortunately grew gradually less and less political. Peel had told the Baron, 'becoming then suddenly emphatic': '. . . that that moment I was to learn that the Queen takes advice upon public matters in another place, I shall throw up; . . . I would not remain an hour, whatever the consequences of my resignation may be.'[1] And when Peel in his turn was asked to continue to correspond, although out of office, he was careful to say:

'I shall be very happy to avail myself of your Royal Highness's kind permission occasionally to write to your Royal Highness . . . I can act in conformity with your Royal Highness's gracious wishes, and occasionally write to you, without saying a word of which the most jealous or sensitive successor in the confidence of the Queen could complain.'[2]

Gladstone and Disraeli were men with characters which were in every respect diametrically opposed. It was natural, therefore, that any third person who had a strong liking for the one, should have had strong dislike for the other. The more dynamic and positive a personality, the more difficult it is to assign that personality to some Limbo, and not to Heaven or Hell. What is surprising is that Queen Victoria should have come with such passion to have admired Disraeli and detested Gladstone. Her preference might reasonably have been expected to have been precisely the opposite, especially as the Prince Consort had held a high opinion of Gladstone,[3] and Gladstone, no less than Disraeli, had been

[1] *L.* i. 362 (23.xi.41), Memorandum: Stockmar to Melbourne.

[2] *L.* ii. 93 (August, 1846), Peel to the Prince Albert.

[3] 'Gladstone is now the real leader of the House of Commons, and works with an energy and vigour altogether incredible. . . .' [Bolitho's *Albert the Good*, 265 (17.iv.60), the Prince Consort to Stockmar.] This is particularly high praise coming from a Prince whose vigour and energy in their turn appear almost incredible to more ordinary mortals.

a great admirer of the Prince.[1] At Windsor in 1845 Gladstone had 'rather a nice conversation' with the Prince about an Anglo-Prussian copyright convention.[2] Indeed, it is hard not to believe that Gladstone was far more likely than Disraeli to have had a real understanding of the Prince's high ideals and sense of public duty. Disraeli was something of an adventurer in life and politics; Gladstone had a high sense of moral purpose both in politics and life. Disraeli was often flippant and frivolous. Gladstone was almost always serious and earnest. Perhaps the root of the trouble psychologically was that neither the Queen nor Gladstone had a keen sense of humour. If they had, they would have been more self-conscious, therefore better able to see their own faults, and so better able to understand one another.

The way in which Disraeli won the favour of the Queen has already been briefly discussed. The way in which Gladstone lost it remains to be explained. Part of the explanation is that the political problems which most interested Gladstone were not the problems which most interested the Queen. She did not share his enthusiasm for great domestic reforms. By contrast she did share Disraeli's desire for 'a spirited foreign policy', and was as subject as he to the romantic fascination of India and of the East. Part of the explanation no doubt is, as Viscount Gladstone suggests, that the Queen's 'lofty isolation kept her apart from the all-essential dynamics of politics'[3]. The fact that she was neither herself actively engaged in the day-to-day rough and tumble of the political battle, nor a trained student of politics, kept her out of touch with progressive movements and unable to understand what

[1] Viscount Gladstone's *After Thirty Years* (Macmillan, 1928), 327–8. The references to this book are to the third and revised impression.

[2] Guedalla, i. 30.

[3] Viscount Gladstone, 375.

lay behind them. Certainly one nineteenth-century statesman joins hands with another from the twentieth in criticizing 'Buckingham Palace': 'I do not know much [wrote Gladstone] of the interior side of court gossip, but I have a very bad opinion of it, and especially on this ground, that while absolutely irresponsible it appears to be uniformly admitted as infallible.'[1]

The explanation is certainly not that Gladstone was in any way disloyal to the Crown. Indeed the man who in the opinion of one writer was 'the most important' of Queen Victoria's Prime Ministers,[2] was also in the opinion of another writer the one who 'had most respect for the throne'[3]. Viscount Gladstone tells us that in his father's diary for January 2, 1898, there was a definite injunction to keep silence about his relations with the Queen in the later years of his life.[4] Viscount Gladstone held himself relieved of this injunction on account of the editorial policy adopted by Mr. Buckle in the publication of the later volumes of Queen Victoria's *Letters*. Lytton Strachey has rightly pointed out that in his intercourse with the Queen Gladstone was not 'in any degree lacking in courtesy or respect. On the contrary, an extraordinary reverence permeated his manner, both in his conversation and his correspondence with the Sovereign.'[5] Mary Ponsonby (in 1886 apparently) noticed in the Temple of Peace, Gladstone's study at Hawarden, a picture of the Queen, a bust of her on Mr. Gladstone's table, and a bust of the Prince Consort in the middle of the room.[6] She had also noticed that Gladstone's '*feeling*' for the Crown 'was always snubbed', and contrasted this feeling of his

[1] Morley's *Life of Gladstone* (cheap edition, 1912), ii. 193.
[2] J. L. Hammond in *Contemporary Review*, April, 1934.
[3] Francis Birrell's *Gladstone* (Duckworth, 1933), 136.
[4] Viscount Gladstone, xxviii. [5] Strachey, 214.
[6] *Mary Ponsonby*, 178.

with Salisbury's 'utter lack of sentimentalism about the Crown'[1].

Gladstone's method of approach to the Queen was psychologically faulty. His intellectual powers were remarkable, his experience of the world wide. She was not an intellectual woman, and her experience of the world was necessarily less wide than his. It was his business rather than hers, both as a man and a subject, to secure the right temperamental relationship between them, and for its absence he must consequently bear a greater part of the blame.

Even if Queen Victoria never actually said of Gladstone: 'He speaks to me as if I were a public meeting', the statement is one which contains a profound truth. It is in vain for Mr. Shaw to say: 'But surely that is the way in which a Prime Minister should address a Queen when affairs of state are on the carpet.'[2] The question of 'should' does not arise. After all a Queen is also only a woman, and in this case not even an 'intelligent woman' in the Shavian sense. Gladstone's mistake was to treat her not as a woman, not even as Queen Victoria, but always as the Crown. To him she was an institution more than a person. Moreover, 'his very awe of the institution made him set an exacting standard for the individual who represented it'[3].

'Speech was the fibre of his being; and, when he spoke, the ambiguity of ambiguity was revealed. The long, winding, intricate sentences, with their vast burden of subtle and complicated qualification, befogged the mind like clouds, and like clouds, too, dropped thunderbolts.'[4] When he explained his resignation on the Maynooth

[1] *Mary Ponsonby*, 69.

[2] Bernard Shaw: *Pen Portraits and Reviews* (Standard Edition), 235.

[3] Morley, ii. 326.

[4] Strachey's *Eminent Victorians* (Phoenix Library Edition), 265.

question: 'What a marvellous talent is this— [exclaimed Cobden] here have I been sitting listening with pleasure for an hour to his explanation, and yet I know no more why he left the Government than before he began.'[1] There is a well-known story, legendary perhaps, of a whispered consultation on the Treasury Bench between Gladstone and Peel: 'Shall I be short and concise?' asks the former. 'No, be long and diffuse,' answers the latter; and Gladstone would seem to have taken that advice to heart for life.

But this manner of speaking was bound to be displeasing to the Queen. In 1841 Melbourne's opinion was: 'If it were possible for any one to advise Peel, he would recommend that he should write fully to Her Majesty, and *elementarily*, as Her Majesty always liked to have full knowledge upon everything which was going on.'[2] That was still as true in the hey-day of Gladstone as it had been in the hey-day of Melbourne. But Gladstone seemed constitutionally incapable of writing elementarily.

We read in his diary for January 13, 1867: 'Wrote out a paper on the plan of the measure respecting the Irish Church, intended perhaps for the Queen. Worked on Homer. We felled a lime.'[3] Disraeli would never have written a paper, 'intended perhaps for the Queen'; he would always have written a paper specially suited to her. Moreover, this extract from Gladstone's diary becomes even more significant when we find that on the 21st Gladstone wrote to the Queen to say that he had prepared two papers for her to explain his Irish Church policy,[4] both of which so bewildered her that she asked Sir Theodore Martin to make a précis of them. Finally, we have

[1] Morley, i. 278.
[2] *L.* i. 305 (30.viii.41), Memorandum by Mr. Anson.
[3] Morley, ii. 197.
[4] *L.* iv. 577 (21.i.69), Gladstone to Queen.

Sir Theodore's opinion: 'That the Queen should have been lost in the fog of the long and far from lucid sentences of her Minister, running, as they did, through upwards of a dozen closely written quarto pages, seemed only natural.'[1]

There must have been many incidents of this kind. There survives, for example, this little note from the Queen to her private secretary: 'Sir Henry has not returned Mr. Gladstone's long paper, nor told her what the drift of it is.'[2] On one occasion Gladstone gave her a memorandum on the Irish situation, covering between thirty and forty pages of foolscap.[3] It was a very able memorandum. It was a striking testimony to his own industry, and to his desire to enlighten the Queen as to his policy. But that kind of paper was bound to contrast unfavourably with Disraeli's letters. Did Gladstone really think that the Queen would be pleased to receive such a document, or would be capable of mastering it? Or did he, unlikely as it sounds, hope to crush her opposition by sheer weight of argument? Once again Lytton Strachey in one sentence cuts to the core of this apple of discord, in saying of Gladstone: '. . . when, in the excess of his loyalty, he went further, and imputed to the object of his veneration, with obsequious blindness, the subtlety of intellect, the wide reading, the grave enthusiasm, which he himself possessed, the misunderstanding became complete.'[4]

It is interesting to observe how another woman reacted to Gladstone in exactly the same way as the Queen, for Emily Eden writing to Clarendon in 1860 says:

'I remember your snubbing Theresa Lewis when she did not think Mr. Gladstone pleasant, and now you may snub me. I

[1] *Queen Victoria as I knew her*, 51.

[2] Sir Frederick Ponsonby's *Sidelights on Queen Victoria* (London, 1930), 190 (22.viii.84), Queen to Ponsonby.

[3] *L.* vi. 84, 1 (23.iii.86).

[4] Strachey, 215.

dare say he *is* very clever and he is good-natured, doing his best to bring his mind down to the level of mine, but fails. He is always above me, and then he does not converse, he harangues, and the more he says the more I don't understand. Then there is something about high-church people that I can't define, but I feel it when I am with them—something Jesuitical—but they never let themselves go[1]—and to complete my list of things, there is some degree of Parvenuism about him,[2] as there was about Sir Robert Peel, something in his tone of voice and his way of coming into the room, that is not aristocratic. In short, he is not frivolous enough for me. If he were soaked in boiling water and rinsed till he was twisted into a rope, I do not suppose a drop of fun would ooze out.'[3]

The Queen had the same distaste for Gladstone's ecclesiastical views as Emily Eden: 'It was always an element in her reticence with regard to Mr. Gladstone, that he was too High Church; "I am afraid he has the mind of a Jesuit," she used to say.' *The Quarterly Review* article also suggests that she objected to Gladstone because she thought he was overworking her: 'Her prejudice against Mr. Gladstone . . . really started in her consciousness that he would never acknowledge that she was, as she put it, "dead beat".'[4] But the whole evidence of the *Letters* in fact shows that her energy must have been almost as volcanic as his. Gladstone himself, apropos of his relations with the Queen, said: '. . . I am a man so eager upon things, as not enough to remember always what is due to persons. . . .'[5]

Gladstone never, even at the end, seems to have understood where and how he had in this matter blundered.

[1] Cf. Birrell, 116: 'His weakness was a certain clumsiness in personal relations, an inability to have it out properly with his interlocutor. . . .'

[2] 'Oxford on top and Liverpool below.'

[3] Maxwell's *Clarendon*, ii. 224.

[4] *Quarterly Review*, April, 1901. We shall see (below, p. 61) that he did not think she had too much work to do.

[5] Guedalla, i. 48 (29.xi.68), Gladstone to Dean Wellesley.

But a remarkable memorandum shows that he was sometimes able to take his failure in a good-humoured fashion:

'The force of a resemblance really compels me to put a word on paper, which I had not intended, which will stand alone, and will never pass the door of my lips on its passage to the ear of any human being.

In the autumn of 1838 I made the *gita* of Sicily from Palermo by Girgenti and Syracuse or Messina in two or three weeks, riding on the back of a mule. The beast was wholly inaccessible to notes of kindness by voice or hand. . . . But we rode usually with little interval from 6 a.m. to 4 p.m. and its undemonstrative unsympathetic service was not inefficiently performed. . . .

But I well remember having at the time a mental experience which was not wholly unlike a turn of indigestion. I had been on the back of the beast for many scores of hours, it had done me no wrong; it had rendered me much valuable service, but it was in vain to argue; there was the fact staring me in the face. I could not get up the smallest shred of feeling for the brute, I could neither love nor like it.

A rule of three sum is all that is necessary to conclude with. What that Sicilian mule was to me, I have been to the Queen; and the fortnight or three weeks are represented by 52 or 53 years.'[1]

But he was not always able to be so good-humoured. The subject was one which seems greatly to have worried and disturbed him. It grieved him 'to be troublesome to any one, especially among women to a Queen, and to an old and much respected Queen. I am very sorry for it; and I should be much more sorry still, but I cannot suspect that I had either by wilfulness or by neglect caused aggravations of the mischief.'[2] In February, 1897, he notes:

'I do not speak lightly when I state my conviction that the circumstances of my farewell, which I think were altogether

[1] Guedalla, ii. 75–6 (No date given).
[2] Ibid. 76 (19.iii.94), Memorandum by Gladstone.

without parallel, had serious causes beyond the operation of political disagreements, which no doubt went for something but which were insufficient to explain them. Statements, whether true or false, must have been carried to her ears, which in her view required (and not merely allowed) the mode of proceeding which was actually adopted.'[1]

Mr. Birrell suggests that this may be a veiled reference to the possibility of the Queen having heard current rumours of Gladstone's relations with prostitutes—evil rumours which were finally silenced by the case of *Wright* v. *Gladstone* (1927).[2]

Thus Gladstone paused from time to time to brood about his bad relations with the Queen. But his loyalty was undeviating. For example:

'. . . taking relations with me since 1844, as a whole, there is in them something of mystery, which I have not been able to fathom, and probably never shall. I hope my duty to H.M. and her family has never in fact, as it has never in intention, fallen short. And I have a new cause of gratitude to H.M. in her having on this last occasion admitted my wife anew to a footing of confidence and freedom.[3] She has too long, I think, been suffering on my behalf. I am glad that this chapter is well closed. God Save the Queen.'[4]

It has been seen that, puzzling as the whole subject appeared to Gladstone, next to the mysterious 'statements' to which he refers as 'serious causes' of his breach with the Queen, he himself places 'political disagreements'. Was he right in doing that? Was the clash between the Queen and Gladstone merely a conflict between two antipathetic personalities, or was it the result of fundamental divergence between two opposing views of politics? Was it

[1] Quoted, Birrell, 137. The reference here is, of course, to the farewell of 1894, and not to the meeting at Cimiez in March, 1897. Cf. below, pp. 101–2.

[2] See *After Thirty Years* (Appendix V), 435.

[3] Cf. below, p. 101.

[4] Guedalla, ii. 76 (10–11.iii.94), Memorandum by Gladstone.

due to a combination of these two factors, and, if so, which was the more important?

These are difficult questions to answer, and questions which for many pages to come we shall be continuously engaged in trying to answer. But, to anticipate, it does on the whole seem true to say that the divergence was more a divergence of policies than of persons. The fundamental fact is that 'while the Queen retained for life the fixed impression of Disraeli's teaching, Mr. Gladstone continued to grow visibly more Radical'[1]. His political development in his old age is really a most astonishing phenomenon. Indeed, his old age itself is a most astonishing phenomenon. For example, in 1884 we find: 'Mr. G. is still bent on retirement immediately after the Seats Bill is through Parliament. It is doubtful whether Andrew Clarke will permit it. He is said to hold that excitement is indispensable to the old man's health.'[2] Eight years later came the incident of the mad cow: 'Mr. G. has been knocked down in Hawarden Park by a mad cow. The papers record it. It seems he said nothing about it on his return home; but at dinner some one observed that there was a strange cow—escaped from somewhere—in the Park, and Mr. G. said "Oh, yes! I met it, and it knocked me down", and then related the circumstances.'[3] After that it is not surprising in the next month to find Lord Rosebery, while discussing his Cabinet colleagues, saying: 'The old man is by far the most susceptible to new influences.'[4]

The upshot of all this is the truth that the main causes of his differences with the Queen are, 'of course, connected with temperament, but they are ultimately differences of

[1] Guedalla, ii. 62.

[2] Esher, i. 102 (9.i.84), Lord Esher to Sir Garnet Wolseley.

[3] Ibid. 161 (7.ix.92), Journal.

[4] Ibid. 163 (5.x.92), Journal.

view'[1]. It was in his northern tour of 1862 that Gladstone first discovered himself as a popular speaker.[2] A central turning-point in his career was his defeat in the election for the Oxford University seat in 1865, and his Manchester speech: 'At last, my friends, I am come among you, and I am come among you "unmuzzled".'[3] Finally, in the Midlothian campaign he appealed to the masses on a moral issue, and his appeal was successful. Thereafter he trusted the people. But the man who put his trust in the people was not the man also to put trust in princes; the man who became 'the people's William' could not also be the Queen's William. If, on the other hand (and it is not so difficult to imagine), from 'the rising hope of the stern, unbending Tories' he had developed into the acknowledged leader of Conservatism—if, in other words, he had come to stand in Salisbury's shoes, it is hard to believe that the battle of wills between him and the Queen would have been at all fierce.[4]

The coldness between the Queen and Gladstone did not exist from the very beginning of their acquaintance. Indeed, the question of the precise moment at which the first signs of a rift appeared is one of great importance. Its importance is not merely on account of the academic interest which a certain school of historians find in origins as such. The answer throws a flood of light on the causes of this estrangement.

Mr. Farrer asserts that: 'The difference began when Mr. Gladstone and other Peelites forsook Lord Palmerston's Ministry in 1855, in the middle of the Crimean War, and, much to the offence of the Court, threw the weight of their influence on the side that wished to stop the war.'[5]

[1] J. L. Hammond in the *Contemporary Review*, April, 1934.

[2] Morley, ii. 60–1.

[3] Ibid. 112.

[4] Cf. below, pp. 113–19 and 242–7.

[5] Farrer's *Monarchy in Politics*, 300.

But this seems to carry the matter too far back.

The biographer of Lord Granville, discussing Gladstone's 1868 Ministry, says that the Queen

> 'was year by year less able to conceal how little she was in harmony with the party to which she had once given her fullest support, and how gradually if unwillingly she was withdrawing the complete confidence which had made Lord Granville her trusted counsellor on more than one important occasion in the earlier portion of her reign. . . . The great knowledge and acquired experience in affairs of the Queen was more and more from this time onward to make itself felt as a serious power . . . there were circumstances then beginning to operate, though as yet only dimly recognized, which tended to increase the weight of the Crown.'[1]

Gladstone's official biographer, John Morley, has remarkably little to say about this whole question of Gladstone's collision with the Crown. He was writing very soon after the actual events, he was in honour and loyalty bound to exercise a certain restraint, and also he was no doubt expecting soon to hold high office again in another Liberal Government. Nevertheless he does give an answer to the question which we have asked: 'Army reform first brought Mr. Gladstone into direct collision with reigning sentiment at Court. The Queen had doubted the wisdom of disestablishing the Church of Ireland, but to disestablish the Commander-in-Chief came closer home, and was disliked as an invasion of the personal rights of the occupant of the throne.'[2] Later, he adds that Gladstone '. . . became more and more conscious that the correspondence and occurrences of 1871–2 had introduced a reserve that was new.'[3] This

[1] *The Life of the Second Earl Granville*, by Lord Edmond Fitzmaurice (London, 1905), ii. 8.

[2] Morley, ii. 275.

[3] Ibid. 326.

judgement is now confirmed as a result of Mr. Guedalla's recent researches. For what in the first volume of *The Queen and Mr. Gladstone* he chiefly seems to prove is that incidents of 1871 and 1872 did place a serious strain on the good relations between them, and prepare the ground for the decisive break which occurred between 1876 and 1880. These incidents will soon be described in their proper place. They were of a personal rather than a political nature, and it is now quite clear that it was to them that Morley was referring.

But if the correspondence and occurrences of 1871–2 introduced a reserve that was new, resulting from personal rather than political differences, none the less 1874 brings one most striking piece of evidence of fundamental political divergence: 'What an important turn the elections have taken! It shows that the country is not *Radical*. What a triumph, too, Mr. Disraeli has obtained, and what a good sign this large Conservative majority is of the state of the country, which really required (as formerly) a strong Conservative party!'[1]

This in its turn in no way discredits the judgement of Viscount Gladstone, who speaks with the authority derived from a son's knowledge of a father's life. According to this account, the father in 1880 told the son that his relations with the Queen were good and friendly during the years from 1868 to 1874, though at one time[2] he had noticed a certain coldness after his proposal for a Royal Residence in Ireland and his proposal that the Prince of Wales should be more constantly employed, had been rejected, but that 'in 1880 he found a complete change, and thought it came from the influence of Lord Beacons-

[1] Martin's *Queen Victoria*, 89–90 (10.ii.74), Queen to Sir Theodore Martin.
[2] 'I think in 1870,' says Viscount Gladstone.

field'[1]. The first entry in Gladstone's own diary concerning his changed relations with the Queen is under the date of July 16, 1881: 'She is as ever perfect in her courtesy, but as to confidence she holds me now at arm's length.'[2]

Viscount Gladstone, therefore, speaks of 'the sudden uprising of the Queen's wrath against Mr. Gladstone in 1876 . . .'[3] and emphatically asserts: '. . . beyond any doubt his relations with the Queen were good and friendly up to 1876. The new-born dislike of Mr. Gladstone synchronized in its development with the rapid growth of Lord Beaconsfield's personal ascendancy over the Queen.'[4] This assertion is supported by an estimate of the tone of the Queen's letters to Gladstone, published and unpublished:

'All the Queen's letters to Mr. Gladstone from 1841 to 1894 are in the possession of his executors. Down to 1876 there is not a single letter which shows a trace of personal dislike. Quite the

[1] Viscount Gladstone, 338. As early as 1868 Granville (who knew the Queen well and was then in high favour with her) thought that Disraeli 'was not above using the Queen's feelings as an instrument of party warfare'. (Guedalla, i. 45). It is interesting to contrast the different ways in which Disraeli and Gladstone spoke of each other in writing to the Queen. Thus the former, for example, says of the latter: 'In a rhetorical point of view he surpassed himself; as a statesman, he threw off the mask. . . .' (*L.* v. 340–1 (10.vii.74), Disraeli to Queen), while Gladstone, for example, says: 'Mr. Disraeli was particularly happy and effective in the tone of banter which he frequently employs' (Guedalla, i. 281 (1–2.v.71), Gladstone to Queen). It is not, of course, suggested that the contrast between these two sentences by itself conclusively proves that Disraeli did poison the Queen's mind against Gladstone; but it does seem clear enough that at Court he was not as scrupulously fair to him as, say, Peel was to Russell (cf. above, p. 41).

[2] Viscount Gladstone, 338; also quoted in Guedalla, ii. 39.

[3] Viscount Gladstone, xxii.

[4] Viscount Gladstone, 320. Sir John Marriott (*Queen Victoria and her Ministers*, 145) says that Viscount Gladstone has 'conspicuously failed to prove that the Queen's "newborn dislike of Mr. Gladstone" was due to the malign influence of Lord Beaconsfield'. But Sir John in his turn conspicuously fails to disprove Lord Gladstone's statements. Indeed, apparently he does not even attempt to do so.

contrary. In 1880 and subsequently, apart from certain peculiarities of style, the letters, in tone and character, might have been written by another person, so great is the contrast.'[1]

Viscount Gladstone's clear and confident judgement of the cause, the influence of Beaconsfield, and the moment, 1876, of the Queen's estrangement from Gladstone, finds confirmation in a letter written by Lady Ponsonby to her husband in 1878:

'I *do* think Dizzy has worked the idea of personal government to its logical conclusion, and the seed was sown by Stockmar and the Prince. While they lived, the current of public opinion, especially among the Ministers, kept the thing between bounds, but they established the superstition in the Queen's mind about her own prerogative, and we who know her, know also perfectly how that superstition, devoid as it is of even a shadow of real political value, can be worked by an unscrupulous Minister to his advantage and the country's ruin. If there comes a real collision between the Queen and the House of Commons (say, for instance, that the country insists on Gladstone for the next Liberal Prime Minister) it is quite possible she would turn restive, *dorlotée* as she has been by Dizzy's high-sounding platitudes, and then her reign will end in a fiasco *or* she prepares one for the Prince of Wales; for I do think in a tussle of that sort, and I do hope and pray it should be so, that the People win the day.'[2]

It is now time to begin a narrative account of the relations between Gladstone and the Queen. It is interesting to note that the first time there is in the *Letters* a faint breath of criticism of Gladstone, it is over a question of policy, when he proposed public examination as a form of selection for the Civil Service.[3] But it is clear enough that in these early years the Queen and Gladstone were good friends. Indeed the Queen and the Prince were largely

[1] Viscount Gladstone, 321.
[2] *Mary Ponsonby*, 144 (M. E. P. to H. F. P, 5.xi.78).
[3] *L.* iii. 10–11 (7.ii.54), Queen to Gladstone.

responsible for Gladstone's being made Chancellor of the Exchequer in 1852 in preference to Sir James Graham.[1] In March, 1862, there is an entry in the Journal: '. . . saw Mr. Gladstone for a little while, who was very kind and feeling,'[2] and it was, perhaps, after this interview that Dean Wellesley wrote to him: 'Of all her ministers she seemed to me to think that you had most entered into her feelings, and she dwelt especially upon the manner in which you had parted from her.'[3]

There were, of course, differences of opinion. In 1864, when Palmerston opposed a project of Gladstone's for a reduction of military expenditure, the Queen read the relevant correspondence and said that she 'must express her cordial and unqualified approval of every word said by Lord Palmerston'[4]. The Queen was always, on principle, opposed to projects of that kind. In 1865 we find Palmerston reporting to the Queen that 'Mr. Gladstone has been as troublesome and wrong-headed as he often is upon subjects discussed in Cabinet'[5]. But this adverse judgement apparently had no lasting influence on the Queen's mind, as the very next year she writes: 'The Queen cannot conclude without expressing to Mr. Gladstone her gratification at the accounts she hears from all sides of the admirable manner in which he has commenced his leadership in the House of Commons.'[6]

A new situation arose in 1868 with Gladstone's reso-

[1] *L.* ii. 421 (22.xii.52), Memorandum by Prince Albert.

[2] *L.* iv. 26 (19.iii.62), Journal.

[3] Guedalla, i. 22 (24.iii.62), Dean Wellesley to Gladstone. To this seemingly high appreciation of Gladstone's sympathy the reservation must be made that at that time Disraeli was not a minister. If the sentence had begun: 'Of all her friends and acquaintances . . .', perhaps it could not have ended in the same way.

[4] *L.* iv. 243 (27.xi.64), Queen to Palmerston.

[5] Ibid. 248 (20.i.65), Palmerston to Queen.

[6] Morley, ii. 119 (19.ii.66), Queen to Gladstone.

lutions for the disestablishment of the Irish Church. About one of these Disraeli, who was then Prime Minister, wrote:

'The third and most violent resolution is an Address to the Crown, praying your Majesty to place at the disposal of Parliament your Majesty's interest in the temporalities of the [Irish] Church. Mr. Disraeli cannot say at present whether there be any precedent for such a dealing with the prerogative, but, if so, it must be in the time of the Long Parliament.'[1]

It was about this time too that Gathorne Hardy 'dined with the Queen who is . . . very anti-Gladstonian. . . . She is clearly alarmed at what is going on, and at dinner spoke to me strongly about her Coronation Oath.'[2]

These resolutions prepared the ground for Gladstone's accession to office. He received from Dean Wellesley a letter of friendly advice, under several heads:

'1st. I know that the Queen has a great regard for you, and believes you to be attached to her & anxious to consult her wishes & comfort, as far as is possible, so that you need have no fear but that you will be received at the outset with the greatest cordiality personally.

'2. She differs however from you on the question of Disestablishment & will probably tell you so frankly. . . .

'3. . . . The F.O.—Upon this you may expect to find repugnance as to some individual whom you may possibly propose. . . . She does not seem to me to object even to advanced Liberals in the Cabinet. But with the F[oreign] Minister next to the Premier, she has intimate personal relations.[3]

'4. Everything depends upon your manner of approaching the Queen. Her nervous susceptibility has much increased since

[1] *L.* iv. 517 (23.iii.68), Disraeli to Queen.

[2] *Gathorne Hardy, First Earl of Cranbrook, A Memoir*, by A. E. Gathorne-Hardy (London, 1910), i. 274 (7.iv.68) Diary.

[3] The Queen struggled very hard to avoid having to take Lord Clarendon as Foreign Secretary: cf. *L.* iv. 555–66.

you had to do with her before & you cannot show too much regard, gentleness, I might even say tenderness towards Her.'[1]

Gladstone answered:

'. . . indeed few things would be more painful to me than the thought in retrospect that I could at any time have caused H.M. one moment of gratuitous pain or trouble. Next you may rely upon it that I do not require even your assurance as to the cordial support which the Queen gives to her ministry. Who could suppose that H.M. could now change the unbroken practice of thirty years?'[2]

The time was to come when Gladstone was often to have the thought in retrospect that he had caused the Queen pain and trouble, and the unbroken practice of thirty years was to be changed. But for the first three years of his first ministry 'he gave almost unfailing satisfaction to his sovereign. Their harmony from 1868 to 1871 was notable and rarely interrupted.'[3]

There were, of course, as before, differences, and very acute differences, of opinion. On the Bill for the disestablishment of the Irish Church the Queen commented: 'Mr. Gladstone knows that the Queen has always regretted that he should have thought himself compelled to raise this question as he has done: and still more that he should have committed himself to so sweeping a measure.'[4] But in the same letter she ends by offering him her assistance, and though she thus made no secret of her own personal opinion of the measure, she worked hard to prevent its causing a collision between the two Houses of Parliament. With this end in view she succeeded in arranging for an interview to take place between Gladstone and the Arch-

[1] Guedalla, i. 47 (27.xi.68), Dean Wellesley to Gladstone.
[2] Ibid. 48 (29.xi.68), Gladstone to Dean Wellesley.
[3] Ibid. 24.
[4] *L.* iv. 578 (31.i.69), Queen to Gladstone.

bishop of Canterbury (Tait) before the Bill was even introduced.[1] The value of this interview was that the Archbishop found the proposals which the Prime Minister then unfolded to him to be so much more moderate than he had anticipated that his opposition from that moment ceased to be uncompromising. His policy for the House of Lords then became to accept the second reading and press for amendments in committee. In a letter to the Queen he pointed out that the question of whether the second reading would be carried depended largely on whether Granville in moving it would indicate that amendments would be respectfully considered: 'The Archbishop cannot doubt . . . that any representation from your Majesty would make it almost impossible for him to avoid adopting this wise and conciliatory tone.'[2] We do find two days later these words from the Queen to Granville: '. . . Lord de Grey is writing to him upon a subject of the gravest importance, and she cannot sufficiently express her anxious hope, that Lord Granville will do *all* he *can* to enable the moderate Conservatives to *prevail*.'[3] Meanwhile the Archbishop had thought it right to 'mention' to Disraeli 'that I have had communications from the Queen, in which Her Majesty expresses the strong hope that the Irish Church Bill may be allowed to pass the second reading in the House of Lords, with a view to its being amended'[4]. After this it is only right to find the Archbishop writing in his diary that '. . . thanks to the Queen, a collision between the Houses has been averted'[5]. The whole incident is interesting as an illustration of the

[1] *Life of Archibald Campbell Tait*, Archbishop of Canterbury, by R. T. Davidson and W. Benham (London, 1891), ii. 9.

[2] Davidson and Benham, ii. 27 (7.vi.69), Tait to Queen.

[3] *L.* iv. 605 (9.vi.69), Queen to Granville.

[4] Davidson and Benham, ii. 27 (8.vi.69), Tait to Disraeli.

[5] Ibid. 42 (25.vii.69).

technique of successful royal mediation between Lords and Commons.

Of the Irish Land Bill the Queen said: 'The only thing the Queen would wish to remark is, the apparent want of sympathy with the landlords.'[1] But that, as Mr. Guedalla has already pointed out, is apt to be the fashion of Land Bills.

The first definite breach between the Queen and Gladstone took place in the summer of 1871. On account of a wave of criticism of the monarchy which will be described later, Gladstone, with the best interests of the monarchy at heart, and acting in accordance with the advice which General Grey had so frequently given, tried—and failed—to persuade her to postpone her departure to Balmoral till the close of the session.[2] Out of such a molehill she was always ready to make a mountain, and the kind of mountain which seemingly no amount of faith could ever have moved. She even took the occasion to threaten the Lord Chancellor with her abdication: 'She must solemnly repeat that unless her ministers support her and state the whole truth she cannot go on and must give her heavy burden up to younger hands.'[3]

> 'We have done all we can [wrote Gladstone to Ponsonby]. She will decide. Of course, if challenged, I shall take the responsibility. But this shield will not wear very long. The whole business is one of the most deplorable I have ever known. . . . And yet the woes of fancy are as real in their consequences as, and far more truly formidable than, the most fearful dispensations of Providence.'[4]

Gladstone was always ready to make reasonable allowance

[1] *L.* v. 7 (29.i.70), Queen to Gladstone.
[2] Cf. above, p. 21 and p. 38, and below pp. 207 ff.
[3] Guedalla, i. 300 (10.viii.71), Queen to Lord Hatherley.
[4] Ibid. 303 (14.viii.71), Gladstone to Ponsonby.

for the Queen's neurasthenia.[1] But he could not help saying

'Upon the whole I think it has been the most sickening piece of experience which I have had during near forty years of public life. *Worse* things may easily be imagined: but smaller and meaner causes for the decay of Thrones cannot be conceived. It is like the worm which bores the bark of a noble oak tree and so breaks the channel of its life.'[2]

The situation was complicated by Disraeli's coming out with a speech in defence of the Queen's seclusion.[3] To Gladstone it savoured of his 'usual flunkeyism. Its natural operation will be to increase her bias against visible public duties . . . he says what is in some part absurdly untrue. The bulk of Her Majesty's official work is certainly not large.'[4]

The next month Gladstone was invited to Balmoral. For some days the Queen said she was not well enough to see him. At last he was received, and he describes the interview thus: 'The repellent power which she so well knows how to use has been put in action towards me on this occasion for the first time since the formation of the Government. I have felt myself on a new and different footing with her.'[5] And, after all this, in January of the next year the Queen gaily announces that she proposes 'to run across to Baden!'[6]

From the character of his reception at Balmoral Gladstone drew a moral:

'On account of her natural and constant kindness as well as her position, I am grieved; and this much the more because of what is to come. For the question [of the royal seclusion]

[1] Cf. below, pp. 197–8.
[2] Guedalla, i. 304 (16.viii.71), Gladstone to Ponsonby.
[3] It is extensively quoted in Monypenny and Buckle, ii. 483–4.
[4] Guedalla, i. 71–2 (28.ix.71), Gladstone to Mrs. Gladstone.
[5] Ibid. 70 (1.x.71), Gladstone to Granville.
[6] Ibid. 327 (18.i.72), Queen to Gladstone.

gathers in gravity. . . . And an instinct tells me, that much will have to be said about it ere long; more probably with reference to putting forward the Prince of Wales, than to forcing duty upon her against which she sets herself with such vehemence and tenacity.'[1]

On this occasion Gladstone also was among the prophets, for in the next year a protracted controversy about employing the Prince of Wales to represent the Crown in Dublin caused an even more serious breach than had the incident of 1871.[2]

But in 1873 Granville was able to report of Gladstone's visit to Balmoral that the Queen 'had never known you so remarkably agreeable'[3], and towards the end of his first ministry 'possibly the half-seen prospect of an early parting eased their relations'[4]. Certainly in the ministerial crisis of that year the Queen showed herself completely impartial as between Gladstone and Disraeli.[5]

When, finally, in 1874 the latter found himself faced by a Front Bench consisting of a 'row of exhausted volcanoes' and the first Gladstone ministry came to an end, the Queen in her account of a discussion at the final interview of the causes of the fall of that Government did indeed write: 'I could, of course, not tell him that it was greatly owing to his own unpopularity, and to the want of confidence people had in him,'[6] but Gladstone wrote in his diary: 'I was with the Queen at Windsor for three-quarters of an hour, and nothing could be more frank, natural and kind, than her manner throughout.'[7]

[1] Guedalla, i. 71 (1.x.71), Gladstone to Granville.

[2] Ibid. 25.

[3] Ibid. 81 (20.ix.73), Granville to Gladstone.

[4] Ibid.

[5] See the account in Sir Frederick Ponsonby's *Sidelights on Queen Victoria*, 88–117.

[6] *L.* v. 318 (17.ii.74), Memorandum.

[7] Morley, ii. 274 (17.ii.74) Gladstone's diary.

He noted, however, 'a letter from the Queen which seemed . . . of scant kindness'[1].

Perhaps this is the right place for a passing reference to an incident which looms large in most text-books of constitutional history, the abolition of Army Purchase by Royal Warrant in 1871. It was an incident more spectacular in character than genuinely indicative of the place of the Crown in the Constitution. The idea that it was one of the causes of the breach between the Queen and Gladstone is disposed of by Morley: 'It has been said or implied that this proceeding was forced imperiously upon the Queen. I find no evidence of this. In the language of Lord Halifax, the minister in attendance . . . the Queen "made no sort of difficulty in signing the warrant" after the case had been explained.'[2] The truth very likely was that the Queen's feelings were divided. On the one hand, she looked with disfavour on the idea of abolishing Army Purchase; on the other hand, she relished the opportunity for an exhibition of her royal power, and the latter feeling triumphed.

The precise constitutional significance of the method of the abolition is sufficiently explained in the Minute of the Cabinet which the Queen demanded and obtained in order that the position might be regularized:

'By the Act of 1809, Purchase became penal, except so far as "fixed regulations made, or to be made, by the Crown". Therefore, for the purpose of abolishing Purchase, nothing more was required than that the Crown should be advised to cancel the existing regulations, and all purchases of commissions would at once become illegal.'[3]

[1] Guedalla, i. 84 (14.ii.74), Gladstone's diary. In this connexion there is perhaps a significance in the omission at the end of the Queen's letter to Gladstone in *L.* v. 317 (14.ii.74).

[2] Morley, ii. 277.

[3] *L.* v. 153 (19.vii.71), Minute of Cabinet. Dicey made great play with this incident to illustrate his point that 'The prerogatives of the Crown have become the privileges of the people . . .' (*Law of the Constitution*, 462–3).

In 1874 Disraeli had at last climbed to the 'top of the greasy pole', and in his old age was for the first time Prime Minister with the support of a parliamentary majority. When in 1875 Gladstone visited Windsor he found the Queen 'kind as usual, but evidently under restraint with me'.[1] But in the first two years of Disraeli's ministry the Queen's criticisms of Gladstone are still of a comparatively moderate and restrained character. Take two examples. In August she writes with reference to the Public Worship Regulation Bill, which, as will be seen later, Disraeli was pushing through Parliament directly at her instigation and at first probably against his own better judgement:[2] 'Mr. Disraeli has had a most difficult task, and has managed it with that tact and temper for which he is so remarkable. She is sorry to see how unwise and unprotestant a line Mr. Gladstone has taken.'[3] This would seem to be the first direct comparison between the two statesmen to Gladstone's disadvantage that appears in the *Letters*, and it is worth remarking that the Queen does not hesitate to make such comparisons to a third person. Again in 1875, for example, with reference to the purchase of the Suez Canal shares, she writes: 'It is *entirely* the doing of Mr. Disraeli. . . . His mind is so much greater, larger, and his apprehension of things great and small so much quicker than that of Mr. Gladstone.'[4] But this is still to criticize Gladstone in much the same tone as she had used on many former occasions.

Viscount Gladstone fixes the first overt sign of a complete change of attitude on the part of the Queen to Gladstone precisely at February 2, 1877, when in a letter

[1] Guedalla, i. 85 (9.vii.75), Gladstone's diary.
[2] See below, p. 135.
[3] *L.* v. 351 (6.viii.74), Queen to Archbishop Tait.
[4] Ibid. 428 (26.xi.75), Queen to Mr. Theodore Martin.

to Beaconsfield she says: '[Sir H. G. Elliot][1] is perfectly astounded at Mr. Gladstone, his wildness, folly, and fury!'[2] But it might be said that here she is only reporting Sir H. Elliot's opinion, and two months previously there is an even more striking example of the use of the wildly abusive language which was in the future to be so regularly employed when the Queen had anything to say about Gladstone. In December, 1876, Gladstone's attitude to Russia (and specifically not that of Hartington and Granville) is condemned as unpatriotic and disloyal.[3] The Queen ends her letter by consenting to open Parliament in person, which throughout her widowhood was always a sign of her special favour. She never saw Gladstone's *Bulgarian Horrors and the Question of the East* as in the line of direct logical succession to his *Two Letters to the Earl of Aberdeen on the State Prosecution of the Neapolitan Government.*

From this time onwards the flow of adverse comment, heavily underlined, is never checked, but it is worthy of extensive quotation. The Queen held Gladstone directly responsible for the War in the Near East: 'I wish . . . to state *solemnly*, that I know that this war . . . *would* have been *prevented*, had Russia not been *encouraged* in the strongest manner by the extraordinary, and, to me, *utterly* incomprehensible, agitation carried on by some Members, and especially by one, of my late Government . . .'[4] This view had been formed before Colonel Wellesley,[5] a British Military Attaché at the Tsar's headquarters, described the Emperor of Russia as being 'most

[1] Sir H. G. Elliot had been British Plenipotentiary at the conference at Constantinople the previous year, and was Ambassador at Vienna at the time of the incident of Gladstone's unauthorized visit to Copenhagen. Cf. below, p. 74, n. 2.

[2] Viscount Gladstone, 326 (14.ii.77), Queen to Beaconsfield.

[3] *L.* v. 504 (18.xii.76), Queen to Beaconsfield.

[4] Ibid. 538 (4.vi.77), Queen to the Duke of Argyll.

[5] For his secret mission, see below, pp. 161–2.

unhappy . . . that he had been forced into it. Gortchakoff and Ignatieff were the promoters, and the Empress and Mr. Gladstone's attitude the chief causes in bringing it about.'[1] That the Queen should have found that attitude '*utterly* incomprehensible' is a revealingly ingenuous touch. But the Queen's hostility to Gladstone was not confined to comment only. It seems that he was omitted from the list of those invited to the wedding of the Duke of Connaught and Princess Louise Marguerite of Prussia.[2]

Finally, in September, 1879, when a dissolution seemed imminent, the Queen writes to the Marchioness of Ely, who was an intimate friend, one of those letters to her which are so valuable on account of their complete frankness. It must be quoted almost in its entirety:

'I wish it were possible for Sir H. Ponsonby to *get at some* of the *Opposition*, and to point *out* the *extreme danger* of binding themselves by foolish, violent declarations about their policy beforehand. I hope and trust the Government will be able to go on after the Election, as change is so disagreeable and so bad for the country; but, if it should *not*, I wish the *principal* people of the Opposition should *know* there *are certain* things which *I never can* consent to.

1. Any lowering of the position of this country by letting Russia have her way in the East, or by letting down our Empire in India and in the Colonies. This *was* done under Mr. Gladstone, quite *contrary* to Lord Palmerston's *policy* . . .[3]

[1] *L.* v. 560 (8.viii.77), Journal.

[2] Esher, i. 59 (14.iii.79), Journal: 'Mrs. Gladstone introduced the topic of the Royal wedding which had taken place in the morning and to which Mr. Gladstone had not been invited, in spite of a private remonstrance to the Queen through Dizzy.' Cf. also Lord Askwith's *Lord James of Hereford* (Benn, 1930), 92–6, where Lord James complains of social discrimination on the part of royalty, consistently maintained till 1891, on account of his opposition to the Royal Titles Bill. It is only fair to add that the Queen herself is not directly charged with adopting this discriminating attitude.

[3] It is interesting to observe the way in which the Queen's old hostility to Palmerston is forgotten in new hostility to Gladstone; in effect she now supports a policy of Palmerstonian imperialism.

2. That I would never give way about *the Scotch Church*, which is the real and true stronghold of Protestantism. . . .

'I never could take Mr. Gladstone or Mr. Lowe[1] as my Minister again, for I never COULD have the slightest *particle* of confidence in Mr. Gladstone *after* his violent, mischievous, and dangerous conduct for the last three years, nor could I take the *latter* after the very offensive language he used three years ago against *me*.[2]

'Sir H. Ponsonby has so many Whig friends that he might easily *get* these things *known*. In former days *much* good was done by Baron Stockmar and Mr. Anson[3] paving the way *for* future arrangements and *preventing* complications at the moment, like Sir R. Peel's failure in '39 about the Ladies. Ever yours affectionately, V. R. & I.

'I never *could* take Sir C. Dilke as a *minister*.'[4]

In 1880 the dreaded change of government took place. Gladstone had in 1874 given out that he was retiring from politics, and consequently was no longer the official leader of the Liberal party. But he had been unable to restrain himself from descending again into the political arena at the time of the Eastern Crisis with his campaign against the 'unspeakable Turk': 'Preserved in the Octagon is a large packet of notes on *Future Retribution*, and on them is the docket, "*From this I was called away to write on Bulgaria*".'[5] The crux of the situation in 1880 was grasped by the Duke of Connaught: 'I am afraid, from what I can hear and from what I read in different papers, that

[1] On three subsequent occasions the Queen did have, with great reluctance, to accept Gladstone as her Prime Minister. Lowe never took office again.

[2] The reference is to Lowe's attitude to the Royal Titles Act, by which the Queen became Empress of India. Cf. below, p. 174, n. 4.

[3] Private Secretary to the Prince Consort, 1839–49.

[4] *L.* vi. 47 (21.ix.79), Queen to the Marchioness of Ely. [5] Morley, ii. 416.

Mr. Gladstone is more popular among the Liberals and Radicals than ever, in fact they are mad about him.'[1] Nevertheless the Queen did all in her power to avoid taking him as Prime Minister:

'What the Queen is especially anxious to have impressed on Lords Hartington and Granville is, firstly, that Mr. Gladstone *she* could have nothing to do with, for she considers his whole conduct since '76[2] to have been one series of violent, passionate invective against and abuse of Lord Beaconsfield, and that *he caused* the Russian War . . .'

Simultaneously she announces that

'she wishes, however, to support the new Government and to show them confidence, as she has hitherto done all her Governments, but that *this must entirely depend* on their conduct. There must be no democratic leaning, no attempt to change the Foreign policy (and the Continent are terribly alarmed), no change in India, no hasty retreat from Afghanistan and *no* cutting down of estimates. In short *no lowering* of the *high position* this country holds, and *ought always* to hold.'[3]

She sent for Hartington, but he 'saw the Queen alone and told her plainly that Mr. Gladstone and no other could form a Government'.[4]

Incidentally it is interesting to note that Lord Hartington also 'said that if *he* were to succeed it would be a more Radical Government than one formed by Mr. Gladstone, as *he* would have to give the lion's share to the Radicals, whereas Mr. Gladstone's Government would be predominantly Whig'[4]. It must have been an extremely

[1] *L.* vi. 79 (11.iv.80), Duke of Connaught to Queen.

[2] Cf. above, p. 54. Here is an admission on the Queen's part that the breach came in 1876, and an admission that it was connected with Beaconsfield, though the Queen sees Gladstone denigrating Beaconsfield and not Beaconsfield denigrating Gladstone. But, of course, in access to the Queen's mind, Beaconsfield between 1876 and 1880 was in a position of advantage.

[3] *L.* vi. 75 (8.iv.80), Queen to Ponsonby.

[4] Esher, i. 69 (April, 1880), Journal.

painful dilemma to have to choose between Radicalism and Mr. Gladstone, when both were disliked so intensely.

Gladstone seems to have thought that the Queen, in sending first for Hartington and not for Granville, had made a minor constitutional mistake. He saw Hartington just after his return from Windsor and wrote in his diary: 'I could not find that she expressed clearly her reason for appealing to him *as a* responsible leader of the party, and yet going past *the* leader of the party, namely Granville. . . .'[1] The Queen's attitude was the more surprising as she had previously written to Granville: '. . . she looks on *him*, and on him *only*, as the real leader of the Liberal party, and on whosoever is chosen as leader of the Liberal party in the House of Commons as under him. Upon *this* head there *can* and *must* be no doubt.'[2] Similarly she later told Sir Stafford Northcote 'that *she* will look on [him] as the Leader of the great Conservative Party, though it may not be necessary to *announce* this *now*. . . .'[3] When that letter was written Salisbury had been elected leader in the Lords, and it was he whom eventually in 1885 she commanded to form a Ministry.[4]

In 1876 Disraeli had described how—it was surely very gracious of him—'I said a good word for Granville and Harty-Tarty [specifically not Gladstone, note]—to whom, I was sure, she might look, if necessary, with confidence.'[5] But four years later one of his lieutenants reports how she '. . . expressed a decided preference for Lord Hartington over Lord Granville. I remarked that the latter was

[1] Morley, ii. 471 (22.iv.80), Gladstone's diary.

[2] *L.* v. 379 (31.i.75), Queen to Granville.

[3] *L.* vi. 219 (15.v.81), Queen to Sir Stafford Northcote.

[4] In 1923, on the resignation of Mr. Bonar Law, Mr. Baldwin was sent for by the King and was only subsequently elected Leader of the Conservative Party.

[5] Monypenny and Buckle, ii. 979 (16.xii.76), Disraeli to Lady Bradford.

the older, and more experienced: but H.M. said she . . . thought he would be too pliable to Radical influence . . .'[1] A wise doctor prescribes in accordance with his patient's whims, and Beaconsfield proceeded to recommend Hartington on the ground that 'he was in his heart a conservative'[2]—in itself a curious recommendation for a Liberal statesman.

Mr. Guedalla suggests that 'Gladstone in 1880 was almost as lost as Palmerston in 1846'[3]. The meaning of this suggestion would seem to be that during Palmerston's spell out of office between 1841 and 1846 the Queen whom Mr. Guedalla dubs 'Victoria I', Melbourne's Queen Victoria, gay and young, disappeared and 'Victoria II' reigned in her stead, the Queen who was the earnest and high-minded wife of Prince Albert; that similarly during Gladstone's years in opposition, 1874–80, 'Victoria II' was superseded by 'Victoria III', a creature of Beaconsfield's creation, and that Gladstone, who had been accustomed to 'Victoria II', knew not 'Victoria III'.

But Gladstone had to some extent been warned of the changed attitude of the Court. In a memorandum dated May 28, 1878, and marked 'Secret' he writes:

'Yesterday I saw Carnarvon, whose conversation was remarkable . . . what I wish particularly to record [is a statement] given in the strictest confidence, which shows how little at present within the royal precinct liberty is safe. . . . It happened repeatedly not only that Cabinet Ministers have been sent for to receive "wiggings" from the Queen—which as he said it is their affair and fault if they allow to impair their independence—but communications have from time to time been made to the Cabinet warning it off from certain subjects and saying she could not agree to this and would not agree to that. . . . I said

[1] Monypenny and Buckle, ii. 1404 (9.iv.80), Sir Michael Hicks Beach to Beaconsfield. [2] Ibid. 1406 (18.iv.80), Memorandum by the Queen.
[3] Guedalla, i. 16.

it recalled James II and the Bill of Rights to which he assented. It is at any rate a position much more advanced than that of George III, who I apprehend limited himself to a case of consistency with the Coronation Oath. But that controversy was decided once for all when George IV after a terrible struggle agreed to the Roman Catholic Emancipation Bill. I said that such an outrage as this was wholly new, totally unknown in every Cabinet in which I had served; and that the correspondence must be regarded as due to Lord Beaconsfield, which he entirely felt.'[1]

Sir John Marriott, who points out that '. . . the general election of 1880 was in fact a plebiscite for Mr. Gladstone', says 'small wonder that the Queen's reception of a Minister thus forced upon her by the Electorate should have been something less than cordial.'[2] It seems a strange doctrine that a constitutional monarch is entitled to resent the popularity of a prominent statesman. Mr. Bolitho very fairly 'reiterates the dismal and appalling incidents [of the Land War in Ireland] only to impress upon the reader the weight of Mr. Gladstone's burden'[3] at this time as an excuse for alleged failures in foreign policy. Mr. Hammond probably comes nearer the mark than any of these three when he says that after 1880: 'Just as Gladstone could not think of Disraeli without thinking of his treatment of Peel, so the Queen could not think of Gladstone without thinking of his treatment of Disraeli'[4]. In 1841, when Melbourne went out and Peel came in, the Queen was young and flexible, with a wise husband at her side to assist and advise her. In 1880 when Beaconsfield went out and Gladstone came in, the Queen was old, obstinate, opinionated, and entirely dependent on her own judgement. The results were disastrous. In 1880, though less successful, she was as anxious to avoid taking Gladstone

[1] Viscount Gladstone, 141–2. [2] *Queen Victoria and her Ministers*, 158.
[3] Bolitho, 208. [4] In *The Contemporary Review*, April, 1934.

as Prime Minister as she had been to avoid taking Peel at the time of the Bedchamber Crisis in 1839. To Lord Beaconsfield she wrote: 'My great hope and belief is, that this shamefully heterogeneous union—out of mere folly—will separate into many parts very soon, and that the Conservatives will come in stronger than ever in a short time. Possibly a coalition first.'[1] Gladstone was soon to assert that 'he would never be surprised to see her turn the Government out, after the manner of her uncles'. But his audience thought this 'the impulsive side of his character. . . .'[2]

It was in fact during Gladstone's second ministry from 1880 to 1885 that the zenith of the Queen's hostility to him was reached. She had never before been so hostile as she was then, nor indeed was she in the years to follow much less hostile. She made no secret of this hostility,[3] she was quick to seize on any suspicion of a suggestion that he was likely to retire,[4] and she had as little to do with him personally as possible: 'I *never* write except on formal *official* matters to the Prime Minister!', she told Beaconsfield, and '. . . [I] see as little of those I *cannot* unfortunately have *confidence in* as possible'[5]. She enumerates those of the Cabinet whom she invited to stay at Balmoral as the Duke of Argyll and Lords Spencer, Dufferin, Granville, and Hartington.[6] The last named at this time found the Queen 'very gracious' but she

[1] Monypenny and Buckle, ii. 1399–1400 (9.iv.80), Queen to Beaconsfield. 'Possibly a coalition first,' cf. below, pp. 90 ff.

[2] Esher, i. 74 (19.ix.80), Journal.

[3] e.g. *L.* vi. 303 (25.vi.82), Journal: 'I told [Lord Hartington] I wished he were at the head of the Government, instead of Mr. Gladstone.'

[4] Ibid. 262 (16.ii.82), Journal; 363 (29.xi.82), Granville to Queen; 399 (20.i.83), Queen to Granville.

[5] Ibid. 143 and 144 (20.ix.80), Queen to Beaconsfield.

[6] Very different from this had been the state of affairs in 1874. When the question arose then as to who was to be Minister in Attendance at Bal-

avoided 'discussing the subject of Kandahar with him, and he has hitherto failed to make her talk. He fears she is getting into the habit of avoiding the discussion of subjects with her ministers which are unpalatable to her.'[1] Such a policy of not 'having things out' could serve only to create an atmosphere of suspicion and mistrust. It is hard to believe that under these circumstances Gladstone deliberately adopted a retaliatory policy of reserve, but towards the close of the ministry she complains of his letters in a way in which he had a right to complain of hers: '. . . he is so reserved and writes such unsatisfying letters, that the Queen never knows where she is. She does not know *who* takes his or other views (which all his predecessors kept her informed of) and she is left powerless to *judge* of the state of affairs!'[2]

Well might Gladstone in 1881 say: 'She is as ever perfect in her courtesy but as to confidence she holds me now at arm's length;'[3] and again: 'much civility . . . but I am always outside an iron ring, and without any desire, had I the power, to break it through.'[4] In 1883: ' "The Queen alone", he said fiercely, "is enough to kill any man". I could not help laughing at his manner [it is Rosebery who tells this tale], but he said, "This is no laughing matter, though it may sound so. . . ." '[5] Gladstone was all too conscious of the state of the Queen's feelings towards him, and a letter from Lord Granville shows that he did his best to spare them: 'Lord Granville remembers Mr. Gladstone once mentioning to him a

moral, the Queen said that 'all her Ministers were agreeable to her'. Zetland, i. 78 (2.v.75), Disraeli to Lady Chesterfield.

[1] Esher, i. 77 (9.x.80), Journal.

[2] *L.* vi. 643 (28.iv.85), Queen to Granville.

[3] Guedalla, ii. 39 (16.vii.81), Gladstone's diary.

[4] Ibid. (30.xi.81), Gladstone's diary.

[5] Crewe's *Rosebery*, 165 (5.i.83), Rosebery's diary.

feeling of delicacy he had, and a dread lest your Majesty should feel, on account of his official position, an obligation to receive him socially, more than your Majesty would otherwise desire.'[1]

But the Queen did not show the same consideration for him. In September, 1883, while he was enjoying a holiday in the form of a sea cruise, a sudden decision was taken to go to Copenhagen, where at the time the Tsar of Russia and the King of Greece happened to be staying. Gladstone thereby broke the rule that a Prime Minister may not set foot on foreign soil without the royal permission, and the Queen's indignation was great: 'The Prime Minister—and especially one *not* gifted with prudence in speech—is not a person who can go about *where* he likes with impunity. . . . The Queen must say she is very indignant.'[2] This is extracted from a letter to Granville. Her communication to Gladstone himself made him 'rather angry . . . I should call the letter—for the first time—somewhat unmannerly'[3]. Subsequently he docketed another missive: 'I shall take no notice of this rather foolish letter.'[4]

She was once again indignant when he made a public speech at Ballater: 'The Queen is *utterly* disgusted with his *stump* oratory—so unworthy of his position—almost under her very nose.'[5] His explanation to Ponsonby was:

'I told you in good faith that I hoped to remain silent, or all but silent, to-day, and for the present. But the unbounded enthusi-

[1] *L.* vi. 159 (29.xi.80), Granville to Queen.

[2] Ibid. 440 (18.ix.83), Queen to Granville. The Queen had some justification for a certain anxiety as to the political effects of the visit to Copenhagen, as will be seen from a letter from Sir H. Elliot to Sir H. Ponsonby (Ibid. 444; 23.ix.83), but the degree of her indignation was beyond all reasonable bounds.

[3] Guedalla, ii. 47 (22.ix.83), Gladstone to Granville.

[4] Ibid. 67 (25.v.86), Gladstone to Granville.

[5] *L.* vi. 539 (16.ix.84), Queen to Ponsonby.

asm all along the line made it impossible for me literally to act upon this intention—which I regret in the interest of my chest and otherwise. I moved however (about five or six times) upon the lines of brevity and commonplace.'[1]

A year later his doctors ordered him not to speak on account of throat trouble, and so he refused an invitation to Osborne because he would 'be as a statue among living people'[2]. It is not surprising that this simile 'made Her Majesty smile'. It is a great pity that Gladstone was not more often able to make her smile. But Mr. Guedalla considers that about 1883 there begins to be 'plain evidence of an admission that, where so many of his colleagues were deplorable, she almost needed Mr. Gladstone'[3].

There was an abundance of possible causes of dispute between the Queen and her Cabinet. The Cabinet proposed to bring to an end the occupation of Candahar. The Queen was in favour of its retention, and a remarkable scene occurred on January 5, 1881, when a Council was postponed from about 10 a.m. to 4 p.m., while the Queen telegraphed to Gladstone her objections to the Speech from the Throne, which the Council had been summoned to approve, because it contained an announcement of the abandonment of Candahar. Eventually, a way out of the difficulty was found with the formula that

'The Queen, in approving the Speech generally, commanded the Minister in attendance to convey to the Cabinet her disapproval of that part of the Speech referring to Candahar, and the Queen can only give her assent to the Speech on the express understanding that the Cabinet will give her an assurance that, should circumstances arise rendering the retention of Candahar desirable, the Government will not hesitate to continue to hold that position.'[4]

[1] Guedalla, ii. 299 (15.ix.84), Gladstone to Ponsonby.
[2] Ibid. 379 (15.vii.85), Gladstone to Ponsonby.
[3] Ibid. 45.
[4] *L.* vi. 180 (5.i.81), Memorandum.

'Dreadfully put out [reads the Queen's Journal], they at length came in, after 4. . . . The business was hurriedly gone through, and the Speech approved. I spoke to no one, and the Ministers nearly tumbled over each other going out.'[1]

It is delightful to think of Sir William Harcourt tumbling over Lord Spencer, but they had really carried the day with the threat 'that to disapprove was to eject the Ministry and that, on the eve of the opening of Parliament, was revolution'[2]. In consequence the Speech was approved, and the Queen was left complaining that she had 'never before been treated with such want of respect and consideration in the forty-three and a half years she had worn her thorny crown. . . . Sir Henry cannot overrate the Queen's indignation. Mr. Gladstone tries to be a Bismarck, but the Queen will not be an Emperor William to do anything *he orders*.'[3] Ponsonby said he had never seen her so angry.[4]

Prince Leopold took the occasion to lay down the doctrine that the Speech was that of the Sovereign and not of the Ministers.[5] Lord Beaconsfield began a letter: 'Madam, and most beloved Sovereign,—The principle of Sir W. Harcourt, that the Speech of the Sovereign is only the Speech of the Ministers, is a principle not known to the British Constitution. It is only a piece of Parliamentary gossip.'[6] This was an extraordinary lapse. As early as the reign of Queen Anne, Swift had observed that it was well known 'that Speeches on these occasions

[1] *L.* vi. 178 (5.i.81), Journal.

[2] Ponsonby's *Sidelights*, 144 (5.i.81), Memorandum by Ponsonby.

[3] Ibid. 145 (5.i.81), Queen to Ponsonby. Cf. also A. G. Gardiner's *Life of Sir William Harcourt* (London, 1923), i, Appendix I, 397 ff., for 'Memorandum for Mr. Gladstone by Earl Spencer and Sir W. Harcourt as to what passed at Osborne on January 5th, 1881, relative to the approval by the Queen of the Speech from the Throne'.

[4] Esher, i. 79 (6.i.80), Journal.

[5] Ponsonby, *Sidelights*, 155 (10.i.81), Lord Sydney, Lord Steward, to Ponsonby.

[6] *L.* vi. 181 (11.i.81), Beaconsfield to Queen.

are ever digested by the advice of those who are in the chief confidence, and, consequently, that they are the sentiments of Her Majesty's Ministers, as well as her own'[1]. Wilkes argued that it was commonly understood that the King's Speech was that of his Ministers when in the famous Number 45 of the *North Briton* (1763) he characterized a passage in that year's Speech as 'the most abandoned instance of ministerial effrontery ever attempted to be imposed on mankind'. As late as 1841 criticisms by the Duke of Wellington of the Queen's Speech led Peel to explain that 'the Speech was that of Her Majesty's Ministers, and did not in any way, as the noble Duke said it would, commit the Sovereign to its sentiments'[2].

So much for Candahar. Equally strong was the Queen's objection to the South African policy of her Government, and before the news of the defeat at Majuba she observed that 'Sir Hercules Robinson [Governor of the Cape Colony] considers a concession of everything before a victory has been won would seriously increase our difficulties in S. Africa'[3]. She condemned the release of Parnell and Davitt. When she heard the news of the murder of Lord Frederick Cavendish and Mr. Burke she said that she considered '*this* horrible event the *direct result* of what she has always considered and has stated to Mr. Gladstone and to Lord Spencer as a most fatal and hazardous step'[4]. This comment anticipates the even more emphatic condemnation of Government policy which was soon to follow on the occasion of the death of General Gordon. She disapproved of the second Irish Land Act for the same reason

[1] *The Examiner*, No. 19, Nov. 30 to Dec. 8, 1710; quoted, C. S. Emden's *The People and the Constitution*, (Oxford, 1933), 282.

[2] Quoted, C. S. Emden, 282.

[3] *L.* vi. 197 (20.ii.81), Queen to Lord Kimberley.

[4] Ibid. 285 (7.v.82), Queen to Granville.

that she had disapproved of the first:[1] 'It is much felt that Mr. Gladstone and the Government, but especially the former, have never expressed any sympathy with the terrible position of the landlords. . . .'[2] Madagascar provided an opportunity for a direct snub, followed by a general condemnation: 'As regards Madagascar . . . the Queen has telegraphed what she meant. What she fears is a growing tendency to swallow insults and affronts and not taking them up in that high tone which they used formerly to be. . . .'[3]

The third Reform Bill not only caused a renewal of differences between the two Houses of Parliament, differences which the Queen played a very large part in composing; it also caused yet further differences between the Queen and Gladstone. The way in which the Queen brought about direct negotiations between Gladstone, Salisbury, and Northcote, negotiations which were successful in preventing a collision between the two Houses, is already well known. But for the resulting compromise credit must also be given to Gladstone who was genuinely, almost desperately, anxious to uphold the House of Lords, and who in consequence had to hold in check many of his own followers who were only too anxious to advance to a mass attack on its privileges. Gladstone's own view of the House of Lords was that it was 'a body . . . unhappily opposed to every Liberal administration (except Lord Aberdeen's under which it showed great wisdom). . . .'[4] None the less his policy was not that of 'mend or end', nor even of reform:

'Mr. Gladstone himself, while he has been sharply sensible of the injurious action of the House of Lords upon all Liberal

[1] Cf. above, p. 60.
[2] *L.* vi. 304 (1.vii.82), Queen to Lord Spencer.
[3] Ibid. 451 (30.x.83), Queen to Gladstone.
[4] Guedalla, ii. 129 (28.xii.80), Gladstone to Ponsonby.

Governments and legislation during the last quarter of a century, desires not that the House of Lords should be reformed, but that it should use its power with moderation; and he deeply deplores its present attitude because he knows how powerfully it tends to precipitate a great organic question.'[1]

Some examples of the Queen's opinions on this question admirably examplify her political outlook in general. She mistook the main trend of the constitutional changes of her time: '. . . the way in which the present House of Commons is allowed to *dictate* and *arrogate* to itself the *power* of the *executive*, disregarding both *the House of Lords and the Crown*, OUGHT to be *firmly* and *strongly resisted*.'[2] The Queen in fact considered that the legislature was gaining power at the expense of the executive. The actual process was precisely the contrary.[3] She condemned Gladstone because he had 'no feeling but for the House of Commons, and the *Upper House* and Opposition generally *distrust* him so very much. . . . That high-handed dictator style of Mr. Gladstone will *not* do. Such collisions *never* happened in Lord Palmerston's time, nor in Lord John Russell's.'[4] 'The House of Commons after all [she had argued] is only *one* out of the *three* parties in the Constitution so much boasted of . . . and it is greatly to be desired that the Government should *not* send up measures so framed, to the Upper House, that the Lords *cannot conscientiously* agree to them.'[5]

In July, 1884, the Queen thought that—

'According to Mr. Gladstone's observations there ought to be a Radical House of Lords . . . as well as the House of Commons,

[1] Ibid. 288 (23.vii.84), Gladstone to Queen.

[2] *L.* vi. 135–6 (4.ix.80), Queen to Granville.

[3] See, for example, Josef Redlich's classical *Procedure of the House of Commons*, i. 73–212.

[4] *L.* vi. 234 (17.viii.81), Queen to Granville.

[5] Ibid. 229 (7.viii.81), Queen to Gladstone.

so that any radical measure should pass! The Monarchy would be utterly untenable were there *no balance* of power left, *no restraining* power! The Queen will yield to no one in TRUE LIBERAL FEELING, but not to destructive, and she calls upon Mr. Gladstone to *restrain, as he can,* some of his wild colleagues and followers.'[1]

The Queen, of course, was quite right. If the House of Lords were to be abolished, there would be little logical justification left for the continued existence of the hereditary Monarchy.

A little earlier she had announced to Gladstone that

'She will not withhold her assent to his proposal for an Autumn Session to reconsider the Franchise Bill; but in doing so she must express her opinion that it would have been a more fair and judicious course to have dissolved Parliament so as to have obtained the opinion of the country on the questions raised in the House of Lords.'[2]

Soon afterwards she sent to Ponsonby the draft of a further letter to Gladstone:

'The Lords are *not* in disharmony with the people, but unfortunately Mr. Gladstone's Government leans so much to the extreme Radical side, instead of to the sound and moderate portion of his following, that measures are presented to the House of Lords which the Conservatives and moderate Liberals do not feel they can with safety agree to. No one is more truly Liberal in her heart than the Queen, but she has always strongly deprecated the great tendency of the present Government to encourage instead of checking the stream of destructive democracy which has become so alarming. This it is that, she must say justly, alarms the House of Lords and all moderate people. And to threaten the House of Lords that they will bring destruction on themselves is, in fact, to threaten the Monarchy itself. Another Sovereign but herself must acquiesce

[1] *L.* vi. 523 (25.vii.84), Queen to Gladstone.
[2] Ibid. 513 (10.vii.84), Queen to Gladstone.

in any alteration of the House of Lords. She will not be the Sovereign of a Democratic Monarchy.'[1]

Apparently Ponsonby was most successful in moderating this tone, for we find that what actually went was: 'She is sorry that she cannot agree with Mr. Gladstone in his opinion of the House of Lords, which has rendered such important services to the nation, and which at this moment is believed by many to represent the true feeling of the country. The House of Lords is in no way opposed to the people.'[2]

Three days later the Queen made the following notes on the draft of a letter from Ponsonby to Gladstone:

'The points the Queen wishes to impress on both sides, but most on that of the Government, are . . .

'(2) Both parties *must* give way a little and it will never do to *dictate to the House of Lords*, or to threaten. Mr. Gladstone speaks of the growing danger of a conflict, but only *thinks* it is the Conservative Party who do the mischief, whereas the violence and dangerous destructive principles of his *Radical* adherents and even colleagues are just as much to blame as the House of Lords.

'(3) Mr. Gladstone must be prepared for the Queen to hold him responsible for the agitation and danger which may be got up by the extreme Liberals and for her calling on him and insisting on a dissolution as the only safe means of putting a stop to it.

'(4) The Queen wishes Mr. Gladstone, if he finds he cannot get on and will not yield, to be brought to resign, to save the country, and Lord Hartington to take the lead.

'(5) Lord Salisbury and others should be asked what they mean to do to avoid this strife.'[3]

Sir Frederick Ponsonby comments: 'Queen Victoria was under the impression that she was holding the scales evenly between the two parties, but it is evident from

[1] Ponsonby's *Sidelights*, 171 (15.vii.84), Queen to Gladstone (Draft).

[2] *L.* vi. 519 (15.vii.84), Queen to Gladstone.

[3] Ponsonby's *Sidelights*, 184 (18.vii.84), Notes by the Queen on draft letter from Ponsonby to Gladstone.

this that she thought all concessions should come from Mr. Gladstone.'[1] In the Queen's attitude to the House of Lords Gladstone was to see something 'in the nature of an argument for the abolition of the House of Commons: not that she means this but it is what her argument leads to. . . . There is no use in a controversy with her infallibility. . . .'[2]

But the Queen's condemnation of Gladstone was most emphatic and most open on the occasion of the death of Gordon. It was a tragedy which caused a great increase in Gladstone's personal unpopularity and so helped to bring about the fall of his second ministry. There can be little doubt that on this issue the Queen shared the feelings of the majority of her people. In fact, the Gordon episode is a good instance of her possession of a certain sixth sense, which has been the valuable possession of other sovereigns, a sense for knowing what were the thoughts of her subjects.[3]

The question is highly controversial, but it is worth noting that in Mr. Guedalla's view: 'The choice of General Gordon was the first (and perhaps the last) mistake in Mr. Gladstone's policy in the Sudan. After that tragic error the rest was almost bound to follow; and since the fatal consequences left an indelible mark on his relations with the Queen, it may be noted that the initial blunder was committed with her complete approval.'[4] Already Egypt had been the occasion of what was perhaps the strongest condemnation of the Queen which Gladstone is known ever to have put on paper:

'I must own that I think the Queen's resolute attempts to disturb & impede the reduction of the army in Egypt, are (to

[1] Ponsonby's *Sidelights*, 185.

[2] Guedalla, ii. 55 (16.vii.84), Gladstone to Granville.

[3] Cf. below, pp. 245–6.

[4] Guedalla, ii. 53.

use a plain word) intolerable. It is my firm intention not to give in, so far as I am personally concerned, for a moment to proceedings almost as unconstitutional as they are irrational; though the unreasonableness of her ideas is indeed such that it is entitled to the palm in comparison with their other characteristics.'[1]

The Queen foresaw the danger to Gordon as early as February, 1884: 'The Queen trembles for General Gordon's safety. If anything befalls *him*, the result will be awful.'[2] In March she says of a telegram from Baring, asking the Government to reconsider its decision not to allow Gordon to be succeeded by Zebehr: 'This is unanswerable. If this is refused the Queen will *hold* the Government responsible for any sort of misfortune which *will* happen. Parliament should be *told* the truth. . . .'[3] Again, to Sir Henry Ponsonby she says, though she may be referring to the proposal to fix a comparatively short time limit to the British occupation of Egypt as well as to the position of Gordon: 'The conduct of the Government in this Egyptian business is *perfectly miserable*; it is universally condemned; and this weakness and vacillation have made us despised everywhere.'[4] To Lord Hartington she writes: 'Gordon is in danger: you are bound to try and save him. Surely Indian troops might go from Aden; they could bear the climate. You have incurred fearful responsibility.'[5]

Just about a year after these warnings came the news of the fall of Khartoum and Gordon's death. On hearing of the first of these two disasters the Queen's comment in her Journal was: 'The Government is alone to blame,

[1] Guedalla, ii. 43 (4.x.82), Gladstone to Hartington.

[2] *L.* vi. 477 (9.ii.84), Queen to Gladstone.

[3] Ibid. 484 (14.iii.84), Queen to Ponsonby. The objection to Zebehr was that he had been a slave trader.

[4] Ibid. 500 (17.v.84), Queen to Ponsonby.

[5] Ibid. 485 (25.iii.84), Queen to Hartington.

by refusing to send the expedition till it was too late.'[1] Lord Cromer's judgement on this point concurred with the Queen's: 'The Nile expedition was sanctioned too late, and the reason why it was sanctioned too late was that Mr. Gladstone would not accept simple evidence of a plain fact, which was patent to much less powerful intellects than his own.'[2]

But the Queen went very much further than mere comment in her diary. She sent to Gladstone, to Lord Hartington, and to Lord Granville, the following telegram *en clair*: 'These news from Khartoum are frightful, and to think that all this might have been prevented and many precious lives saved by earlier action is too frightful.'[3] The same point is made even more explicit to Sir H. Ponsonby: 'Mr. Gladstone and the Government *have*—the Queen *feels it dreadfully*—Gordon's innocent, noble, heroic blood on their consciences.'[4] But the telegram *en clair* very nearly produced most serious consequences, as the Queen was informed that 'Mr. Gladstone had sent to enquire if the message had been made known by the telegraph clerks to others; and he evidently wished to bring the matter forward again as a question of whether he could remain in office if publicly condemned by the Queen'[5]. The constitutional importance of the whole Gordon episode and the Queen's affixing of responsibility for the disaster on Gladstone lies, therefore, mainly in this, that it opened up the very distinct possibility of a Government resigning, not because it no longer possessed the confidence of the House of Commons, but because

[1] *L.* vi. 597 (5.ii.85), Journal. [2] Cromer's *Modern Egypt*, ii. 17.

[3] *L.* vi. 597 (5.ii.85), T. *en clair* to Gladstone, Hartington, and Granville.

[4] Ibid. 608 (17.ii.85), Queen to Ponsonby.

[5] Ibid. 603 (7.ii.85), Ponsonby to Queen. Referring to this telegram, Gladstone told Morley: '. . . he had resolved never to set foot in Windsor Castle again . . .' (Morley's *Recollections*, i. 278).

it no longer possessed the Crown's confidence. That so late as 1885 there should have been this possibility is a most striking piece of evidence of its continued political power.

A little later the Cabinet showed itself to be against a proposal of Lord Wolseley's that he should be made Governor-General of the Sudan, and at once the Queen telegraphed: 'If you refuse to grant Lord Wolseley's wise suggestion, you run the risk of increasing difficulties and bloodshed. Remember the example of Gordon.'[1] This reminder seems to have had its effect, for Sir Henry Ponsonby is able to report a concession on this point by the Government, which he attributes directly to the pressure brought to bear by the Queen.[2]

Lord Wolseley does not appear to have been very favourably disposed to Gladstone,[3] and perhaps the Queen knew this and took advantage of the fact when she wrote to Lady Wolseley a confidential letter so remarkable for its unconstitutional character that it must be fully quoted:

> '*In strict confidence* I *must* tell you I think the Government are *more incorrigible* than ever, and I do think that your husband should hold *strong* language to them, and *even* THREATEN to resign if he does *not* receive strong support and liberty of action. I have written very strongly to the Prime Minister and others, and I tell *you* this; but it *must never appear*, or Lord Wolseley *ever let out* the *hint* I give *you*. But I really think they *must be frightened*. ... Pray *either* destroy this, or lock it up, but I cannot rest without asking you to tell Lord Wolseley.'[4]

Many examples could be given of remarks on the Government of a generally depreciatory kind. Before

[1] *L.* vi. 613 (26.ii.85), C. T. Queen to Granville.
[2] Ibid. 618 (5.iii.85), Ponsonby to Queen.
[3] Ibid. 630–1 (22.iii.85), Lord Wolseley to Queen.
[4] Ibid. 619 (3.iii.85), Queen to Lady Wolseley.

taking leave of this topic, one of them must serve for all:

'She has no doubt that Lord Granville feels as Lord Palmerston did; who with all his many faults, had the honour and power of his country strongly at heart, and so had Lord Beaconsfield. *But* she does *not* feel that Mr. Gladstone has. Or at least he puts the House of Commons and party *first*; thinking *no doubt* that he *is* doing what is best by keeping this country out of everything and swallowing offences like the conduct of the French at Madagascar.'[1]

Here Gladstone's sincerity at any rate is fully admitted.

The extent of the control over appointments which was exercised by the Queen during this Ministry is of the highest importance. At the moment of its formation she was anxious to know why Mr. Goschen was not included.[2] She accepted the appointments of Lord Ripon as Viceroy and of Lord Selborne as Lord Chancellor only under protest, and made a merit of that.[3] She objected to the appointment of Leonard Courtney as Under-Secretary to the Home Office on the ground that the last appointment of a similar character, that of George Otto Trevelyan as a Civil Lord of the Admiralty, was also of a Radical.

'The position of the Crown, and also of the Prime Minister [Gladstone explained] with regard to these appointments, is peculiar. They are the appointments of the Secretary of State. I learn from Granville that he was sent for by Lord Palmerston, not by Lord Melbourne, when he was made Under Secretary in the Foreign Office. Sir W. Harcourt [the Home Secretary] expressed his wish in this case with a view to the efficient transaction of the difficult business of his office. Had I taken an objection on the ground that Mr. Courtney belonged to the extreme section of the party, he might have said with truth that

[1] *L.* vi. 447 (22.x.83), Queen to Granville.

[2] Guedalla, ii. 88 (27.iv.80), Ponsonby to Gladstone.

[3] Ibid. 93 (30.iv.80), Queen to Gladstone.

it is at the least as necessary to have regard to personal efficiency and activity in selection for secondary offices, as to the sectional position of individuals. . . .'[1]

To most people this would seem to have closed the question. From Queen Victoria came a last word: 'The Queen hopes the next appointment to a place in your Government will be made from the party of the Moderate Liberals.'[2]

The next year there was a remarkable sequel when the Queen objected to Leonard Courtney being transferred to the Under-Secretaryship for the Colonies. On Ponsonby's letter is written:

'To Ld. Gr[anville]
Sir W. H[arcourt]
Ld. K[imberley]

Lord Granville.

I think this intolerable. It is by courtesy only that these appointments are made known to H.M.

W. E. G.'[3]

But during these years it was not only Gladstone who gave trouble to the Queen, it was also his colleagues, and particularly Joseph Chamberlain. She thought him Gladstone's 'evil genius'.[4] However, Chamberlain's desire for a more active policy in Egypt raised her opinion of him: 'Found Mr. Chamberlain very sensible and reasonable about the question of Egypt, which he thought most distressing and almost hopeless. I think him decidedly pleasanter and more unobtrusive in manner than Sir C. Dilke.'[5] But Chamberlain's reputation with the Queen sank again when he made a speech in which he raised the

[1] Ibid. 130–1 (29.xii.80), Gladstone to Ponsonby.
[2] Ibid., ii. 132 (31.xii.80), Ponsonby to Gladstone.
[3] Ibid. 165 (3.viii.81), Ponsonby to Gladstone.
[4] *L.* vi. 298 (21.v.82), Queen to Granville.
[5] Ibid. 485 (15.iii.84), Journal.

question of the 'future prospects' of the House of Lords. To Gladstone this appeared 'to be an isolated expression, due probably to inadvertence, but Mr. Gladstone will, without naming Your Majesty's intervention (unless Your Majesty's pleasure be otherwise) point this out to Mr. Chamberlain. . . .'[1] So far as can be seen Her Majesty's pleasure was not otherwise, so Gladstone was left chivalrously to shield his colleague from knowledge of the source of the reproof he had undertaken to administer. Gladstone, however, simultaneously lays it down as a matter of general principle that in this matter the Queen

> 'gives him credit for power or influence, of which he is desirous that Your Majesty should graciously bear in mind the necessary limitations . . . as all Cabinet Ministers are in a most important sense equals, and all members of the House of Commons have a representative as well as an official character to sustain, it is but a limited and rare power of expostulation that Mr. Gladstone's office allows him to claim.'[2]

But when the Queen continued to remonstrate with him about Chamberlain's speeches his answers became a little sharper: '. . . I have no general jurisdiction over the speeches of my colleagues, and no right to prescribe their tone and colour. When they offend against an assurance which with their authority I have given to the Queen, they then afford me a title to interfere, upon which I have been, I hope, not unduly slow to act.'[3] It was just at this moment that the Queen said of him in a note to Ponsonby: 'He is very shifty about Mr. Chamberlain', and on that ground refused to invite him to a meeting of the Privy Council at Osborne.[4] Her complaints about Chamberlain's speeches continued to fall thick and

[1] Guedalla, ii. 291 (26.vii.84), Gladstone to Queen.
[2] Ibid. 292 (26.vii.84), Gladstone to Queen.
[3] Ibid. 294 (7.viii. 84), Gladstone to Ponsonby.
[4] Ponsonby's *Sidelights*, 187 (8?viii.84).

fast upon Gladstone: 'It is, the Queen thinks, absolutely necessary for the honour of the Govt. that Mr. Gladstone sh$^{d}$ take a firm stand & separate his name from Mr. Chamberlain—with w$^{h}$ unfortunately it is too often wrongly no doubt—connected. Mr. Chamberlain *must* restrain his language—or *not* remain in the Cabinet. In any other Cabinet such freedom of language has not been tolerated.'[1] No wonder that a little later: 'The Queen says she is tired of complaining to you about Mr. Chamberlain's speeches. . . .'[2]

But Gladstone not only denied that he had any general jurisdiction over the speeches of his colleagues, he also denied her right to know what were their individual opinions in Cabinet:

> 'Mr. Gladstone always held that the Queen ought not to be told about dissensions in the Cabinet; that Cabinets existed for the purpose of differing—that is, for the purpose of enabling Ministers who differed to thrash out their differences—and that the Queen was only concerned with the results which were presented to her by, or in the name of, the Cabinet as a whole. This seems reasonable [concludes Dilke] and ought, I think, to be the constitutional view; but the Queen naturally . . . hates to have personal differences going on of which she is not informed. . . .'[3]

Disraeli's practice had been precisely the opposite.[4]

Five years later a letter from Ponsonby shows that the question had been raised once again:

> 'She listened carefully to all I repeated respecting the reporting of the opinions of members of the Cabinet but insisted that most Prime Ministers had fully informed her on the points.
>
> 'When I told her about Lord Palmerston she said it was true

[1] *L.* vi. 558 (27.x.84), Queen to Gladstone; and Guedalla, ii. 309.
[2] Guedalla, ii. 324 (20.i.85), Ponsonby to Gladstone.
[3] Gwynn and Tuckwell, i. 346–7 (19.xi.80).
[4] Monypenny and Buckle, ii. 1326.

that he had never given her this information or if ever he did it had never been very accurate.

'Her Majesty still maintains that Lord Melbourne, Sir Robert Peel, Lord John Russell and Lord Beaconsfield always gave her an insight into the opinions of the Ministers.'[1]

John Morley in the famous seventh chapter of his *Walpole* states the position on this point thus:

'The Cabinet is a unit—a unit as regards the sovereign, and a unit as regards the legislature. Its views are laid before the sovereign and before Parliament, as if they were the views of one man. It gives its advice as a single whole, both in the royal closet, and in the hereditary or representative chamber.'[2]

In 1885 the question of Home Rule for Ireland came to the front. It was a proposal about which it was inevitable that the Queen and Gladstone should take completely opposite views. Three years previously the Queen had expressed her disapproval of some remarks of Gladstone's which seemed to countenance a revival of the Home Rule movement,[3] and had dubbed Home Rulers 'rebels'[4]. On December 22, 1885, Ponsonby called on Harcourt and

'said that the Queen was much alarmed at the reports of Gladstone's Home Rule scheme, but recognised that the present Government could not last long, and admitted that its successor should be a Liberal one. Her idea was that "extremes" (meaning Gladstone and R. Churchill) should be got rid of, that Hartington should be Prime Minister and Salisbury Foreign Secretary under him, the whole of the rest of the Cabinet being Liberal and Whig.'[5]

Harcourt, of course, said this was utterly impossible. Possibly it was something of this which she had in mind

[1] Guedalla, ii. 352 (8.v.85), Ponsonby to Gladstone.
[2] John Morley's *Walpole* (1889), 157.
[3] *L.* vi. 259 (11.ii.82), Queen to Gladstone.
[4] Guedalla, ii. 199 (13.vi.82), Queen to Gladstone.
[5] A. G. Gardiner's *Harcourt*, i. 552.

when as early as 1880 she had said somewhat obscurely: 'Possibly a coalition first.'[1] The idea of a coalition was one with which, as we are about to see, her thoughts were very much occupied in 1884 and 1885.

When in 1886 Gladstone did finally introduce his Home Rule Bill her objections were amplified: 'The Queen cannot deny that she looks forward with anxiety to the further development of a measure which does not appear to command the approval of the majority of her subjects in the United Kingdom.'[2] In this instance her objection to the Home Rule Bill is based on the same kind of doctrine as that put forward on many occasions by the majority in the House of Lords to justify its rejection of measures submitted to it by the House of Commons, the doctrine that it is legitimate to reject a measure which it is reasonable to suppose does not command the support of a majority of the people.[3]

The controversy over Irish Home Rule led to a great revolution in British party politics. At one time the Queen was anxious for the formation of a third party of moderates, excluding Conservative and Liberal extremists alike, with the object of 'saving the country and the Constitution', and she pressed on the Duke of Argyll[4] the idea of his leading such a party in the Upper House:

'I long for the moderates of both sides to form a third party which would be a check to both the others and prevent this mischief the violents are making. This might eventually lead to the formation of a third Party in the House of Lords, and is what Mr. Goschen was very eager for, under possibly *your*

[1] Cf. above, p. 72.

[2] *L.* vii. 93 (27.iii.86), Queen to Gladstone.

[3] Cf. above, p. 80, where she states the same doctrine with regard to the Franchise Bill of 1884.

[4] His son (who succeeded him as ninth Duke in 1900) had married the Queen's fourth daughter, the Princess Louise, in 1871.

Leadership. . . . We must save the country and the Constitution.'[1]

But later the Queen did her best to accelerate the process by which a section of the Liberal party split from the main body on the Home Rule issue and became the Liberal Unionist party. Her intermediary and agent was Goschen. As early as 1881 she had found out that he shared her antipathy to Gladstone's Near East policy: 'I said how much harm Mr. Gladstone had done by his speeches, in which Mr. Goschen quite agreed.'[2] In December, 1885, when it seemed likely that the fall of Salisbury's first Government was at hand, she appealed to Goschen to promote an alliance between the Liberal dissentients and the Conservatives against Gladstone and Home Rule:

'I appeal to *you* and to all moderate, loyal, and *really patriotic* men, who have the safety and well-being of the Empire and the Throne at heart, and who wish to save them from destruction, with which, if the Government again fell into the reckless hands of Mr. Gladstone, they would be threatened, to rise above party and to be true patriots! You must convince Lord Hartington of what is at last *his duty* and of what he owes to his Queen and country, which really goes before allegiance to Mr. Gladstone, who can persuade himself that *everything* he takes up is right, even though it be calling black, white, and wrong, right.

'Let me urge and implore you by *all* the sense of honour you so strongly possess . . . to do *all* you can to gather around you all the moderate Liberals, who indeed ought to be called "*Constitutionalists*", to prevent Mr. Gladstone recklessly upsetting the Government without being able to form a Government himself, which could stand, and which I could accept, for I should firmly refuse Mr. Chamberlain, and Sir Ch. Dilke, for different reasons, as you can understand.

'I am sure that you with Lord Hartington and many other

[1] *L.* vi. 547 (7.x.84), Queen to Duke of Argyll.

[2] Ibid. 178 (3.i.81), Journal. Goschen had just returned from Constantinople.

moderate Liberals would save the country by standing aloof from Mr. Gladstone, who is utterly reckless, and whose conduct at this moment, in proposing what would be *Home Rule*, is most mischievous and incomprehensible.

'Out of this might grow a Coalition in time.'[1]

Out of that there did in time grow a Coalition, but not so quickly as the Queen might have wished, and not in time to prevent the overthrow of Salisbury and his replacement by Gladstone. But even if the Queen thus failed to secure her immediate object, this very active intervention in the realm of party politics was almost certainly not without effect in bringing about the fusion of the Unionist and Liberal Unionist parties, and credit must be given to the Queen for her prescience in advocating so early what was later seen to be inevitable.[2]

The same ideas were pressed on another independent Liberal, W. E. Forster, who, as Chief Secretary for Ireland, had resigned from the second Gladstone Cabinet rather than sanction 'the Kilmainham treaty':

'The Queen desires me to say her Majesty hopes that you are prepared to stand by the moderate patriotic and loyal men,

[1] *L.* vi. 712 (20.xii.85), Queen to Goschen.

[2] Goschen's position as a royal confidant at this time was responsible for Lord Salisbury's enunciating a constitutional doctrine of some importance, the doctrine that during a ministerial crisis the consultations of the Crown with political leaders should take place on the responsibility of the retiring Prime Minister: 'I expressed a wish to talk with Mr. Goschen to hear what he could suggest. . . . Lord Salisbury entirely agreed, thought it right, and wished that it should be done *by his advice* to *relieve me from all responsibility*—very kindly. In former days old Lord Lansdowne and the great Duke of Wellington had been consulted in this way, in '51 and in '55.' (*L.* vii. 24, 28.i.86, Memorandum.) Actually, on this occasion Mr. Goschen refused to commit himself by giving advice.

At a later time Mr. Goschen's appointment to be First Lord of the Admiralty was criticized by the Queen: '. . . cannot help being anxious regarding your nominee for Admiralty. . . . Fear Mr. Goschen was not altogether popular in same capacity from 1871–1874.' (*L.* viii. 527, 26.vi.95, Queen to Salisbury.) This might be interpreted to mean that the Queen's opinion of Goschen was not so high in 1895 as in 1885.

who will not agree with the wild plans of Mr. G., and that you will not join in trying to drive out the present Government to let Mr. G. come in again. The Queen considers that would be a real misfortune for the country and for the whole world.'[1]

In January, 1886, the pressure on Goschen is renewed:

'Mr. Gladstone is supposed to wish to make an attempt to drive the Government out very shortly. The Queen trusts that, at this moment, he will not be supported. These are not times for mere party attacks.'[2]

And again:

'Why can you, moderate, loyal and patriotic Whigs, not join, and declare you will not follow Mr. Gladstone, and not support him? He will ruin the country if he can, and how much mischief has he not done already! . . . I hope and think Mr. Gladstone could not form a Government.'[3]

But these hopes and thoughts proved of no avail. In February, 1886, Gladstone became Prime Minister for the third time. Even in the negotiations for the formation of the new Government the Queen did her best to discredit it. The Duchess of Roxburghe had refused the offer of the post of Mistress of the Robes, and the Queen wrote to her mother:

'I think your son might put into the papers that the post had been offered to Annie, and, tho' she was greatly honoured and would willingly have accepted it, the Duke felt he could not support Mr. Gladstone's Irish policy, and she had therefore declined it. Something of this kind I should like to appear.'[4]

She commended a speech by Lord Hartington in opposition to her Government:

'As this is no party question, but one which concerns the safety, honour, and welfare of her dominions, the Queen wishes to express personally to Lord Hartington, not only her admira-

[1] *L.* vi. 714 (22.xii.85), Lady Ely to Mr. Forster.
[2] *L.* vii. 17 (24.i.86), Queen to Goschen.
[3] Ibid. 23 (27.i.86), Queen to Goschen.
[4] Ibid. 51 (11.ii.86), Queen to Dowager Duchess of Roxburghe.

tion of his speech on Friday night, but also to thank him for it. . . . And she trusts, with certainty now, that these dangerous and ill-judged measures for unhappy Ireland will be defeated.'[1] She accepted from Lord Salisbury the advice that it would be best to let Gladstone dissolve, in which case a majority hostile to his would probably be returned, and the Home Rule project quashed.[2] But it was at this time too that Gladstone himself for once rose to the height of a direct rebuke to the Queen: 'Your Majesty's argument [he told her—the subject was the House of Lords] might doubtless have been used with great force from the Opposition Bench. . . .'[3] Gladstone's record of his conversation with the Queen when in August, 1886, he laid down his office, shows an absence of bitterness and a forbearance, which do him the greatest possible credit:

'The conversation at my closing audience on Friday was a singular one, when regarded as the probable last word with the sovereign after fifty-five years of political life, and a good quarter of a century's service rendered to her in office. . . . I remember that on a closing audience in 1874 she said she felt sure I might be reckoned upon to support the throne. She did not say anything of the sort to-day. Her mind and opinion have since that day been seriously warped.[4] . . . Only at three points did the conversation touch upon anything even faintly related to public affairs. The rest of the conversation, not a very long one, was filled up with nothings. It is rather melancholy. But on neither side, given the conditions, could it well be helped.'[5]

[1] *L.* vii. 102 (11.iv.86), Queen to Hartington.

[2] Ibid. 129 (15.v.86), Memorandum by Salisbury.

[3] Guedalla, ii. 398 (8.iii.86), Gladstone to Queen. This letter is also to be found in *L.* vii. 76–7, but with this particular passage omitted.

[4] Of course it might well be argued on behalf of the Queen that there was not the same danger to the throne in 1886 as in 1874, and that therefore some statement similar to that which she had made in 1874 would not have been apropos in 1886.

The three points on which she touched which did relate to public affairs were of very minor importance.

[5] Morley, iii. 263.

Much less has been said on the subject of the relations between the Queen and Gladstone between the years 1880 and 1886 than might have been said. It was the period in which their mutual misunderstanding reached its climax. The period from 1886 to 1898, the year of Gladstone's death, must receive still more summary treatment, if only because it was a period in which this misunderstanding might almost be said to have become a matter of routine. In 1887 there is another indication of social discrimination against Gladstone:[1] '. . . Lord Salisbury still thinks it would be a gracious act, and tend to allay the bitterness of feeling which exists, if your Majesty were to include Mr. Gladstone in your Majesty's invitations.'[2] In the same year the Queen wrote to Lord Lansdowne: 'He will have followed with interest and disgust the accounts of the debates on the Crimes Bill and the language and conduct of the Irish, and not only of them, but of Mr. Gladstone and a few others. It is dreadful to see a man who was three times Prime Minister fall so low.'[3] There is a certain maliciousness in the remark that: 'The Queen is glad that Mr. Gladstone is determined about his Home Rule, as that is sure to bring him into great difficulties. . . . Mr. Gladstone has brought so much personal violence into the contest, and used such insolent language, that the Queen is quite shocked and ashamed.'[4]

In 1892 the Court Circular announced that: 'Lord Salisbury tendered his resignation, which Her Majesty accepted with great regret.' The Queen's opinion was that: 'By an incomprehensible, reckless vote, the result of most unfair and abominable misrepresentations at the elections, one of the best and most useful Governments

[1] Cf. above, p. 66 and pp. 73–4.
[2] *L.* vii. 280 (4.iii.87), Salisbury to Queen.
[3] Newton's *Lansdowne*, 45 (3.vi.87), Queen to Lansdowne.
[4] *L.* viii. 132 (23.vii.92), Queen to Ponsonby.

have been defeated. . . . The Queen Empress can hardly trust herself to say what she feels and thinks on the subject.' None the less she goes on to speak of the very great 'danger to the country, to Europe, to her vast Empire, which is involved in having all those great interests entrusted to the shaking hand of an old, wild and incomprehensible man of 82½'[1]. To the Prince of Wales she referred to 'this iniquitous Government'[2], even before its formation was completed. When on this occasion she received Gladstone: 'On his coming out he said the interview was such as took place between Marie Antoinette and her executioner.'[3]

'After the Council was over [this is Harcourt's note three days later] Rosebery, Spencer and W. V. H. were told that they were to have audiences. W. V. H. asked Ponsonby what the Queen was going to say. He replied, "She wants to know who will communicate with her and tell her what is going on, as, of course, Gladstone cannot do so and she wants to know if you will do it". W. V. H. said this was very awkward and he should not know what to say, as he could not possibly undertake this except at the wish of Gladstone and by his request.'[4]

The Queen commanded Ponsonby 'to express a hope that the name of Lord Ripon will not be submitted to her for the appointment of Secretary of State for India'[5]. Lord Ripon was made Colonial Secretary.

This fourth ministry of Gladstone's, from 1892 to 1894, involved the same sort of disputes as previously, and they arose over the same sort of questions. The royal opposition to proposals for Home Rule was as strong as ever. The Queen wired to her Prime Minister: 'I cannot say

[1] Newton's *Lansdowne*, 100.

[2] *L.* viii. 143 (13?viii.92), Queen to Prince of Wales.

[3] *Private Diaries of the Rt. Hon. Sir Algernon West*, edited by H. G. Hutchinson (London, 1922), 51 (15.viii.92).

[4] Gardiner, ii. 185 (18.viii.92), Harcourt's Journal.

[5] Guedalla, ii. 438 (14.viii.92), Ponsonby to Gladstone.

that the measure will be for the *better* government of Ireland. Can you leave out "better". . .'[1] 'Better' was left out, so as late as 1893 the Queen's Speech was still up to a point her own speech and not that of her Ministers.[2] She wrote in her Journal: 'This unfortunate Home Rule Bill was read a first time on Friday . . . but it is sad to think it will be [read] a second time! Please God, in committee it will be much altered.'[3] The Egyptian question was still prominent. The Cabinet after some hesitation decided, on the advice of Lord Cromer, to send another Battalion to Egypt, and Sir Henry Ponsonby ascribed this decision entirely to the 'pressing remonstrances' of the Queen.[4]

But Gladstone was not slow to defend himself. In October, 1892, he sent the Queen a long memorandum on the general political situation, which showed that even in his old age he had a really remarkable insight into the nature and strength of current social forces. In places in this memorandum he even suggests the existence of what would now be described by some such term as class struggle. In one particular passage, for example, he openly claims that the Crown derives its knowledge of politics exclusively from contact with one class, and so is kept in ignorance of the political views of other classes: 'At the present juncture, the views of your Majesty's actual advisers, although now supported by a majority of the people . . . are hardly at all represented, and as Mr. Gladstone believes are imperfectly known, in the powerful circles with which your Majesty has ordinary personal intercourse. . . .'[5] This is another, stronger way of putting Viscount Gladstone's point that the Queen's

[1] Guedalla, ii. 462 (28.i.93), T. to Gladstone.
[2] Cf. above, pp. 75 ff.
[3] *L.* viii. 227 (19.ii.93), Journal.
[4] Ibid. 214 (23.i.93), Ponsonby to Queen.
[5] Ibid. 172 (28.x.92), Memorandum by Gladstone.

'lofty isolation kept her apart from the all-essential dynamics of politics'. The Queen's comment on this document is short, simple and characteristic: 'Reading a long Memorandum, from Mr. Gladstone about the political situation, which is very curious.'[1]

Gladstone's papers show that his audiences with the Queen in these years were pure formalities. A memorandum of his of November, 1892, details the topics of conversation in an audience with the Queen, thus:

'1. Inquiry for the Queen's health.
2. The fogs of London & Windsor.
3. The Laureateship. W. Watson.
4. The Dowager Duchess of Sutherland. . . .
5. The Roumanian Marriage. . . .
6. Lord Acton; not yet personally known to the Queen.
7. Condition of Lady Kimberley.
8. Has Mrs. Gladstone still a nephew who is a master at Eton?
9. Dean Wellesley. . . .
10. The Dean of Peterborough.
11. Health of the Bp. of Rochester.
12. Agricultural distress (H.M. seemed half inclined to lay it upon "large importations").
13. Commission thereupon (not desired).

'These are all or nearly all the topics of conversation introduced at the audience to-night. From them may be gathered in some degree the terms of confidence between H.M. and her Prime Minister. Not perhaps with perfect exactitude, as she instinctively avoids points of possible difference. But then it seems that such are now all points.'[2]

Again the next year he notes: 'Audience of the Queen at 3.30, a form as usual, indeed I fear a sham.'[3] For this

[1] *L.* viii. 176 (1.xi.92), Journal.
[2] Guedalla, ii. 71 (25.xi.92), Memorandum by Gladstone.
[3] Viscount Gladstone, 341 (8.iii.93), Gladstone's diary. Cf. above, p. 73, for Lord Hartington's similar experiences in the second Gladstone ministry.

restraint the Queen was apparently inclined to lay the blame on Gladstone, for we find him explaining to Ponsonby:

'Sir W. Harcourt tells me that the Queen, in conversation with him at Windsor last Saturday, remarked that I did not when admitted to the honour of an audience introduce into the conversation any matter of business. This is certainly so; and my rule has been not to refer to any subject of a *class* different from such as Her Majesty might have selected. But if the Queen allows a greater latitude I shall be ready to regard myself as at liberty to refer to any matter of business which so far as I can judge is not likely to be otherwise than agreeable to Her Majesty.'[1]

The pity of it was that there were next to no matters of business which were likely to be agreeable to the Queen.

There is evidence to show that in February, 1894, the Queen was making inquiries as to whether it was not possible for Gladstone to be replaced by Lord Salisbury. We have a letter from Sir Henry Ponsonby to the Queen, saying: 'If your Majesty sent for Lord Salisbury or the Duke of Devonshire, it would probably be a fortnight before they could form a Government, and then would probably ask for a dissolution',[2] and a letter from the Queen to Lord Rowton: 'The Queen is most anxious that Lord Salisbury should *not* think she is wanting in openness towards him, or doubt that her wish to see him again at the head of affairs is as great as ever; but she feels she could not act differently than she has done at the present time. It must be remembered that the present Government have still a majority in the House of Commons.'[3] It certainly was awkward that the Queen's Ministers

[1] Guedalla, ii. 467 (16.iii.93), Gladstone to Ponsonby.

[2] *L.* viii. 365 (28.ii.94), Ponsonby to Queen.

[3] Ibid. 369 (2.iii.94), Queen to Lord Rowton. As Montague Corry he had been Private Secretary to Disraeli from 1866 to 1881.

possessed the confidence of the elected representatives of the nation, even though they did not possess the confidence of the Crown, and that this fact could not be allowed to escape the royal memory.

In March, 1894, the official relationship finally terminated, and a pathetic account of an interview between the Queen and Mrs. Gladstone tells us more than much of the correspondence between the Queen and Gladstone himself:

'She was very much upset, poor thing, and asked to be allowed to speak, as her husband "could not speak". This was to say, which she did with many tears, that, whatever his errors might have been, "his devotion to your Majesty and the Crown were very great". She repeated this twice, and begged me to allow her to tell him that I believed it, which I did: for I am convinced it is the case, though at times his actions might have made it difficult to believe.'[1]

Very different had been the Queen's parting from one of her Conservative Ministers. Then it was she who had wept: 'I shall not forget [wrote Lord Cranbrook] my last interview as Minister. The Queen exclaimed, "Oh, my dear Lord Cranbrook, I cannot tell you how sorry I am to lose you or part from you," [and] burst into tears . . .'[2] It is impossible not to feel sorry for Gladstone as he hands to his secretary the Queen's letter on his resignation, 'with a sigh', saying: 'And this is the only record that will remain of 51 years as Privy Councillor'[3]; and two years later records in retrospect that: 'It was the kind and generous farewell from Ponsonby which had to fill for me the place of a farewell from my Sovereign.'[4]

To complete the story of the relations between the

[1] Ibid. 370 (3.iii.94), Journal.
[2] *Life of Cranbrook*, ii. 334 (19.viii.92), Cranbrook's diary.
[3] West, *Diaries*, 289 (4.iii.94).
[4] Viscount Gladstone, 348 (2.i.96), Gladstone's diary.

Queen and Gladstone. His great loyalty continued to be exploited: 'Hope your friends will oppose attempt to reduce Duke Coburg allowance',[1] reads a little later a telegram from the Queen. In November of the next year, however, the Queen once more returned to the attack on Gladstone in a communication about the Armenian massacres: 'One great difficulty and misfortune is the impression of England's being opposed to the Mohammedans, and which is encouraged by the impolitic half-mad attitude of Mr. Gladstone. . . .'[2] But at their final meeting at Cannes in 1897 her manner to him was 'decidedly kind . . . and she gave me her hand . . . which had never happened with me during all my life.'[3] He died the next year and the Queen's absolute love of truth made it difficult for her to strike the correct note of sympathy in her letter to Mrs. Gladstone: 'How can I say that I am sorry when I am not?' she asked one of her ladies.[4] An observer reported that—

'The Queen was very angry at the attempts made to induce her to write in praise of Mr G. It would have been in the nature of a recantation. She absolutely refused to be dictated to by the newspapers. Salisbury backed her. The message to Mrs G. she had already written in her own hand. She was willing to put something in the Court Circular, but only if not to do so "would hurt the Ministry!". She was displeased with the Prince of W. acting as Pall Bearer, and kissing Mrs G.'s hand! She said, "I am sorry for Mrs Gladstone; as for him, I never liked him, and I will say nothing about him!" '[5]

In saying that she had *never* liked him the Queen's memory seems to have failed her.

[1] Guedalla, ii. 499 (30.iii.94), T. Queen to Gladstone.

[2] *L.* viii. 572 (5.xi.95), C.T. Queen to Salisbury.

[3] Guedalla, ii. 77.

[4] Bolitho, 305.

[5] Esher, i. 217 (2.vi.98), Journal. The observer in question was the Rt. Hon. Akers Douglas, subsequently Lord Chilston.

Her summing-up may fitly bring this part of the narrative to a close:

'He was very clever and full of ideas for the bettering and advancement of the country, always most loyal to me personally, and ready to do anything for the Royal Family; but alas! I am sure involuntarily, he did at times a good deal of harm. He had a wonderful power of speaking and carrying the masses with him.'[1]

[1] *L.* ix. 246 (19.v.98), Journal.

## III

# THE INFLUENCE OF THE QUEEN ON HOME AFFAIRS; FROM GLADSTONE'S LAST MINISTRY

WHEN Gladstone resigned in 1894, the Queen, having had from Lord Kimberley an assurance that '. . . he thought he could answer for his colleagues being ready to give every assistance, and to act loyally under any Prime Minister I might choose', apparently entirely on her own initiative, and without consulting any one but herself, 'wrote a few lines to Lord Rosebery, urging him to accept the Premiership. . . .'[1] Gladstone was not asked for his advice as to who his successor should be, except in an unofficial and roundabout way by Sir Henry Ponsonby. Upon which Gladstone, laying emphasis on the fact that he was not speaking in an official capacity, 'presuming that the Queen would send for one of the present Ministers, . . . said that he could not agree that a Peer was impossible.'[2] He mentioned Rosebery, Ripon, Harcourt, Morley, and Asquith, but did not specially recommend any one of them. Gladstone subsequently told Morley that if he had been formally and officially consulted he would have advised the Queen to send for Lord Spencer,[3] whom he had not mentioned. An editorial footnote to the *Letters* tells us that: 'Neither the Queen's Journal nor the Windsor Archives give any support to the picturesque story that, at this crisis, while her Majesty was awaiting Lord Rosebery to entrust the Government to his charge, Sir William Harcourt was ushered into her presence by

[1] *L.* viii. 370 (3.iii.94), Journal.

[2] Ibid. 369 (3.iii.94), Ponsonby to Queen.

[3] Ibid. 369 n. Apparently Gladstone wished to have a peer as Prime Minister in order to strengthen the Liberal interest in the House of Lords. Cf. *After Thirty Years*, 344.

mistake instead.' But the footnote adds that Sir Algernon West, who was Gladstone's private secretary, records in his diary (20. iv. 94) how Gladstone told him that 'an awkward incident had occurred at Windsor when he gave in his resignation; the Queen told Acton to send in Kimberley, and Acton by mistake sent in Harcourt, who thought he was going to be commanded to form a Government'.[1]

It has been shown that the selection of Rosebery to succeed Gladstone was the Queen's personal selection. There is evidence that in 1886, when Rosebery was Foreign Secretary, she held him in high esteem: 'I urged Lord Rosebery not to bring too many matters before the Cabinet as nothing was decided there, and it would be far better to discuss everything with me and Mr. Gladstone,'[2] and, more emphatic: 'The *only* really *good* appointment (and that is *my* doing, for *I* asked for him and *insisted* on having him) is Lord Rosebery.'[3] He had in effect assumed Granville's mantle as the Queen's favourite among Liberal statesmen. But in 1892 criticism is heard:

'. . . she must say how dreadfully disappointed and shocked she is at Lord Rosebery's speech, which is radical to a degree to be almost communistic. Hitherto he always said he had nothing whatever to do with Home Rule, and only with foreign affairs;

[1] *L.* viii. 371, n. 1.

[2] *L.* vii. 48 (6.ii.86), Journal. Cf. the Queen's C.T. to Salisbury (Ibid. 211, 21.ix.86): 'You told me when you left office in February that I should impress on Lord Rosebery importance of bringing as few subjects on *foreign affairs* before the *Cabinet* as possible. Trust you will follow this course now.' In other words, the Queen, the Prime Minister, and the Foreign Secretary are as far as possible to manage foreign affairs between them and to consult the Cabinet as little as possible.

[3] Ibid. 58 (14.ii.86), Queen to Prince of Wales. In connexion with his appointment to the Foreign Office in 1892 Rosebery recorded in a note (11.viii.92) a conversation with Gladstone: 'He said the Queen had insisted on it and offered to press it personally on me, but had not. "Can you guess why?" I said "No." "Because she thought this affair seemed loosely hung together and hoped it might fall through." Crewe's *Rosebery*, 403.

and *now* he is as violent as anyone. . . . In case of the Government's defeat the Queen meant to send for him first, but after the violent attack on Lord Salisbury, this attempt to stir up Ireland, it will be *impossible*; and the G.O.M. at eighty-two is a very *alarming look-out*.'[1]

In 1893, however, Rosebery is apparently once more restored to the royal favour. There is a hint of the Queen having besought him not to leave the Foreign Office for the Viceroyalty of India,[2] and at one point an indication that he is sending the Queen reports of proceedings in the Cabinet: 'With regard to your Majesty's strictly confidential enquiries, he may say that he receives cordial co-operation from Mr. Bryce, and that he has, he believes, the silent support of some other members of the Cabinet.'[3]

Rosebery was not at all anxious to become Prime Minister.[4] He saw quite clearly that even with mutual goodwill his relations with the Queen would be bound in time to become strained: 'One main reason for his wishing to avoid this heavy and thankless succession was that he sets the greatest value on the character of his relations with your Majesty.'[5] The Queen did not admit the danger: 'She is sorry to hear that he apprehends any trouble which might alienate him from her. The Queen can hardly think this possible or at any rate probable.'[6] But she hoped that he would act as a check and a drag upon his Cabinet,[7] and whether or not he himself held

[1] *L.* viii. 119 (30.v.92), Queen to Ponsonby. Clearly, the Queen did not properly understand the meaning of the word 'communistic'. Cf. below, p. 138.

[2] Ibid. 299 (9.viii.93), Rosebery to Queen.

[3] Ibid. 211 (22.i.93), Rosebery to Queen. Egyptian policy was the question under consideration.

[4] 'In after years, Rosebery was fond of saying that the only two people who had thoroughly frightened him were Queen Victoria and Prince Bismarck.' Crewe's *Rosebery*, 240. And Queen Victoria in her turn was to frighten Bismarck.

[5] *L.* viii. 375 (4.iii.94), Rosebery to Queen.

[6] Ibid. 375 (4.iii.94), Queen to Rosebery.

[7] Ibid. 403 (8.vi.94), Queen to Rosebery.

the same conception of the nature of his task, it was a task in which he failed. In short, his apprehensions were justified by the event, though a dispute over the House of Lords was his only direct collision with the Queen. When in 1895 he ceased to be Prime Minister his claim was: 'I can say with absolute truth that my only regret in laying down my office is the cessation of my personal relations with your Majesty.'[1] To him the Queen gave parting advice of a kind that was customary with her: 'The Queen seizes this opportunity of saying a few parting words of kindly advice. . . . It is that he should in his public speeches be very careful not to commit himself by strong expressions which would hamper him hereafter.'[2] A little earlier she had been pressing on him good advice of another kind. This was in his speeches out of Parliament to 'take a more serious tone and be, if she may say so, less jocular, which is hardly befitting a Prime Minister. Lord Rosebery is so clever that he may be carried away by a sense of humour, which is a little dangerous.'[3] 'To that danger'—Sir John Marriott acidly comments—'the Queen was not exposed.'[4]

There was during Rosebery's ministry a most violent dispute over the position of the House of Lords. The Queens' view was that 'The House of Lords might possibly be improved, but it is *part* and *parcel* of the *much vaunted* and *admired British Constitution*, and CANNOT be *abolished*.'[5] This was needless panic. Rosebery was in favour of reform, not abolition, and his actual proposal in October, 1894, was to bring before the House of Commons a resolution declaring the 'impossibility of the

[1] Ibid. 523 (23.vi.94), Rosebery to Queen.
[2] Ibid. 533 (5.vii.95), Queen to Rosebery.
[3] Ibid. 404 (8.vi.94), Queen to Rosebery.
[4] *Queen Victoria and Her Ministers*, 180.
[5] *L.* viii. 384 (17.iii.94), Queen to Rosebery.

elected representatives of the people allowing their measures to be summarily mutilated and rejected by the House of Lords'[1]. In fact, the resolution would not have been very different from that which was passed on the initiative of the Liberal Government on June 26, 1907: 'That, in order to give effect to the will of the people as expressed by their elected representatives, it is necessary that the power of the other House to alter or reject bills passed by this House should be so restricted by law as to secure that within the limits of a single parliament the final decision of the Commons shall prevail.'

On this question the Queen wrote to Lord Salisbury, marking her letter 'Very Private', to ask him for his advice: '. . . would it not be right to warn Lord Rosebery that she cannot let the Cabinet make such a proposal without ascertaining first whether the country would be in favour of it . . .?' and, '. . . is the Unionist party fit for a dissolution *now*?'[2] To the Prince of Wales she telegraphed: 'I am inclined to favour a dissolution sooner than consent to any step which implies tampering with the Constitution, but I must first ascertain what the chances of the Unionists are. . . . Can you not convey your feelings on this dangerous policy to him? I think he behaved very ill to me.'[3] Lord Salisbury's advice fell into two parts. In the first place he laid it down that: 'On a matter of this vital importance [Rosebery] has no constitutional right to announce a totally new policy without first ascertaining your Majesty's pleasure on the subject, and if he is unable to convince your Majesty, it is his duty to tender his resignation.' Of course, Salisbury was something of an interested party in giving this advice, as, if Rosebery

[1] *L.* viii. 429 (24.x.94), Rosebery to Queen.
[2] Ibid. 431 (25.x.94), Queen to Salisbury.
[3] Ibid. 431 (25.x.94), C.T. Queen to Prince of Wales.

did resign, he clearly stood next in the order of succession. But assuming that he was speaking in perfect good faith, and there need be no real difficulty in making the assumption, here once again as late as 1894 we have an ex-Prime Minister, the Leader of one of the two great parties in the State, giving it as his considered judgement that it is the duty of a Prime Minister, who possesses the confidence of the House of Commons, but not the confidence of the Crown, to tender his resignation.[1]

The second part of Salisbury's advice is of far less sensational character than the first, but still it is sensational enough: 'Lord Salisbury humbly submits that your Majesty will be entirely within your constitutional rights . . . in requiring, if you think fit, that the country shall be consulted before a decision on so grave a matter is taken.'[2] In other words, the monarch may impose a dissolution upon a Prime Minister, who enjoys the confidence of the House of Commons, perhaps even of a newly elected House of Commons, but who announces on some grave matter some departure of policy with which the monarch is unable to agree. In the third place Salisbury was able to state:

> 'As far as it is possible to ascertain, the Unionist Party is quite prepared for a dissolution, and would be likely to fare well, if one should now take place. Some think it would be better for them now than later, when a lengthened agitation against the House of Lords has banished the Irish question from men's minds.'[2]

[1] It is not surprising after this to read that Salisbury 'held it as a paramount duty to maintain [the Crown's] prerogatives, and would gladly have seen them extended had that been possible. In his younger days, he used to lament that he had not been born under a more actively monarchical constitution; he should have far preferred service to a king than to a parliament.' *Life of Robert Marquis of Salisbury*, by his daughter, Lady Gwendolen Cecil (Hodder & Stoughton, 1921), iii. 180.

[2] *L.* viii. 433 (27.x.94), Salisbury to Queen.

Salisbury's constitutional views were vigorously rebutted by Rosebery:

'... he would never dream of proposing a constitutional resolution to the House of Commons without submitting it after mature consideration by the Cabinet to your Majesty. But he would humbly deprecate the view that it is necessary for a Minister, before laying a question of policy before a popular audience, to receive the approval of the Crown. Such a principle would tend to make the Sovereign a party in all controversies of the hour, and would hazardously compromise the neutrality of the Sovereign.'[1]

From this view the Queen in her turn dissents:

'The Queen cannot agree with what Lord Rosebery says, in his letter of the 1st, as to the announcement of this policy. It is *not* a "mere question of policy" [Rosebery had not used the word "mere"], but as he himself said, "*a question of enormous importance*", a "*question of the revision of the entire constitution*", and, as such, she maintains her sanction for its public declaration should have been obtained.'[2]

The constitutional doctrine enunciated by this letter seems to be that on questions of 'enormous' or fundamental constitutional importance the consent of the Crown should be obtained, before a Minister makes a public declaration of policy. Presumably this rule would not apply to more ordinary political questions. But who was to draw the line, and where was the line to be drawn, between questions which were and questions which were not of 'enormous importance'? And what was to happen if the Minister failed to obtain the permission of the Sovereign to make an announcement of a policy?

In this case, however, the Queen did apparently decide to insist on a dissolution. Sir Henry Ponsonby is informed that the Queen 'now thinks you should see Prime Minister,

[1] *L.* viii. 440 (1.xi.94), Rosebery to Queen.
[2] Ibid. 449 (13?xi.94), Queen to Rosebery.

and say cannot consent to Resolution without appeal to the country . . .'[1], and a Memorandum by Sir Henry James, later Lord James of Hereford, shows that the Queen was taking another opinion in addition to that of Salisbury, and that Salisbury's opinion was not his alone: '. . . if Lord Rosebery were to refuse to acquiesce in a Dissolution, he would constitutionally be within his right in doing so. Of course the Ministry would under such circumstances resign and the Queen would have to seek new advisers.'[2] We have already seen that in Salisbury's view the Sovereign had a perfect constitutional right to insist on a dissolution. Sir Henry James in effect adds the proviso that the Ministers have a right to refuse to accede to this demand, but that they must then resign. In short, he gives yet another set of circumstances in which it becomes the duty of a Government to resign because it has lost the confidence of the Crown, though he was himself perfectly well aware of the dangers of forcing Ministers into a position where that was the only course open to them.[3]

The advice given by Salisbury on this particular occasion was not the same as and seemingly less wise than the advice he had given the previous year in answer to the question whether, in the probable event of the Home Rule Bill being rejected by the House of Lords, the Queen should be asked by a Petition or an Address from that House to grant a Dissolution. His advice then was the same so far as the strictly constitutional point was concerned, but he looked beyond that to probable political consequences:

'A Dissolution by the Queen, against the advice of her Ministers, would, of course, involve their resignation. Their

[1] Ibid. 442 (3.xi.94), T. Bigge to Ponsonby.
[2] Ibid. 444 (5.xi.94), Memorandum by Sir Henry James.
[3] See his own account of the matter, Askwith, 232.

party could hardly help going to the country as the opponents of the royal authority; or at least, as the severe critics of the mode in which it had been exerted. . . . There must be *some* hazard that, in the end, such a step would injure the authority of the Queen.'[1]

In saying this he was in substantial agreement with the view which we have seen Rosebery later expressed, that this kind of proceeding 'would hazardously compromise the neutrality of the Sovereign'. No doubt there are differences of circumstances between a Monarch agreeing to grant a Dissolution in response to an Address from a House of Lords, which has just rejected the principal Bill in a Government's programme, and a Monarch insisting on a Dissolution because a Prime Minister insists on making an announcement of policy in defiance of his Sovereign's wishes. But it is still not at all clear why in 1894 Salisbury should have contemplated without concern a step which had caused him grave misgivings in 1893, unless indeed he had in the interval become surer of success for the party which would go to the country as the supporters of the royal authority.

A kind of precedent for incidents of this character is to be found in 1859. The Queen had then expressed her 'firm determination not to sanction, under any form, the creation of a British Army [in India], distinct from that known at present as the Army of the Crown'[2]. She had taken the initiative in thus expressing her views on this question before it had in any way been formally brought to her notice, and the Prime Minister of the day, Lord Derby, seems almost, as subsequently was Gladstone, to have been prepared to see her turn his Government out 'after the manner of her uncles!': '. . . unless Lord Derby

[1] *L.* viii. 297 (8.viii.93), Memorandum by Salisbury.
[2] *L.* iii. 316 (5.ii.59), Queen to Derby.

misconceives the purport of your Majesty's letter, he fears that it may leave him no alternative but that of humbly entreating to be relieved from a responsibility which nothing should have induced him to undertake but . . . the conviction that he might rely with confidence upon your Majesty's continued support'[1].

Incidentally it is worth noting that Salisbury justified his giving the sort of constitutional advice we have just seen him offering on the ground that '. . . though he is very anxious to avoid even the appearance of obtruding his opinions upon your Majesty, it will always be his duty and his pleasure as a former servant of your Majesty, and as a Privy Councillor, to answer any questions which you may think fit to put to him'[2]. Maitland, a few years earlier, speaking of the right of a Privy Councillor to have his advice heard by the Queen, had pointed out that '. . . obviously, if this right were really insisted on, our constitution would soon be topsy-turvy: as, for instance, while the present ministry remains in power [Salisbury's second ministry] Gladstone insisted on constantly having the Queen's ear'[3]. But Gladstone never had the Queen's ear when he was in opposition; that was Salisbury's privilege.

At this point the reader may well stop to wonder why so much attention is given to the relations between the Queen and Gladstone, and between the Queen and Rosebery, and so little to the relations between the Queen and Salisbury.[4] The answer can be put in one sentence. From 1876 to 1901 the Queen was quite undoubtedly a political partisan, a supporter of the Conservative party, an

[1] *L.* iii. 317–18 (6.ii.59), Derby to Queen.

[2] *L.* viii. 434 (27.x.94), Salisbury to Queen.

[3] *Constitutional History of England*, 401.

[4] For an excellent discussion of Salisbury's relations with the Queen, see Lady Gwendolen Cecil's *Life*, iii. 179–92.

opponent of the Liberal party. It is even arguable that this was the case from the moment when, after Palmerston's death, there came into being a Liberal instead of a Whig party.[1] Therefore, when Conservative Governments under Salisbury were in power, the state of affairs, so far as the relations between the Queen and the Cabinet were concerned, was mainly like that of a happy nation having no history; happy indeed was the Prime Minister whose relations with the Queen were uniformly good. Strife has been said to be the parent of all things, and it was when Liberal Governments were in power that strife between the Crown and the Cabinet produced incidents which are of importance in the history of the Queen's political influence.

Queen Victoria's two immediate predecessors, George IV and William IV, were both recognized as Whigs before their accession, but both as Sovereigns in fact behaved as partisan Tories.[2] In particular the latter was, after 1832, exactly like Queen Victoria during the years of the rule of Gladstone and Rosebery in the second half of her reign, in the position of an out-and-out Tory, forced against his will into uneasy alliance with a Liberal Government. In the early part of the Queen's reign she had been so much under Melbourne's influence as positively to dread the advent of a Tory Government, and of Peel who seemed to her so cold and odd. During the election of 1841 she made a royal progress round the chief Whig houses,[3] and five years later these are her reflections about this election:

'She considers the power of dissolving Parliament a most valuable and powerful instrument in the hands of the Crown, but which ought not to be used except in extreme cases and

[1] Cf. above, p. 52.
[2] *L.* i. 5.
[3] Lee's *Queen Victoria*, 133–4.

with a certainty of success. To use this instrument and be defeated is a thing most lowering to the Crown and hurtful to the country.[1] The Queen strongly feels that she made a mistake in allowing the Dissolution in 1841; the result has been a majority returned against her of nearly one hundred votes . . .'[2]

By 1851, however, the Queen was almost as much in favour of a coalition between Whigs and Peelites as in 1885 she was in favour of a coalition between Unionists and Liberal-Unionists, and in the early part of her reign Aberdeen's Ministry almost certainly was the one which was most to her taste. But in 1851 she showed impartiality in saying: '. . . it would be very desirable that there should be a strong Conservative Party'[3]. But by 1880 the wheel had come full cycle since 1841. She would not then have thought it in the least desirable that there should be a strong Liberal party.

That the Queen's outlook, in the later years of her life at any rate, was predominantly Conservative is a fact which, in the light of the foregoing narrative account of her relations with Gladstone and Rosebery successively, would be hard to deny. But it is a fact of such importance that it deserves further illustration. The result of the

[1] In 1841 Melbourne had enlarged on this point in an interesting historical fashion; see *L.* i. 276 (15.v.41), Journal. He told the Queen: 'We know that Charles I and Charles II, and even Cromwell, appealed to the country, and had a Parliament returned into their very teeth, and that produced deposition, and convulsion, and bloodshed and death; but since then the Crown has always had a majority returned in favour of it. Even Queen Anne, who removed Marlborough in the midst of his most glorious victories and dissolved Parliament, had an immense majority. . . . William IV, even though he had a majority against him which prevented him from keeping his Ministers, had a much stronger feeling for him in that Parliament than he ever had before. [Cf. below, p. 234.] But I am afraid that for the first time the Crown would have an Opposition returned smack against it; and that would be an affront to which I am very unwilling to expose the Crown.'

[2] *L.* ii. 91 (16.vii.46), Queen to Lord John Russell.

[3] Ibid. 315 (4.iii.51), Queen to King of the Belgians.

General Election of 1880 moved her to declare: 'The Queen cannot deny she (Liberal as she has ever been, but never Radical or democratic) thinks it a great calamity for the country. . . .'[1] The same sentiment is echoed five years later: 'There are many persons who are becoming greatly alarmed by the destructive doctrines which are taught, who would welcome warmly any words of Mr. Gladstone's which affirmed that liberalism is not socialism and that progress does not mean revolution.'[2] Her comment on the next General Election was:

'The Queen has been much distressed, she must say, at the unsatisfactory turn the Elections have taken. But it must be observed that the extreme Radicals have *not* succeeded . . . and that Conservatives have gained many seats since '80. The feeling of the country is therefore very healthy in *that* respect. The Queen thinks, however, *most* of the country and of our *foreign relations*, and of the *absolute* NECESSITY of having strong and able and safe men to conduct the government of the Empire, such as is the case in Lord Salisbury's hands.'[3]

To Goschen in 1886 she wrote:

'It is sad, and I cannot help saying *not* creditable or pleasant fact that the Liberals do *not* wish to *unite* with the Conservatives at such a *supreme* moment of danger to the best interests of my great Empire. However, we must *not* mind this narrow party view (which is, moreover, NOT shared by the Conservatives!)'[4]

In other words, the Liberal point of view is a 'narrow party view', but the Conservative point of view is a truly national point of view. Her attitude towards Liberalism is explained to Rosebery on his taking office as Prime Minister: 'She does not object to Liberal measures which are not revolutionary. . . .'[5] The difficulty was that most

[1] *L.* vi. 73 (3.iv.80), Queen to Ponsonby.
[2] Ibid. 696 (2.x.85), Queen to Gladstone.
[3] Ibid. 706 (3.xii.85), Queen to Salisbury.
[4] *L.* viii. 111 (25.iv.86), Queen to Goschen.
[5] Ibid. 375 (4.iii.94), Queen to Rosebery.

of the Liberal measures which were brought forward after 1880 were in her view revolutionary.

'The fiction that the Crown is of no party [comments Mr. Farrer] has somehow survived the direct proof to the contrary afforded by every reign in greater or less degree since 1760.'[1] Disraeli was wrong in a famous speech in defence of Conservative principles to speak of the Crown as an intelligence 'superior to all party, and entirely free from all influence of that character'[2].

It was the clash between the Queen's Conservatism and Gladstone's Liberalism which, as has already been suggested, was almost certainly the main cause of their personal differences. After all Gladstone after 1876 was the same personally as before 1876, but very different politically. Rosebery was almost as chivalrous, as gallant, as flattering in his method of approach to the Queen as had been Disraeli, but like Gladstone he failed to secure good relations with her. It is hard to see how this can be explained if not in terms of his Liberalism. We have already seen that in 1880 not only did she never write except on formal official matters to her Prime Minister, but also that she avoided discussing with her other Ministers subjects which were unpalatable to her.[3] We have seen how she disapproved of Joseph Chamberlain in his Radical days.[4] Sir William Harcourt in 1881 took it as a matter of course that his principles were bound to be displeasing to the Queen, for after a visit to Balmoral he wrote to Ponsonby: 'I fear I can hardly hope to give satisfaction *politically*, but if I suit *personally* it is as much as can be expected.'[5]

'When he went in to have his audience [on being appointed to the 1892 Ministry] the Queen said, "How do you do, Sir

[1] Farrer, 120.

[2] *Selected Speeches of Lord Beaconsfield*, ii. 493 (3.iv.72).

[3] Cf. above, pp. 72–3.

[4] Cf. above, pp. 87–9.

[5] Gardiner, i. 417 (8.xi.81), Harcourt to Ponsonby.

William, I hope you are well?" W. V. H. replied he was, and added, "I hope, Madam, you will feel that our desire is to make matters as easy and as little troublesome to you as we can possibly do." She bowed, but said nothing, and then added, "How is Lady Harcourt? Terrible weather, is it not? and so oppressive." And that was all!'[1]

Moreover, one last piece of evidence, we shall see that the Queen's political opinions were shared by her sons, by the Prince of Wales in slightly lesser degree, by Prince Leopold, the Duke of Albany, if anything, in greater degree.[2]

In fact, it was most fortunate for the Queen personally, and perhaps fortunate also for the monarchy as an institution, that at the close of the reign when the Queen was old, and doubly obstinate, both with the obstinacy of old age and with her own natural obstinacy, that with the exception of the three years from 1892 to 1895, the country should have been continuously ruled from 1886 to 1901 by a Conservative Prime Minister. But it was even more fortunate that the Queen never had to work with a Radical Prime Minister. After all in comparison to Dilke, or to Chamberlain in his early days, Gladstone was almost a Whig. In any case his deep loyalty was, as we have seen, a fixed point in a changing world: 'Had he wished [Mr. Birrell points out] he could have shaken the throne to its foundations ...'[3] and Mary Ponsonby as early as 1871 had made the same point: 'If they don't take care Gladstone will show his teeth about Royalty altogether, and I wouldn't answer for its lasting long after that'.[4] No care was, in fact, taken, but then none needed to be taken.

But it was not only Queen Victoria who never had to work with a Radical Prime Minister. No English Sove-

[1] Gardiner, ii. 185 (18.viii.92), Harcourt's journal.

[2] Cf. below, pp. 188–93.

[3] Francis Birrell's *Gladstone*, 121.

[4] *Mary Ponsonby*, 68 (27.ix.71), M. E. P. to H. F. P.

reign has yet had to make that experiment. Lloyd George was the first Radical to become Prime Minister, but his case only serves to illustrate the old truth that a Radical as Minister is not necessarily a Radical Minister. It is instructive to observe that in retrospect the experience of the war fascinates him more than the social and political reforms of 1906–14, for it is about the former that he writes his volumes of autobiography. So to a great extent he will have only himself to thank if, as seems likely, he goes down to history not as a great social reformer but as the man who won the war.

This consideration of the Queen's view of party politics leads naturally to a consideration of her own view of the Constitution and of her place in it. It seems not unreasonable to suppose that here the predominant factor in the formation of her views was that she had, as it were, a vested interest in the preservation of the monarchy: 'Much as she loved her country, she loved the Monarchy more ... she accepted, rather than assented to, representative Government.'[1]

'Monarchy to be carried on [her experienced uncle had told her at the very beginning of her reign] requires certain elements, and the occupation of the Sovereign must be constantly to *preserve these elements*, or should they have been too much weakened by untoward circumstances, to contrive by every means to *strengthen them again*. You are too clever not to know, that it is *not* the being *called* Queen or King, which can be of the *least consequence*, when to the title there is not also annexed the power indispensable for the exercise of these functions.'[2]

It was not, therefore, to be expected that she would look with favour on any Radical movements which might ultimately have a republican tendency. The Crown of

[1] Farrer, 175.
[2] *L.* i. 105 (16.i.38), King of the Belgians to Queen.

England might have been said to be her family property. Did not Maitland describe it as 'a chattel entailed upon the Hanoverian dynasty'? She was determined to hand on to her successors, unimpaired and undiminished, all the rights and privileges which she had acquired at her accession. By her cleansing of the Court she had done much to secure them. It is difficult to exaggerate the moral contrast between the monarchy under Victoria and the monarchy under George IV. She was determined that the institution which she and Albert had raised so high should not again be brought low; and one of the many reasons for her hatred of Gladstone was that she thought she could detect in his policies a tendency of which that could only be the final result.[1]

So she seems always to have seen herself as fighting a rearguard action in defence of the institution of monarchy. In consequence she was always on her guard against anything in the least likely to cause any decrease of the powers of the Crown. For example, she tells Gladstone: '. . . She cannot read his remarks on the disposition evinced by the House of Commons to usurp the authority heretofore exercised by the Crown in making & ratifying Treaties with Foreign Powers without much apprehension, that sh[ld] they succeed in establishing their power in these matters, very great injury will result to the Country . . .'[2] And almost any attack on any royalty was resented as an indirect attack on herself. For example: 'The Queen has been g[ty] shocked and disgusted at the success of Mr. Briggs' motion & at . . . the want of feeling and chivalry shown towards the memory of the young Prince [Imperial]. . . . But where is chivalry and delicacy of feeling to be found in these days among many of the members of

[1] Cf. above, pp. 80–1.

[2] Guedalla, i. 341 (17.iii.72), Queen to Gladstone.

Parl^t?'[1] 'The age of chivalry' seems always to be on the point of death.

But on most other questions her views were thoroughly Conservative. For example: 'The House of Lords have thrown the Bill for the abolition of the paper Duties *out* by a very large majority, which is a *very good thing*;'[2] and again, she was 'horrified at the motion for payment of M.P.'s being carried'[3]. More generally, she stated that 'No one can be more *truly* liberal at heart than the Queen is, but she also thinks, that the great *principles* of the *Constitution* of this *great country* ought to be maintained and preserved, and that too many alterations and changes (and there have been so many) should be avoided . . .'[4] She put the same point to Gladstone: '. . . The Queen must earnestly impress on Mr. Gladstone the importance of maintaining the constitutional balance, and of opposing the demands of those who desire to wreck existing institutions.'[5] Again, she asserts that she '. . . *cannot* and will not be the Queen of a *democratic monarchy*; and those who have spoken and agitated, for the sake of party and to injure their opponents, in a very radical sense must look for *another monarch*; and she doubts they will find one.'[6] She adds that the Government is following 'the dreadful example of France'[7]. She had, in fact, never learnt to distinguish between the people and the mob.

[1] Guedalla, ii. 106 (18.vii.80), Queen to Gladstone. The Queen was very fond of the Prince Imperial personally.

[2] *L.* iii. 400 (22.v.60), Queen to King of the Belgians.

[3] *L.* viii. 488 (23.iii.95), Queen to Bigge.

[4] *L.* v. 315 (11.ii.74), Queen to W. E. Forster.

[5] *L.* vi. 516 (13.vii.84), Queen to Gladstone.

[6] Ibid. 166 (25.xii.80), Queen to W. E. Forster.

[7] Another instance of the Queen's antipathy to Republican France, cf. below, pp. 168–9. It is only fair to point out that by 1880 it had not become clear that in the Third Republic France had found a form of government more enduring than any of those with which experiments had been made since 1789.

But in the next year Beaconsfield unconsciously demonstrated that this threat of abdication was likely to remain only a threat: 'The unfortunate state of parties at this moment limits the power of the Throne, but that is no reason why the constitutional prerogative of the Crown should be treated as non-existing.'[1] It is interesting to observe that Beaconsfield, however unwittingly, has laid his finger on the real reason why, however great Queen Victoria's protestations, the monarchy was bound to become more and more of a democratic monarchy, if indeed it was to survive at all. He calls it 'the unfortunate state of parties at this moment' (1881). It would be more true to say that the increase in the size of the electorate, brought about by successive Reform Bills, meant that the Crown was more and more likely to find itself confronted, as it was in this case confronted, by a ministry fully conscious of having the support of a majority of the nation. Such a ministry, while it would have to defer to the Crown and carefully weigh its scruples, was not likely in the last resort to yield to it. Ultimately, the only effective weapon in the Crown's constitutional armoury was the threat of abdication, and it was not a threat which was very likely to be carried into effect. For this reason a king's threat of abdication is of far less importance as a move in the political game than a Minister's threat of resignation. It is even open to doubt whether abdication is legally possible.[2] In any case here you have the explanation of why on the surface Queen Victoria was only able in practice to prevent, to such an astonishingly small extent, changes to which she was opposed. But that is not to say

[1] *L.* vi. 182 (11.i.81), Beaconsfield to Queen. He was referring to the incident of the postponed Council of Jan. 5, 1881; cf. above, p. 75.

[2] F. W. Maitland's *Constitutional History of England*, 344: 'Even the king's power to abdicate, except by giving his assent to a statute declaring his abdication, may, as it seems to me, be doubted.'

that her opposition was not a let and hindrance to successive Liberal Governments, greatly increasing the burden of the Ministers' work and to some extent delaying the process of change: 'The failure of the 1880 administration can be largely attributed to the time wasted quarrelling with the court.'[1]

At the same time it must be remembered that Gladstone in particular was a man of enormous energy, some of which he could perhaps afford to dissipate in controversial correspondence with the Queen, and also that the pressure of business on Ministers was not then so great as it is now. But even Salisbury, whose difficulties with the Queen were infinitely less than Gladstone's, had to admit: '. . . I could do very well with two departments: in fact I have four—the Prime Ministership, the Foreign Office, the Queen, and Randolph Churchill—and the burden of them increases in that order.'[2]

Further, it is always important to remember that in any controversy with the Crown, Ministers were under the grave disadvantage of having always to be restrained and respectful, and unable to speak with the frankness and easy familiarity with which an equal speaks to an equal. This, of course, was especially the case when the Sovereign was a woman. Gladstone had pointed out that the prerogative of the Sovereign as against the Ministers is partly that 'of exercising an influence over their deliberations'[3], and that though the decisions of Ministers 'must ultimately conform to the sense of those who are to be responsible for them, yet their business is to inform and persuade the sovereign, not to over-rule him'. The existence and the extent of the prerogative of influencing the decisions of Ministers is largely due to their being under this

[1] Francis Birrell's *Gladstone*, 104. [2] Cecil, iii. 180.

[3] Gladstone's *Gleanings of Past Years*, i. 78 and i. 232.

obligation to persuade, and not to overrule, the Sovereign. The point is strikingly developed by Bagehot. He points to the case of Lord Chatham who might have been expected as 'a proud tribune of the people to be dictatorial to his sovereign . . . on the contrary he was in the habit of kneeling at the bedside of George III while transacting business. Now no man can *argue* on his knees.'[1] One may recall that at the time of the case of Commendams in 1616, all twelve Judges simultaneously threw themselves upon their knees and implored the King's pardon. Coke alone ventured, while in that posture, to argue. But this argument was the immediate prelude to his dismissal from office.[2]

During the Great War the strategy of the defence of the East Anglian coast in the event of a German invasion was to have been that the enemy in his landing was to be delayed and harassed as much as possible, but that the defending forces were in the end to fall back on the main railway and make that their real line of resistance. The strategy of Queen Victoria's repeated campaigns against Liberal Governments seems in practice to have been not dissimilar. She delayed and harassed as much as she possibly could the forces of Liberalism in their attack on the forces of privilege and vested interest, but she could not hope effectually to prevent the attack occurring, nor could she hope (and here the analogy ends) to prevent its ultimate success. The whole subject is tenuous in the extreme, but this does seem to be the reason why there is in a sense so comparatively little to show in the way of visible, concrete results for all the immense political activity of the Queen, with the extremely important

[1] Bagehot, 70. The whole passage on pp. 70–1 is unfortunately too long to be quoted. But it deserves an attentive reading.

[2] J. R. Tanner's *English Constitutional Conflicts of the Seventeenth Century*, 40.

exception of her great influence over appointments. But that is not to say that at the time it was exercised her influence was not of the very greatest importance.

Before finally leaving the question of the Queen's influence on Home Affairs it is profitable to collect some of her stray judgements on the political leaders of her time. To take first the Conservative leaders. She was from the first greatly impressed by Balfour. When the question arose as to who was to succeed Hicks Beach as Irish Secretary 'Lord Salisbury named his clever and agreeable nephew . . . and I was just going to make the same suggestion'[1]. Later, when she knew him better, she valued him even more highly: 'I am much struck, as is everyone, by Mr. Balfour's extreme fairness, impartiality, and large-mindedness. He sees all sides of a question, is wonderfully generous in his feelings towards others, and very gentle and sweet-tempered.'[2] She thought very differently of Lord Randolph Churchill, speaking of him as odd, mad, impertinent, disloyal, and unreliable.[3] She was particularly annoyed at the manner of his resignation:[4] 'Lord Randolph dined at my table on Monday evening, and talked with me about the Session about to commence, and about the *procedure*, offering to *send me* the proposed rules for me to see! And that *very night at the Castle*, he wrote to Lord Salisbury resigning his office! It is unprecedented!'[5] Lord Randolph defended himself in a letter to Ponsonby:

'It would have been a source of immense relief to me if I had

[1] *L.* vii. 279 (2.iii.87), Journal.

[2] *L.* ix. 74 (11.ix.96), Journal.

[3] *L.* vii. 166 (25.vii.86), Journal, and Ibid. 259 (20.i.87), Queen to Salisbury.

[4] 'It was one of those exquisite moments in which excited politicians enjoy the ineffable sensation that the end of the world has come.' Morley, iii. 275.

[5] *L.* vii. 234 (24.xii.86), Queen to Goschen.

been able to acquaint Her Majesty with what was passing when I had the honour of dining at Windsor, but my great want of experience of official life led me to believe that had I initiated so grave a matter in the conversation which Her Majesty was graciously pleased to hold with me I should have been guilty of a most unusual breach of etiquette and of Ministerial practice and decorum: all the more as no opening presented itself for bringing up the subject, though in truth my mind was entirely absorbed by it.'[1]

The Queen considered Sir R. Cross to be 'an excellent Home Secretary'[2] and in 1895 insisted that '. . . whatever changes may be necessary the Queen must ask for Lord Cross to be *in the Cabinet*'[3]. At the same time Lord Salisbury wrote: 'Her Majesty was very anxious that Mr. Matthews should not again be Home Secretary; and I have obeyed her Majesty's wish.'[4]

Of Liberal statesmen she had more to say, because she had more unfavourable comments to make. She described Palmerston and Russell as 'two dreadful old men'[5]. When the former died she wrote in her usual blunt way: 'I *never* liked him, or could ever the least respect him, nor could I forget his conduct on certain occasions to my Angel. He was very vindictive, and *personal* feelings influenced his political acts very much.'[6] She expressed herself as not quite trusting Lord Clarendon,[7] and in 1868 General Grey informs her that he 'always bears in mind the wish so strongly expressed by your Majesty, that, in case of a change of Government, some means might be found of averting, what would be unpleasant to your

[1] *Lord Randolph Churchill*, by Winston Churchill (London, 1906), ii. 269.
[2] *L.* vii. 167 (28.vii.86), Journal.
[3] *L.* viii. 523 (22.vi.95), Memorandum.
[4] Ibid. 529 (28.vi.95), Salisbury to Bigge.
[5] *L.* iv. 168 (25.ii.64), Queen to King of the Belgians.
[6] Ibid. 279 (20.x.65), Queen to King of the Belgians.
[7] Ibid. 280 (25.x.65), Queen to King of the Belgians.

Majesty—namely: Lord Clarendon's re-appointment to the Foreign Office'[1].

Lord Granville was for a long time a favourite, and an intermediary with Liberal Governments—certainly in 1859 he was reporting Cabinet proceedings to the Prince[2]—but he was unwise enough to speak against the Royal Titles Bill, and after 1880 completely fell from grace: 'Saw Lord Granville, and talked over most of the topics of the day, but with no satisfactory result. He lamented over things, shrugged his shoulders, but is weak as water . . .'[3], and, again: 'Lord Granville behaves miserably; he is the only one *I know well* and he never *even answers* my remarks!!'[4] In the same way she became disappointed with Lord Hartington,[5] until he redeemed himself by leading the forces of Liberal Unionism. Lord Halifax at one time played the same kind of part as a medium of contact

[1] *L.* iv. 555 (undated: November 1868), General Grey to Queen. Cf. above, p. 57.

[2] *L.* iii. 364–7; 377.

[3] *L.* vi. 219 (17.v.81), Journal.

[4] Ibid. 299 (27.v.82), Queen to Prince of Wales. With the Queen's judgement on Lord Granville, compare that of another eminent woman, Beatrice Webb, in *My Apprenticeship*, 304. She quotes from her diary for October 21, 1888: 'He is an inconsiderable man, pleasant enough. But mental insignificance, joined to great political position is irritating to a democratic mind. Like most "society men" he does not care for the likes of me; and until last night he has not spoken to me. But I having appeared in a pretty black gown, he came up to me while I was discussing vehemently labour questions with Mr. Cross. . . . Lord Granville listened with a puzzled air; and when I tried, out of politeness, to bring him in, explaining to him the actual point we were thrashing out, he looked still more utterly at sea, as if I asked him to join in a discussion on Chinese metaphysics. What could a woman, who really by night-light looked quite pretty, want with such questions: still less, how could she expect a polished man of the world to know what she was talking about? So the noble Earl stood silently gazing in mild surprise—I remember Chamberlain on Lord Granville "One does not expect to sit next an old nurse in Cabinet Council" and turned away to tell a little story to some more congenial party.'

It is not surprising after this to learn that to his contemporaries Granville was known as 'Puss'. (Guedalla, i. 59.)

[5] *L.* vi. 548 (7.x.84), Queen to the Duke of Argyll.

with Liberal governments as Lord Granville, and when he died she wrote: 'I truly grieve at his loss. He has always been a true and loyal friend and servant of mine, and in '59, when Lord Russell and Lord Palmerston did, and wanted to do still more, mischief, he was a great and real help.'[1]

But it was over the question of the appointments to the second Gladstone ministry in 1880 that the Queen's attitude towards certain Liberal leaders bordered on the hysterical: 'Mr. Lowe she could *not* accept as a Minister. Sir C. Dilke she would only and unwillingly consent to having a *subordinate office* if absolutely necessary.'[2] But two years later she changed her tone towards Dilke, when she was faced with the prospect of Lord Derby as Secretary of State for India: 'The Queen would far rather see Sir C. Dilke in the Cabinet than Lord Derby, for the former *has right* views on *foreign* politics.'[3] This was the Lord Derby whom as early as 1866[4] she had decided not to be fitted for the Foreign Office, the department in which she always took most interest. She was extremely displeased by his conduct of foreign policy during the Eastern Crisis of 1877–9, and said he 'was *the* most difficult and unsatisfactory Minister she or indeed anyone had to deal with'[5]. In 1880 she announced that she did not 'wish to confer this 1st Vacant Garter on Lord Derby'[6]—it was given instead to the Duke of Bedford—and in 1882 she successfully induced Gladstone to persuade Derby to take the Colonial and not the India Office.[7]

[1] *L.* vii. 689 (11.viii.85), Journal.
[2] *L.* vi. 76 (8.iv.80), Queen to Ponsonby.
[3] Ibid. 378 (14.xii.82), Queen to Gladstone.
[4] *L.* iv. 353 (30.vi.66), Queen to General Grey.
[5] *L.* vi. 105 (30.v.80), Queen to Granville.
[6] Guedalla, ii. 111 (26.viii.80), Queen to Gladstone.
[7] *L.* vi. 379 (14.xii.82), Gladstone to Queen.

In 1886 the same kind of difficulties as to the personnel of the Liberal Government arose as in 1880. The Queen said:

'. . . if Mr. Gladstone came in I would refuse objectionable people. Sir C. Dilke, of course, I must and would never accept on account of his dreadful private character:[1] Mr. Chamberlain, Lord S. advised me *not* to refuse, for it would not be understood and make him a martyr; nor Mr. Morley, a clever and extreme man; but, on observing I did not wish, and meant to object to, Lord Granville as Foreign Secretary, he said I should be "perfectly justified" in doing so, and thought Lord Rosebery would do very well—tho' he was inexperienced; Lord Kimberley would not do. . . . I omitted to state that he [Lord Salisbury] said I naturally would object to Mr. Labouchere as a Minister (if Mr. Gladstone *dared* propose him) and to any Separatist (Home Ruler).'[2]

When the actual moment for making appointments came, the Queen did very largely get her own way. Gladstone said he 'would give up Mr. Childers and would select the gentleman named by your Majesty, Mr. Campbell-Bannerman, for the War Office. He was also ready to obey your Majesty's wishes as regards Lord Rosebery . . .'[3]

The Queen's prejudice against Labouchere continued to be very active, and she described him as horrible and lying, in a message which incidentally affords yet another example of her ignorance of constitutional usage: 'I am quite horrified to see the name of that horrible lying Labouchere and that rebel Parnell in the Committee for the Royal Grants. I protest vehemently against both. It

[1] 'Dreadful private character' is, of course, a reference to his being cited as co-respondent in a divorce case. In 1893 Sir Henry Campbell-Bannerman as Secretary for War suggested that Dilke was largely responsible for public criticism of the appointment of the Duke of Cambridge to the Aldershot Command, attributing to Dilke 'a great underground influence in the Press'. (*L.* viii. 308; 2.ix.93.) So perhaps Dilke had his revenge.

[2] *L.* vii. 24 (28.i.86), Memorandum.

[3] Ibid. 42 (3.ii.86), Ponsonby to Queen.

is quite indecent to have such people on such a Committee.'[1] Lord Salisbury explained that they were bound to be in a minority on the Committee and that therefore the question was not really of any great importance.

In 1892 the Queen '. . . positively refused to take either Sir C. Dilke or . . . Mr. Labouchere. To these, however, she must add Lord Ripon not to have *anything* to do *with India*. Lord Kimberley she is also much against for India, and certainly on no account as Viceroy. She hopes they would *not* change Lord Lansdowne. . . .'[2] Afterwards she recorded her satisfaction that after being refused office 'Mr. Labouchere had expected to be made a great fuss of by everyone, and that there would be a great sensation, "quite a revolution", whereas nobody cared at all. . . .'[3] She made it clear that: '. . . H.M. did not object to his holding an appointment which would not bring him into personal communication with the Queen, on condition that he gave up all connection with the newspaper *Truth*.'[4]

But 1892 provided an opportunity not only for further animadversion on Labouchere, but also for a general condemnation of the Liberal statesmen of the later part of the reign for being ungentlemanly: 'In former times, when there were changes of Government, though often painful to part with those one liked and esteemed, it was to have to do with gentlemen like Lord Russell, Lord Palmerston, Sir G. Grey, Sir R. Peel, Lord Aberdeen, Lord Grey, etc., etc., but now it is with utter disgust that the Queen thinks of it. . . .'[5]

She did not 'tread delicately' in giving her opinion of Bradlaugh: 'The Queen has read with interest the dis-

[1] *L.* vii. 509 (9.vii.89), C.T. to Salisbury.
[2] *L.* viii. 120 (30.v.92), Queen to Ponsonby.
[3] *L.* vii. 157 (11.ix.92), Journal.
[4] *L.* viii. 150 (22.viii.92), Ponsonby to Gladstone.
[5] Ibid. 132 (23.vii.92), Queen to Ponsonby.

cussion on . . . Mr. Bradlaugh & she cannot help rejoicing in the feeling of indignation exhibited ag$^{st}$ such a man's sitting in the House. It is not *only* his known atheism but it is his other horrible principles w$^{h}$ make him a disgrace to an assembly like the House of Commons.'[1]

On the other hand she found that 'Mr. Bryce is one of the best informed men on all subjects I have ever met . . . and he seems to be an impartial and certainly not violent politician'[2]. She thought that Sir William Harcourt as Prime Minister would have commanded neither respect nor confidence.[3] She found Mr. Asquith 'pleasant, straightforward, and sensible'[4].

From the preceding pages it is suggested that one conclusion very clearly emerges, and that is the enormous extent of the Queen's influence over political appointments. Lowell held that it might be said that with 'Peel's appointment to office in 1834 the principle was definitely established that the Prime Minister chooses his colleagues, and is responsible for their selection'[5]. If Lowell meant that from 1834 onwards the Prime Minister chose his colleagues independently of the wishes of the Sovereign, then clearly that was far from true. Maitland was equally wrong in saying that: 'The most important choice that a king can have to make is now the choice of a Prime Minister; the other ministers are practically chosen for him by the Prime Minister. . . .'[6]

[1] Guedalla, ii. 96 (22.v.80), Queen to Gladstone.
[2] *L.* viii. 178 (7.xi.92), Journal.
[3] Ibid. 120 (30.iii.92), Queen to Ponsonby.
[4] Ibid. 156 (26.viii.92), Journal.
[5] *Government of England*, i. 35.
[6] *Constitutional History of England*, 397–8.

## IV

## THE INFLUENCE OF THE QUEEN ON RELIGIOUS AND SOCIAL AFFAIRS

QUEEN VICTORIA was aware that her constitutional position in relation to the Church was one of importance, but does not always seem to have been quite clear as to what exactly that position was. Indeed on one occasion she had to be corrected for ascribing to herself an ecclesiastical title which had been Henry VIII's, but was certainly not Queen Victoria's. She complained to Disraeli of 'an observation of Mr. Hardy's the other night, which if it was correctly reported, would be very extraordinary. It was reported in the newspapers that he had said the Queen was *not* the *Head of the Church.* Now the Sovereign of this country has always been considered the Head of the Church, and also of the Scotch Church, but still more so of the English.'[1] After all, while she was still a Princess at Kensington her Uncle Leopold had said: 'You know that in England the Sovereign is the head of the Church. . . .'[2] But Disraeli answered:

'Mr. Hardy maintains the title "Head of the Church" was waived by Queen Elizabeth, and has never been revived; and that your Majesty's title is "Supreme Governor" or something in that vein. With respect to the Scotch Church, the Lord Advocate informs Mr. Disraeli that the Sovereign has never adopted or claimed the Headship; that the connection of the Sovereign with the Kirk is purely civil.'[3]

[1] *L.* v. 348 (21.vii.74), Queen to Disraeli.

[2] *L.* i. 51 (11.xi.36), King of the Belgians to Princess Victoria.

[3] *L.* v. 349 (25.vii.74), Disraeli to Queen. Mr. Hardy seems to have been a little vague on the point. In the Oath of Supremacy contained in Clause IX of the Act of Supremacy of 1559 Queen Elizabeth is described as 'the only supreme governor of this realm . . . as well in all spiritual or ecclesiastical, things or causes as temporal. . . .' See G. W. Prothero's *Statutes and Constitutional Documents, 1558–1625*, 7.

But the Queen's real influence on the Church was through appointments. On one occasion this led to a brush with Palmerston. We shall see[1] that as a member of an older generation of statesmen he was not afraid of encounters with the Crown, though he did not always emerge victorious from them. The occasion for this particular exchange of sharp words was a vacant canonry at Westminster, of which Palmerston wrote: 'Your Majesty wished to have more than one name submitted for your Majesty's approval, for the appointment . . . this in some degree implies a reference of a recommendation by one of your Majesty's responsible advisers to the judgement of your Majesty's irresponsible advisers in such matters. . .'[2] The Queen's defence against this charge was that the Sovereign had the right, 'as everyone else has, to ask anyone she chooses about any person who is recommended for an appointment to her. The Queen makes it a rule, as the Prince did, to make inquiries in various quarters about the qualifications of those who are recommended to her, whether high or low, for appointments, public or private, and then to take her decision accordingly.'[3]

The Queen was directly responsible for the appointment of Tait to the Archbishopric of Canterbury in 1868 against the advice of Disraeli.[4] But he was in the false position of having no alternative candidate to propose.[5] She claimed a prescriptive personal right to appoint the Dean of Windsor, taking particular pains to have this

[1] Cf. below, pp. 151–2.

[2] *L.* iv. 236 (5.vii.64), Palmerston to Queen.

[3] Ibid. 239 (7.vii.64), Queen to Palmerston. The Queen might well have made the retort that notoriously Palmerston was himself under the influence of an irresponsible adviser in these matters, his son-in-law, Lord Shaftesbury, who had, on this account, been termed the 'Bishop-maker'. Cf. Guedalla's *Palmerston*, 387–91.

[4] *L.* iv. 544–51 (29.x.68–6.xi.68).

[5] Monypenny and Buckle, ii. 407–13.

made clear to Gladstone: 'The Queen is glad to hear that Mr. Gladstone understands that the appointment of Dean of Windsor is a *personal*, and not a *political* appointment; she will therefore not expect Mr. Gladstone to suggest names to her.'[1] Her strong Protestantism led her to do all in her power to prevent Anglo-Catholics obtaining that share of the higher positions in the Church which was their proper due, if only in relation to their numbers and energy. She took strong exception to Liddon's name as a possible Bishop, and even stronger exception to the possibility of his becoming Bishop of Oxford on the ground that 'he might ruin and taint all the young men as Pusey and others did before him. . . .'[2] Similarly, her strong views on the undesirability of Disestablishment led her in the case of a vacant bishopric at Hereford to proclaim that she would 'on no account appoint a Disestablisher'[3]. Indeed, Queen Victoria's conscience would have been almost as much of a hindrance to Ministers determined to carry through a Disestablishment policy as was George III's to the younger Pitt when he proposed Catholic emancipation.[4]

The orthodox theory is that Queen Victoria was easy-going in her attitude to Gladstone's Bill for the Disestablishment and Disendowment of the Irish Church because she recognized this policy to be in accordance with the will of the people. More probably the explanation is that the Irish Church was not near her heart in the same way as was the Scottish. Thus when in 1894 there was a proposal to insert in the Queen's Speech a mention

[1] *L.* vi. 341 (26.ix.82), Queen to Ponsonby.
[2] *L.* vii. 427 (6.vii.88), Queen to Ponsonby.
[3] *L.* viii. 468 (22.i.95), Queen to Bigge.
[4] Farrer, 331: 'Under no republican system, with frequently changing Presidents, would it have been possible for Catholic Emancipation to have been deferred from 1801–1829. . . .'

of Bills to disestablish the Welsh and Scottish Churches, she was firm in her refusal not to allow this: 'I told Sir H. Ponsonby to say I could not mention such a thing, after having promised at my accession to maintain the State Churches....'[1] She told Lord Rosebery the same: '... at her accession, on the Throne in the House of Lords, she solemnly swore to "maintain the Protestant Reformed Religion established by law", and one of the principal provisions of the Act of Union *in* 1707 is that "the *Established Presbyterian Church of Scotland shall be maintained*", and the Queen will do all that lies in her power to be true to this promise.'[2]

The most striking example of the Queen's influence in ecclesiastical affairs is the passing of the Public Worship Regulations Act of 1874, a piece of legislation which was carried at her instigation by Disraeli, and on which the best comment is his own comment: 'If this blow is dealt against the Sacerdotal school, it will be entirely through the personal will of the Sovereign. The Lords were not well disposed at first to the measure; the Cabinet has always been adverse to it; and the House of Commons hesitating and ambiguous.'[3] He had at first taken a cautious line on the Bill, but when he observed the unexpected fervour with which it was received by the House of Commons he waxed enthusiastic in its favour, supporting it in an impassioned speech, as a Bill, 'to put down Ritualism', though it was nothing of the kind.[4] The Queen had earlier pressed the same policy on Gladstone:

'The Queen urged the Archbishop to propose to the Govt. some means by w$^{h}$—*assisted* by the laity—the Bishop shld have

[1] *L.* viii. 379 (9.iii.94), Journal.

[2] Ibid. 452 (21.xi.94), Queen to Rosebery.

[3] *L.* v. 343 (12.vii.74), Disraeli to Queen. Allowance must as usual be made for a possible element of flattery.

[4] Cf. Davidson and Benham, ii. 213.

the power of checking practices which are most dangerous & objectionable & totally foreign to the spirit & former usages of the English Church—but wʰ at present they have *no power* to stop. The Queen must *most earnestly* urge the consideration & she hopes adoption of a proposal to Parliament of some such measure as the Archbishop will, she knows, propose.'[1]

The Queen's influence on Church affairs must be considered in relation to the forces which influenced her religious outlook. She was always a strong Protestant, and in consequence succumbed easily to the cry of 'No Popery': 'The Govt. & many people in this country seem to the Queen to be totally blind to the alarming encroachments & increase of the R. Catholics in England & indeed all over the world. The Pope was never so powerful & the Queen is quite determined to do *all* in her power to prevent this.'[2] Typical of her is her comment on the Positivists: 'How very curious, and how very sad! What a pity somebody does not explain to them what a mistake they are making. But do tell me more about this strange M. Comte.'[3] She declared of the Broad Church position that really it was 'the only true enlightened, Christian & intellectual view of religion wʰ exists. . . .'[4] None the less spiritually she seems to have been most at home in the simple services of the Established Church of Scotland.[5] Her Uncle Leopold on becoming King of the Belgians had been converted easily enough from Lutheranism to Roman Catholicism. It was only too easy for Queen Victoria to make, as she was required by law to do, a less sweeping change in her creed each time she crossed the Scottish Border.

[1] Guedalla, i. 435 (20.i.74), Queen to Gladstone.
[2] Ibid. 201 (24.viii.69), Queen to Granville.
[3] *Quarterly Review*, April, 1901.
[4] Guedalla, ii. 273 (28.v.84), Queen to Gladstone.
[5] Cf. above, p. 67, for the Queen's description of the Scottish Church as 'the real and true stronghold of Protestantism'.

Two Anglican churchmen in turn had a great influence on her. Of these, the first was Dean Wellesley of Windsor, and when he died she wrote: 'The last of my four intimate and confidential friends has now been taken.'[1] We are told that he was 'the latest survival of all those men who were grouped around the Queen in her early youth' and that he 'exercised a paramount authority in matters of Church preferment'[2]. His place in her confidence was quickly filled by Randall Davidson. She first met him in December, 1882, and confided to her diary: 'Saw Mr. Davidson, the Archbishop's son-in-law, and was seldom more struck than I have been by his personality.'[3] The next day she wrote to Gladstone: 'The Queen was vy much struck by Mr. Davidson with whom she had a long interview yesterday. He is singularly pleasing both in appearance & manner; very sympathetic & evidently intelligent, wise & able.'[4] Thereafter Davidson became her most trusted adviser on Church affairs, and was appointed Dean of Windsor in 1882, Bishop of Rochester in 1891, and Bishop of Winchester in 1895. For a time Dr. Norman Macleod played the same kind of part in the affairs of the Established Church of Scotland.

It has already been said that the Queen's interest in foreign affairs exceeded her interest in domestic affairs. Nevertheless, her attitude to social questions is not uninteresting, and at one time, expressing her distress at what she had heard and read about working-class housing conditions, she went so far as to add: 'She cannot but think that there are questions of less importance than this, which are under discussion, and might wait till one involving the very existence of thousands—nay millions—

[1] *L.* vi. 335 (18.ix.82), Journal. [2] *Quarterly Review*, April, 1901.
[3] *L.* vi. 368 (9.xii.82), Journal.
[4] Guedalla, ii. 220 (10.xii.82), Queen to Gladstone.

had been fully considered by the Government.'[1] It is a fair criticism to say that this was not her normal attitude. There is remarkably little evidence to show that she took any interest in the social legislation which is now widely held to be the chief title to fame of the second Disraeli Ministry. But she cannot justly be blamed for not taking a closer and more constant interest in social questions. In this respect her attitude—one of innocent ignorance—was the same as that of most of her contemporaries. It was only at the very end of the century that the work of men like Arnold Toynbee, Charles Booth, and Samuel Barnett brought 'the Social Question' to the front.

It should, however, be recorded that Queen Victoria gave her miniature to Mr. Peabody as a mark of recognition for his work in rehousing the poor, and that she took some interest in housing conditions at Windsor. In 1871 she denounced a proposed match tax because its burden would 'in fact be only severely felt by the poor, which would be very wrong and most impolitic. . . .'[2] In 1899, when the question arose of how to finance the Boer War, she expressed a hope that the increased taxation would not fall upon the working-classes, and a fear that they would be most affected by the extra sixpence on beer.[3] On the other hand, Death Duties were denounced as 'fatal'[4]. She never had any conception of the real meaning of the word 'Socialism' and apparently confused it with rioting: 'The Queen cannot sufficiently express her *indignation* at the monstrous riot which took place the other day in London, and which risked people's lives and was a *momentary* triumph of socialism and disgrace to the capital.'[5] By

[1] *L.* vi. 452 (30.x.83), Queen to Gladstone.
[2] *L.* v. 131 (23.iv.71), Queen to Gladstone.
[3] *L.* ix. 409 (20.x.99), C. T. to Salisbury.
[4] *L.* viii. 414 (13.vii.94), Queen to Rosebery.
[5] *L.* vii. 52 (11.ii.86), Queen to Gladstone. For a vivid description of this

contrast her father, the Duke of Kent, had been a friend of Robert Owen and has been described as 'the first patron of Socialism'[1].

The Queen had strong views on education, firmly holding the opinion that what the people wanted were technical and not humane studies. To Gladstone in 1880 she observed that she had '*long* been of opinion that the elementary Education was of too high a standard,—& useless in consequence, & thus a modification was desirable'[2]; and again in 1886 she 'spoke of education, it being carried too far, and he [Gladstone] entirely agreed that it ruined the health of the higher classes uselessly, and rendered the working classes unfitted for good servants and labourers[3].' To this theme she returned on at least two other occasions.[4] In 1896 she begged Lord Salisbury to call a second Cabinet in order to reconsider a decision to drop an Education Bill.[5] Here, her motive was not zeal for education, but zeal for the prestige of a Conservative Government. Another Cabinet was actually held in accordance with her wishes, but the original decision was upheld.

The Queen was unsparing in her denunciation of the agitation for Woman's Rights. She described this movement as 'dangerous and unchristian and unnatural'.

'The Queen is a woman herself [she wrote]—& knows what an anomaly her *own* position is. . . . But to tear away all the

riot see Godfrey Elton's *England Arise* (Jonathan Cape, 1931), 123–30. It is true that H. M. Hyndman and John Burns, who spoke at the demonstration in Trafalgar Square on February 8, 1886, were both professing Socialists, but the breaking of club windows in Pall Mall and St. James's Street was no part of their plans.

[1] Roger Fulford's *The Royal Dukes* (London, 1933), 197.

[2] Guedalla, ii. 105 (20.vi.80), Queen to Gladstone.

[3] *L.* viii. 168 (30.vii.86), Journal.

[4] Ibid. 380 (10.iii.94), Journal; *L.* ix. 43 (13.v.96), Journal.

[5] Ibid. 54 (20.vi.96), Queen to Salisbury.

barriers w$^{h}$ surround a woman, & to propose that they sh$^{ld}$ study with *men*—things w$^{h}$ c$^{ld}$ not be named before them—certainly not *in a mixed* audience—w$^{ld}$ be to introduce a total disregard of what must be considered as belonging to the rules & principles of morality. Let woman be what God intended; a helpmate for a man—but with totally different duties & vocations.'[1]

Again:

'The Queen is most anxious to enlist every one who can speak or write to join in checking this mad, wicked folly of "Woman's Rights", with all its attendant horrors, on which her poor feeble sex is bent, forgetting every sense of womanly feeling and propriety. Lady —— ought to get a *good whipping*.

'It is a subject which makes the Queen so furious that she cannot contain herself. God created men and women different —then let them remain each in their own position. Tennyson has some beautiful lines on the difference of men and women in *The Princess*. Woman would become the most hateful, heathen, and disgusting of human beings were she allowed to unsex herself; and where would be the protection which man was intended to give the weaker sex? The Queen is sure that Mrs. Martin agrees with her.'[2]

And yet, anti-feminist as Queen Victoria was, her mere presence on the throne served to encourage the growth of feminism. Thus H. G. Wells writes:

'I do not think it is on record anywhere, but it is plain to me from what I have heard my mother say, that among schoolmistresses and such like women at any rate, there was a stir of emancipation associated with the claim of the Princess Victoria . . . to succeed King William IV. There was a movement against that young lady based on her sex and this had provoked in reaction a wave of feminine partisanship throughout the country. It picked up reinforcement from an earlier trouble between George the Fourth and Queen Caroline.'[3]

[1] Guedalla, i. 227 (6.v.70), Queen to Gladstone.

[2] Martin's *Queen Victoria*, 69–70 (29.v.70), Queen to Sir Theodore Martin.

[3] *Experiment in Autobiography* (Victor Gollancz and Cresset Press, 1934), 45–6.

It is a little surprising to find a woman of Queen Victoria's general outlook denouncing vivisection as 'a disgrace to humanity & Christianity'[1]. But her customary moderation in matters of this kind reasserted itself when she asked the ever-patient Gladstone to 'communicate with the Dean of Westminster on the subject of checking Mr. Wilberforce in his desire (if he manifests any) of preaching teetotal sermons in Westminster Abbey'[2].

[1] Guedalla, ii. 152 (16.iv.81), Queen to Gladstone.
[2] Ibid. 489 (14.ii.94), Ponsonby to Gladstone.

## V

# THE INFLUENCE OF THE QUEEN ON FOREIGN, IMPERIAL, AND MILITARY AFFAIRS

THE interest of the Queen in foreign affairs was largely a family interest. In the nineteenth century the royal princes and princesses of Europe were generally permitted to marry only among themselves. The consequence of this perpetual intermarriage was an increasing difficulty in making valid lineal distinctions between the different, national royal Houses. It would not be altogether untrue to say that before the Great War, at the close of which the government of vast areas of the Continent was suddenly changed from a monarchial to a republican form, the titular rulers of Europe (with the exception of France) were all members of a single family.

The House of Saxe-Coburg had in the nineteenth century a remarkably chequered history. On the death of Duke Francis in 1806, its territories were in the possession of the Napoleonic armies, its revenues were non-existent, and it seemed, in short, destined to complete obscurity or even actual extinction. On the death of Queen Victoria in 1901 it had gained a foothold in half the reigning Houses of Europe. The German Emperor was the Queen's grandson. The Tsar of Russia, Nicholas II, had married her granddaughter. Four of her other granddaughters became Queens of Greece, Roumania, Norway, and Spain. The network of these royal relationships extended all over Europe.[1]

Queen Victoria, being richly endowed with a keen human sympathy which led her to take an unfailing interest in all the events of family life, in marriages, births,

[1] On this question see the genealogical tables at the end of *L.* ix.

illnesses, and deaths, came to play to the Royal Family of Europe the same kind of part as was played by Aunt Ann, the classic creation of Galsworthy, to the family of the Forsytes. Family tradition and family life meant more to the Victorians than they do to the present generation, and in most Victorian families there was some one person, usually some matriarch, exercising a kind of planetary influence, a person around whom the whole family circle revolved, a person at whose home the family met on the rare occasions when all its members gathered together, a person who was, in short, the head of the family. Such a person was Aunt Ann Forsyte, and such a person, also, it is claimed, was the Queen-Empress herself.

It was not surprising, therefore, that the Queen should take an interest in the affairs of Europe, since they were so largely her family affairs. But at the same time it was probably true that she was naturally predisposed to take a closer interest in foreign than in domestic politics.[1] Given her personality, the largely personal processes of diplomacy were bound to be of greater interest to her than the details of reforming legislation, and her most notable intellectual attainment was her mastery of French and German.[2] She also spoke a little Italian. It is Professor Laski's opinion 'that the supposed influence of the Monarch upon foreign affairs is mainly a legend without even

[1] Cf. Lady Gwendolen Cecil's *Life of Salisbury*, iii. 289: '. . . She had accommodated herself [to a remarkable degree] to a convention which forbids the Sovereign to have opinions on home politics. The result had been to destroy her interest in them, and to concentrate it almost wholly upon questions of external and national [international?] policy.' This suggestion is an interesting one, and, no doubt, contains a truth. But it has been seen that the Queen was in fact very far indeed from accommodating herself to any such alleged convention.

[2] She told Rosebery that she always had her German letters overhauled before they were sent. She could rely on her own French. The popular supposition that she usually spoke German in her own domestic circle is untrue. (Crewe's *Rosebery*, 434.)

the power to edify'[1]. But this, surely, is very much open to question. Certainly in the opinion of another expert, great as was the influence of Edward VII on foreign policy, it fell far short of that of his mother.[2]

A state of affairs in which almost all Europe was thus ruled by one family had advantages and disadvantages. Among the disadvantages was the danger of a quarrel between relatives, an event which is common enough, becoming a quarrel between nations. It is arguable, for example, that between 1914 and 1918 Englishmen and Germans who had no real grievances against one another, indulged in an orgy of mutual slaughter, partly at any rate because of a certain coldness in the attitude of Queen Victoria to the Emperor William II on account of the latter's treatment of his widowed mother, and partly because of a more open conflict between the Emperor and his uncle, Edward VII, which had broken out as early as 1888.[3] This is an extreme example, but the biographer of Edward, 'the Peacemaker', was no doubt well advised to speak of 'the common experience that advances in private cordiality between the royal families of different countries give small guarantee of improved political relations between governments and peoples'.[4]

On the credit side, however, there was a certain international advantage in the existence of this great and powerful family in that it did enable political differences which Foreign Ministers had been unable to settle to be composed by an exchange of letters, at once personal and private as between relatives, and political and public as between crowned heads. As Gladstone said: '. . . Personal and domestic relations with the ruling families abroad

[1] Laski, *The Crisis and the Constitution*, 31.

[2] *Cambridge History of British Foreign Policy*, iii. 615 (Algernon Cecil).

[3] Cf. below, p. 165.

[4] Lee's *King Edward VII*, i. 269.

give openings, in delicate cases, for saying more, and saying it at once more gently and more efficaciously, than could be ventured in the more formal correspondence, and ruder contacts, of Governments.'[1] One modern writer expresses the opinion that

> 'The Queen's contribution was invaluable in identifying and illuminating [the] personal element in European politics. . . . Drawing her facts from her large private correspondence, illuminated by old experience, she would discuss the characters and motives of the sovereigns and statesmen of Europe much in the same way that an intelligent and observant county gentleman's wife might discuss those of her county neighbours.'[2]

This finds confirmation in Lord Rowton's having said that the Queen 'has selected all over Europe the most intelligent member of the royal family of every Court, and upon any question, domestic or foreign, which arises, she obtains by letter an opinion'[3].

The first important incident in British foreign policy after 1861 was the decision not to support the Poles in their revolt in 1863. Here the full weight of the royal influence was in favour of this decision, and the determining factor so far as the Queen was concerned was the desire on no account to be involved in a war with Germany. Bismarck and Prussia had placed a cordon round Poland in order to prevent foreign aid reaching the insurgents, and so to earn the gratitude of Russia. But in this context the Queen does not speak merely of Prussia. She begins by speaking of Germany, because the Prince Consort had always been in favour of German unification: 'The Queen is terribly alarmed at the French language and proposals respecting Poland, and thinks *we* must, on NO account, let ourselves be dragged into what *may* be a war with Germany! . . .

[1] Gladstone's *Gleanings*, i. 41.

[2] Lady Gwendolen Cecil's *Life of Salisbury*, iii. 186.

[3] Esher, i. 160–1 (23.viii.92), Journal.

The proposals of France would inevitably bring us into collision with Prussia, and we should have a French Army on the Rhine before we could turn round.'[1] The Crown Princess of Prussia is reported as being in despair at the Prussian attitude to Poland.[2] But even if the Queen herself had some sympathy for the rebels, the governing consideration in her mind was a determination to prevent a war in which France would be the ally and Germany the enemy. A war of this kind was indeed avoided, with the consequence that our difficulties over the Schleswig-Holstein question the very next year were considerably increased by the fact that France, partly through annoyance at our refusal to help the Poles, gave us tit for tat by refusing to help the Danes.

It might have been thought that in the Schleswig-Holstein question conflicting family ties would have made it difficult for the Queen to make up her mind on the issues involved. On the one hand, her eldest daughter was Crown Princess of Prussia: on the other, her eldest son's newly wedded wife was a Danish princess. But the Queen's attitude was not in the least affected by this latter relationship and we find her writing to Lord Clarendon: 'It strikes the Queen that it would be *very* useful, if Lord Clarendon would take an opportunity of seeing the Prince of Wales, and *preparing* him for what the Danish Government, in *all* probability, will have to consent to. . . .'[3] This letter indicates the extent to which the heir to the throne was at that time normally kept in the dark as to the course of public events, and also shows some fear on the Queen's part that her son, under the influence of his wife, might become so strongly pro-Danish as actively to oppose the

[1] *L.* iv. 66 (23.ii.63), Queen to Granville.
[2] Ibid. 69 (24.ii.63), Queen to King of the Belgians.
[3] Ibid. 190 (17.v.64), Queen to Clarendon.

Government. That this fear was not justified is proved by Lord Clarendon's answer[1] in which he says that he has seen the Prince, who had already written to the King of Denmark advising compliance with the British proposals, and was anxious to be employed as an intermediary with Denmark. His offer to act as intermediary was accepted, on the condition that it was only to be made use of sparingly and with extreme caution.[2]

As has been seen, Queen Victoria had on most questions such decided views that it was never easy for her not to be a partisan, and in this question she was a partisan of Germany. In October, 1863, Gladstone found her 'intensely interested' in the Schleswig-Holstein affair '. . . because the Prince thought it a great case of justice on the side rather opposite to that of Palmerston and the government policy. She spoke about this with intense ernestness, and said she considered it a legacy from him.'[3] She told 'Vicky' (the Crown Princess of Prussia) with one breath that in this sad Schleswig-Holstein question she could really speak with more thorough impartiality than any one, and almost with the next that her heart and sympathies were all German.[4]

The Queen's opinions were, therefore, made crystal clear in the very early stages of this episode: 'She does not believe any attack is intended upon either the integrity or independence of Denmark; and neither Prussia nor Austria seem inclined to give effect to the threatened Federal Execution, but, if they do, it will be the fault of Denmark, and not of Germany.'[5] The issue is in effect prejudged. Germany is bound to be right and Denmark

[1] Ibid. 194 (20.v.64), Clarendon to Queen.
[2] Ibid. 195 (22.v.64), Grey to Clarendon.
[3] Morley, ii. 78 (7.x.63), Gladstone's diary.
[4] *L.* iv. 153 (27.i.64), Queen to Crown Princess of Prussia.
[5] Ibid. 86 (19.v.63), Queen to Russell.

wrong, and, as was natural enough, the real spirit of Prussian policy, and the influence of Bismarck, escape comment or criticism. Three months later the Queen is insisting on her right to be consulted about this question, and is indulging in further condemnation of Denmark: '. . . She wishes to state once more her desire that *no step* is taken in foreign affairs *without* her *previous sanction* being obtained. This applies especially to the Polish question, but the Queen applies it equally to all others of importance and in particular to Schleswig-Holstein, about which the shameful bad faith of the Danes may lead to serious mischief.'[1] Later still: 'She urges the Government *most* strongly to do *nothing* without *consultation* with the other *Powers*, but *especially* with Germany.'[2]

The views of Palmerston and Russell on this question were almost precisely the opposite of the Queen's. The first sign of an acute difference of opinion between the Crown and its Ministers on this question appears in a letter from Lord Russell to the Queen, written in November, 1863:

'Lord Russell feels very confident that, if Austria and Prussia are persuaded that your Majesty's Government feels a serious interest in the integrity of Denmark, peace may be preserved. . . . Any surrender of the integrity of Denmark would be very unpopular in this country. Lord Derby and Mr. Disraeli have hitherto reproached your Majesty's Government with being too favourable to Germany. . . .'[3]

Perhaps these opinions were to a certain extent based on a semi-romantic desire to be on the side of the small boy in his fight against the big boy, and this point is actually made by Palmerston in picturesque and typically Palmer-

[1] *L.* iv. 102 (11.viii.63), Queen to Palmerston.
[2] Ibid. 115 (16.xi.63), Queen to Russell.
[3] Ibid. 120 (23.xi.63), Russell to Queen.

stonian language, which would have horrified the Prince Consort by its unscientific character:

'The Germans are acting like a strong man who thinks he has got a weak man in a corner, and that he can bully and beat him to his heart's content. But that is not the conduct of brave or generous minds, and it sometimes happens in real life, as it does in a romance, that the wicked giant finds that his intended victim meets with unlooked-for support.'[1]

In February, 1864, however, Lord Granville was able to report to General Grey[2] that Russell had accepted the proposition, which Palmerston had also a short time previously accepted, that there was no question of England going to war single-handed. But that did not end the matter. The smallness of the English army meant that it was not really possible for England, without an ally, to aid the Danes against the Germans. But later in the same month, on a rumour, to which there can hardly have been any solid foundation, that the Austrian Fleet was to sail from the Mediterranean to the Baltic, Palmerston eagerly embraced the project of sending the English Fleet into battle against the Austrian,[3] and in April the Queen was directly responsible for the withdrawal by Palmerston and Russell of a proposal to send the Fleet to the Baltic in the event of Austria and Prussia not agreeing to an armistice:[4] '. . . though all this anxiety is wearing her out it will not shake her in her firm purpose of resisting any attempt to involve this country in a mad and useless combat.'[5] And again: 'She can only repeat that she is so thoroughly convinced of the awful danger and recklessness of our stirring up France and Russia to go to war, that she would be

[1] Ibid. 145 (8.i.64), Palmerston to Queen.
[2] Ibid. 157 (13.ii.64), Granville to Grey.
[3] Ibid. 163 (22.ii.64), Palmerston to Queen.
[4] Ibid. 174 (19.iv.64), Russell to Queen.
[5] Fitzmaurice, i. 459 (12.ii.64), Queen to Granville.

prepared to make a stand upon it, should it even cause the resignation of Lord Russell.'[1] But it is hard to see who she could then have found to take his place, and of that difficulty she was no doubt aware.

The general question of how far the Queen really was responsible for English neutrality and the abandonment of Denmark to her fate is extremely difficult to determine. Mr. Farrer sums up to the effect that '. . . the Queen did more than express opinions adverse to those of her chief Ministers and of a large section of public opinion; she insisted on their prevailing. She saved the country from war in spite of itself. . . .'[2] Probably this is going too far. Strachey gave it as his opinion, for what it is worth, that 'on the whole . . . it seems probable that the determining factor in the situation was the powerful peace party in the Cabinet[3] rather than the imperious and pathetic pressure of Victoria'[4]. It is, at any rate, quite clear, admittedly weak as is the conclusion, that her opinions and the pressure she exerted were important factors, though exactly how decisive factors it is difficult to ascertain, in the pacifist policy pursued by England in the Schleswig-Holstein dispute.

It was a dispute which is also of domestic constitutional interest on three grounds, two minor and one major. The first minor point is that early in 1864 the Queen summoned Lord Derby, the Leader of the Opposition, to Osborne and impressed on him the danger of making the

[1] Fitzmaurice, i. 460 (14.ii.64), Queen to Granville.

[2] Farrer, 282.

[3] Gladstone in his diary (7.v.64; Morley, ii. 90) noted that the war party consisted of Palmerston, Russell, Lord Westbury, and Lord Stanley of Alderley (the first two being for war even if it had to be fought single-handed). This leaves as the peace party, Gladstone himself, Duke of Argyll, Earl de Grey and Ripon, Earl of Clarendon, Sir C. Wood, Bt., Sir George Grey, E. Cardwell, T. Milner Gibson, and C. P. Villiers.

[4] Strachey, 198.

Schleswig-Holstein question a party one.[1] The warning would seem to have been superfluous, for as we have already seen, Derby and Disraeli were as much pro-Danish as Palmerston and Russell. The Queen, in fact, was on this issue as much opposed to Her Majesty's Opposition as to Her Majesty's Government. But this is the first of many occasions[2] during the period under review on which the Queen advised opposition leaders to take up a national and non-party attitude, though her own outlook was by no means devoid of a strong party bias for most of the time.

The second minor point is that Lord Russell received a reprimand for sending off telegrams which had not received the royal approbation.[3] This reprimand had many precedents, and was to be one of the precedents for many similar reprimands in the future. The third point is more important and more interesting, a rebuke which Lord Palmerston, undeferential as always, administered to the Queen. He sent the Queen a copy of a certain newspaper and said of it:

'. . . This paper, and others which have been mentioned to Viscount Palmerston, tend to show, that an impression is beginning to be created that your Majesty has expressed personal opinions on the affairs of Denmark and Germany which have embarrassed the course of the Government. . . . It would be a great evil if public opinion were to divest your Majesty of that proper and essential protection which the Constitution secures for the Sovereign by making the responsible Ministers answerable for all that is done or not done; and if your Majesty's

[1] *L.* iv. 154 (2.ii.64), Queen to Palmerston.

[2] For other instances of this technique of contact with the Opposition, cf. Ibid. 89 (10.vi.63), Queen to Derby; Ibid. 329 (29.v.66), Queen to Derby; Ibid. 389 (10.i.67), Derby to Queen; Ibid. 603 (7.vi.69), Queen to Derby; *L.* v. 345 (16.vii.74), Granville to Queen; *L.* vi. 100 (21.v.80), Queen o the Duke of Richmond; Ibid. 187 (28.i.81), Journal; Ibid. 320 (4.viii.82), Queen to Salisbury; Ibid. 358 (14.xi.82), Salisbury to Sir Richard Cross; Ibid. 511 (3.vii.84), Journal.

[3] *L.* iv. 120 (23.xi.63), Russell to Queen.

personal opinions and views were to become the objects of criticism or attack. Your Majesty has no doubt been duly careful as to the degree and manner in which your Majesty's opinions and views have been expressed, but it might be well that no indiscreet expression from persons about your Majesty should give any countenance to such remarks as those in this newspaper.'[1]

Two days later the Queen tells her Uncle Leopold, the King of the Belgians, that 'Pilgerstein is gouty, and extremely impertinent. . . .'[2] No subsequent Prime Minister ever dared to address such language to the Queen.

In August, 1865, the Queen 'somewhat obtrusively'[3] consented to the engagement of her daughter Helena to Prince Christian of Schleswig-Holstein-Sonderburg-Augustenburg. He was the younger brother of the Duke Frederick whose claim to Schleswig-Holstein had been supported by the Crown Prince and Princess of Prussia. Prince Christian had just been deprived of his commission in the Prussian army, and the incident was a cause of annoyance to Bismarck.

Taking up again the narrative story of the Queen's influence on British foreign policy, it is extremely interesting to observe that it was only after the Schleswig-Holstein War that she began to be informed of the importance of the part played in German politics by Bismarck. In August, 1865, she received a letter from the Countess Blücher, in which Bismarck was condemned in no uncertain tones: 'The Queen [Queen Augusta of Prussia] says the King's *personal* feelings to your Majesty are what they *ever* were; that he is under the influence of a clever, unprincipled man, who has completely changed him. . . .'[4] The next

[1] *L.* iv. 186 (10.v.64), Palmerston to Queen.
[2] Ibid. 187 (12.v.64), Queen to King of the Belgians.
[3] Lee's *Edward VII*, i. 257–8.
[4] *L.* iv. 273 (27.viii.65), Countess Blücher to Queen.

year Bismarck is described by the Crown Princess of Prussia as 'the wicked man'[1].

Apart from this growing realization of the sinister influence of Bismarck, the Queen's sympathies, though always German, were not necessarily always Prussian. In the year of revolutions she had said: 'I do not either at all agree in [Stockmar's] wish that Prussia should take the lead; his love for Prussia is to me incomprehensible, for it is the country of all others which the *rest* of Germany dislikes.'[2] Again, in August, 1865, she said: 'Prussia seems inclined to behave as atrociously as possible, and as she *always has done*! Odious people the Prussians are, *that* I *must* say.'[3] For this reason Queen Victoria at first upheld the Austrian cause during the Seven Weeks War, even to the extent of advocating an English-Austrian-French alliance against Prussia. She sent a memorandum to Lord Russell, 'showing the absolute necessity of our attempting to do something, in conjunction with France, to arrest the misfortunes a war would entail'[4]. But after the Battle of Sadowa in July, 1866, had altered the situation, the Queen's tone changed, and the traditional policy of the House of Saxe-Coburg which as a smaller House in contrast to, say, the House of Hanover, was in favour of German unification,[5] reasserted itself: 'Germany's great wish is to be *united* under the supremacy of Prussia . . . a strong, united, liberal Germany would be a most useful ally to England.'[6] That had also been the wish of the Prince Consort.[7] It was the supreme tragedy of German

[1] *L.* iv. 305 (20.iii.66), Crown Princess of Prussia to Queen.

[2] *L.* ii. 192 (29.viii.48), Queen to King of the Belgians.

[3] *L.* iv. 271 (3.viii.65), Queen to King of the Belgians.

[4] Ibid. 314 (30.iii.66), Journal.

[5] *L.* i. 2.

[6] *L.* iv. 364 (7.viii.66), Queen to Lord Stanley.

[7] Cf. *The Empress Frederick*, by Princess Catherine Radziwill (Cassell, 1934), 112, quotation from the Crown Prince Frederick's war diary (14.xii.70): 'My thoughts are busied in a very special way to-day with my beloved,

history in the nineteenth century, and a supreme misfortune for the world as a whole, that a Germany united under the supremacy of Prussia and a liberal Germany, which would be the ally of England, proved to be mutually exclusive.

The years between the close of the Austro-Prussian War in 1866 and the outbreak of the Franco-Prussian War in 1870 yield many examples of the Queen's remarkable foresight as to the future course of events in foreign affairs. Broadly speaking the Queen saw clearly enough that war was likely, and argued strongly that if its outbreak was to be prevented England must declare herself in advance to be on the German side. General Grey, obviously acting as the royal mouthpiece, wrote to Disraeli:

'If we keep up an enormous force of volunteers, if we incur a frightful expense to create an Iron-clad Navy, . . . it is caused by fear of the *possible* designs of *France*. With *Prussia* we have no clashing interests—no possible point of collision. . . . The fear of a German Army on the Rhine would probably have more effect than the fear either of our Volunteers or Army of Reserve, in deterring France from attacking us; while we could come effectually with our fleet to the assistance of Prussia in the Baltic, in case of French aggression upon her. While, therefore, we cultivate the most friendly relations with all other Powers, including France, the *principle* of our Foreign Policy (and this was also the opinion of the Prince Consort) should be a thorough understanding for mutual support, in the interests of Peace,

never-to-be-forgotten father-in-law, who this very day nine years ago was taken from us . . . it would have been a subject of congratulation in his case if only he could have witnessed the restoration of the Empire, the complicated questions involved in which so often formed the subject of his talks with me. In particular, I recall perfectly a conversation we had during a stroll in the gardens of Buckingham Palace, in which he more especially stressed the point that we Prussians would have to give up the idea of playing a decisive role without assistance from Germany. His notion was not that of gaining by force of arms the ends the attainment of which was hindered by the stupidity of the Princes and the narrow-mindedness of the nation. . . .'

with North Germany; and of this it would be well that Germany should feel assured.'[1]

The argument is one which was subsequently elaborated in another letter from General Grey to Disraeli, in which it is explained that the Queen's real reason for wanting a German alliance is the danger of France and Prussia fighting an inconclusive war and then joining hands to threaten 'the independence of the rest of Europe'. The Queen's demand was that it should be clearly laid down that England would come into the field against any violation of the neutrality of Belgium or Luxemburg: 'Such an assurance . . . would in fact be directed rather against France than against Prussia.'[2]

The same kind of arguments were repeated in April, 1869, in a very remarkable correspondence with Clarendon,[3] which was finally sent to Gladstone as Prime Minister. This correspondence arose out of a demand from Portugal for a definite guarantee of English support in the event of her being attacked by Spain. The Queen was in favour of such a pledge being given. Clarendon objected to being committed in advance to any such definite course of action, and he prevailed against the Queen. Lord Stanley had taken up a similar attitude with regard to the prospect of a Franco-Prussian War: 'If war does break out, we have only one course; that of a rigidly impartial neutrality.'[4] But a month before this pronouncement Disraeli, in answer to the first of the two letters from General Grey which have just been quoted, made a very different kind of statement:

'You may assure the Queen . . . of my constant efforts to sustain her Majesty's policy. Lord Stanley, of late, acting, I

[1] *L.* iv. 452–3 (29.vii.67), Grey to Disraeli.
[2] Ibid. 456 (5.viii.67), Grey to Disraeli.
[3] Ibid. 589–92 (April, 1869).
[4] Ibid. 458 (9.viii.67), Stanley to Grey.

hope, in some degree under the influence of my reiterated representations, has entirely dropped the phrase, and, I hope, the abstract policy, of what is called 'non-intervention'. . . . I think the general bias of Lord Stanley's mind is to lean towards Prussia, and I have always encouraged and enforced that tendency.'[1]

As always with Disraeli's letters to the Queen, allowance must be made for a flattering feint of compliance with the royal wishes. But if these remarks are in any sense genuine indications of a sincere opinion (and we have seen that so far as Lord Stanley was concerned they were shortly proved mistaken) it becomes interesting to speculate whether in the event of Disraeli having been Prime Minister in 1870 England might not have formed a German alliance and fought against France. Such a war would have been a more than adequate gratification of his taste for a 'spirited foreign policy'.

Be that as it may, it is clear that between 1866 and 1870 the Queen was fighting a losing battle, and that her strong expressions of her point of view did not affect the conduct of her Ministers. The situation is curiously similar to that of the years immediately preceding 1914. We know, from Harold Nicolson's biography of his father,[2] how strongly in those years Lord Carnock, Permanent Under-Secretary of State at the Foreign Office, pressed for a definite decision that in the event of France being attacked by Germany, England would take the French side, and that this should be made known to France and Germany, and how Lord Grey resisted this pressure and refused to commit his country to this policy. Queen Victoria prior to 1870 held the same point of view as Lord Carnock prior to 1914, though he demanded a French alliance, and she, a German alliance. But in both cases the argument was

[1] *L.* iv. 455 (31.vii.67), Disraeli to Grey.

[2] *The First Baron Carnock*, Hon. Harold Nicolson (London, 1930).

broadly the same, that war could be prevented only by general knowledge of the fact that the full weight of England was to be thrown into one of the scales. That this policy in either case might have prevented that particular war is arguable; that it would have prevented war in the long run is very much open to doubt.

In March, 1870, the coming event of the Franco-Prussian War cast its shadow before it. 'Vicky' wrote very urgently to her mother to ask for her opinion on the candidature of Leopold of Hohenzollern for the vacant throne of Spain.[1] On this point Lord Clarendon advised the Queen 'that it would not be expedient for your Majesty to give any advice upon a matter in which no British interest is concerned'[2]. This was very bad advice, for a very vital British interest happened to be concerned, the British interest in the preservation of peace. But in July, having been asked to do so by the King of the Belgians and by Lord Granville (who had succeeded Lord Clarendon as Foreign Secretary after his death in June), the Queen did write to the Count of Flanders,[3] a brother-in-law of Leopold of Hohenzollern, and he did withdraw his candidature. Lord Granville was right in telling the Queen that she had contributed 'to put an end to the substantial cause of dispute'[4].

When war still seemed imminent, although the substantial cause of dispute had thus apparently been removed, the Queen naturally felt reluctant to continue her efforts to avert the catastrophe: 'The Queen, having interfered as requested, feels that this persistence of the French in seeking for further grounds of quarrel places her in a humiliating position.'[5] Nevertheless, she did continue her

[1] *L.* v. 10 (12.iii.70), Crown Princess of Prussia to Queen.
[2] Ibid. 11 (14.iii.70), Clarendon to Queen.
[3] Ibid. 28 (11.vii.70), Queen to Count of Flanders.
[4] Ibid. 35 (15.vii.70), Granville to Queen.
[5] Ibid. 32 (14.vii.70), C. T. to Granville.

efforts. Two telegrams of July 15, 1870, deserve quotation. First, '. . . Might it not be desirable for the Queen, the Emperors of Russia and Austria, and the Kings of Holland, Belgium and Italy to make a combined appeal to the King of Prussia and the Emperor of the French . . . ?'[1] 'It has been suggested to the Queen that a personal appeal from her to the French Emperor might avert war. If you think so, telegraph such an appeal at once, dating it from Osborne.'[2]

We have already seen that after the Schleswig-Holstein crisis there had been a growing realization of the importance of Bismarck's influence, and yet it was not in the least suspected that he was responsible for the outbreak of the Franco-Prussian War. Gladstone tells the Queen: 'It is evident that the sentiment of the House on both sides generally condemns the conduct of France . . .'[3]; and Granville dogmatically asserts: 'France is morally unpardonable.'[4] Apparently the first English official to arrive at a true view of the matter was Sir Robert Morier, who, in 1870, was Secretary of Legation at Darmstadt; and though he deserves every credit for his perception of the truth, he was himself at first hardly credited: 'Colonel Ponsonby . . . begs leave to express his surprise at Mr. Morier's statement, which is so confidently made as to lead one to believe Mr. Morier has no doubt of the case.'[5] It was some time after Mr. Morier had made statements which surprised Colonel Ponsonby that the Queen noted in her Journal that 'Fritz' (the German Crown Prince) 'has the intensest horror of Bismarck, says he is no doubt energetic and clever, but bad, unprincipled, and *all-powerful*.'[6] In 1875, at the time

[1] *L.* v. 33 (15.vii.70), C. T. to Granville.
[2] Ibid. 34 (15.vii.70), C. T. to Granville.
[3] Ibid. 34 (15.vii.70), Gladstone to Queen.
[4] Ibid. 35 (15.vii.70), Granville to Queen.
[5] Ibid. 75 (12.x.70), Ponsonby to Queen.
[6] Ibid. 154 (31.vii.71), Journal.

of a bad Franco-Prussian war-scare, she herself described him as 'so overbearing, violent, grasping and unprincipled that *no one* can stand it, and *all* agreed that he was becoming like the first Napoleon whom Europe had to join in PUTTING down . . . indeed *no one* will stand the overbearing insolent way in which he acts and treats other nations, Belgium for instance.'[1]

The Queen made another attempt at mediation towards the close of 1870, when she telegraphed to the King of Prussia: 'The Queen asks the King of Prussia as a friend whether, in the interests of suffering humanity, he could so shape his demands as to enable the French to accept them.'[2] The reply was evasive. But the Queen before sending this telegram stated that: 'The great danger for *us* in *interfering* is to have the *appearance* of *wishing* to *prevent* Germany from making a lasting peace and from obtaining such securities from her [France] as may *really* prevent the recurrence of a *similar war*. . . .'[3]

The interest of the Franco-Prussian War in relation to the Crown's political influence is that it offers a good example of the technique by which Queen Victoria made use of her personal contacts with foreign rulers in an attempt to preserve peace. She was successful (so far as her part in the matter went) in securing the withdrawal of the Hohenzollern candidature. She failed in her attempt to put pressure on the King of Prussia to moderate the terms of peace which he was offering to France. The failure was not due to any lack of respect on the King's part for the personality or the views of Queen Victoria, but to the fact that he was under the domination of Bismarck, and to the fact that the issues at stake were those

[1] Ibid. 405–6 (8.vi.75), Queen to German Crown Princess.
[2] Ibid. 71 (19.ix.70), T. to King of Prussia.
[3] Ibid. 62 (9.ix.70), Memorandum.

of *Realpolitik.* Under other circumstances the Queen's influence was sometimes enough to turn the scales.

The Queen's conception of the policy England should adopt at this juncture was in accord with that of her Ministers. It might have been expected that she would have advocated active participation on the German side, and the Crown Princess of Prussia, for once sharing the public opinion of her adopted country, seems to have counted on such an alliance: 'I think in the *main* grievance Germany is right and her feeling *legitimate*; for in my mind I cannot help thinking England *could* have and should have prevented the war—by a rebuke and a threat to the party who was the aggressor.'[1] In fact the English policy of neutrality made England very unpopular in Germany, while at the end of the war English sympathy for the losing side caused an increase of the popularity of France in England.

The part played by the Queen in the Eastern Crisis of 1876–8 is already so well known that it requires little description or comment:[2] 'Never in her life, not even in the crisis over the Ladies of the Bedchamber, did she show herself a more furious partisan.'[3] In the days of Palmerston the Queen had disliked both him and his foreign policy. It was very different when a Palmerstonian foreign policy was carried out by Disraeli. The consequence was that he had to complain that: 'The Faery writes every day, and telegraphs every hour; this is almost literally the case.'[4]

[1] *L.* v. 80 (7.xi.70), Crown Princess of Prussia to Queen. The same argument is also expressed ibid. 48 (25.vii.70), Crown Princess of Prussia to Queen.

[2] Cf. 'The Victorian Monarchy', by Kingsley Martin, *Edinburgh Review*, April, 1926, 381–2: '. . . the vigour of the royal pressure, both in the Schleswig-Holstein crisis of 1864 and the Russo-Turkish embroglio of 1876–8, seems to pass beyond the bounds of constitutional "warning" and "encouragement".'

[3] Strachey, 230.

[4] Monypenny and Buckle, ii. 1022 (June, 1877), Disraeli to Lady Bradford.

The quantity of this correspondence is so great that it has not been possible to include a fully representative portion of it in the *Letters*.[1]

But the Queen's attitude was at first quite moderate. When in 1870 Russia repudiated the Black Sea clauses of the Treaty of Paris of 1856, she wrote that '. . . . a war at the present moment [against Russia] might be very disastrous to *us*, and do great harm to Turkey instead of good', and that it was essential to avoid 'a war for so unsatisfactory a cause—as in fact the upholding of a Mohammedan State with so little real intrinsic power. . . .'[2] She criticized our refusal to agree to the Berlin Memorandum from 'a fear that Turkey will look to us to help her against the rest of Europe, and that we shall thus precipitate rather than prevent the catastrophe'[3].

The key to her attitude, however, is to be found in the question of Constantinople: 'It is clear England *cannot fight for* the Turks, but we also cannot fight against them. The much abused policy of *upholding* the Turkish Empire was merely to prevent Russia having Constantinople! This we still never could allow!'[4] The Queen's vision was not obscured by love for Turkey; but it was obscured by hatred of Russia, and this is especially apparent in her point of view of the Bulgarian atrocities: 'Hearing as we *do* all the undercurrent, and knowing as we do that Russia *instigated* this insurrection, which *caused* the cruelty of the Turks, it *ought* to be brought home to Russia, and the world *ought* to know that on *their* shoulders and *not* on *ours* rests the *blood* of the murdered Bulgarians!'[5] There is also in the Journal an account of an interview with Colonel

[1] *L.* v. 437 (G. E. Buckle).
[2] Ibid. 85 (20.xi.70), Queen to Granville.
[3] Ibid. 453 (16.v.76), Ponsonby to Disraeli.
[4] Ibid. 488 (17.x.76), Memorandum.
[5] Ibid. 480 (28.ix.76), Queen to Beaconsfield.

Wellesley, who had just returned from the Russian Court, and reported that the Tsar 'said and believed that the Prince of Wales and I were anti-Russian, which I said was not untrue, for we felt strongly the way in which Russia had behaved all along, and how they had instigated the Bulgarian insurrection which had led to the massacres'[1]. Colonel Wellesley, it is interesting to note, had been sent on a secret mission to the Tsar by the Queen and Disraeli, unofficially to warn him that a second Russian campaign against Turkey was likely to bring England into the field against him: 'The natural safeguards of the constitution were thus swept away by excluding from the management and even the cognisance of foreign affairs both the minister responsible to Parliament and the expert advisers whom he was understood to consult.'[2]

The Queen's policy in this Eastern crisis is perhaps best summed up when she wrote to Beaconsfield: '. . . The Queen thinks great progress is being made with respect to a Congress, though she must own to disbelieving any *permanent* settlement of Peace until we have fought and beaten the Russians. . . .'[3] It was peculiarly fortunate that at this moment of crisis, the Queen's views being what they were, her favourite minister was in power. Is it altogether unfair to describe the foreign policy which she and he favoured as the policy of 'dazzling strokes . . . of baffled rivals and discomfited opponents; of perpetual shouting of challenges and waving of flags', which in 1922 Curzon was specifically to condemn in a minute to the Prime Minister?[4] At any rate it is difficult not to admire her when she gives Disraeli unstinted support, saying: 'It has gone on for six months—this noise; and suppose a

[1] *L.* v. 561 (8.viii.77), Journal.

[2] *Cambridge History of British Foreign Policy*, iii. 601–2 (Algernon Cecil).

[3] *L.* v. 625 (31.v.78), Queen to Beaconsfield.

[4] Hon. Harold Nicolson's *Curzon; The Last Phase*, 42.

mistake had been made, what then? But I will never admit that any mistake has been made from first to last.' Well might Disraeli cry 'Bravo!'[1] He succeeded in influencing her when no one else could have done so. If any other Prime Minister had been in power, it is easy to imagine that one of two things might have happened. Either we should have been driven into war and once more 'put our money on the wrong horse', or the Queen might quite probably have abdicated. Certainly on four distinct occasions during the crisis even Disraeli was threatened with her abdication: 'Another Sovn. [she told him] must be got to carry out Ld. Derby's policy.'[2] She announced that if the Russians appeared before Constantinople she would be 'so humiliated that she thinks she would abdicate at once'[3]. On other occasions she feels that 'she cannot, as she before said, remain the Sovereign of a country that is letting itself down to kiss the feet of the great barbarians'[4]; and that '. . . her own first impulse would be to throw everything up, and to lay down the thorny crown. . . .'[5] She does not seem to have understood that her threat of resignation could not with effect be employed as freely and frequently as a minister's threat of resignation.

The most interesting feature of the *Letters* after the Treaty of Berlin, so far as foreign affairs are concerned, is the signs of a growing estrangement from Germany, apparently almost wholly due to personal causes. Queen Victoria's eldest daughter married Frederick, Crown Prince of Prussia. In historical perspective the figure of the Crown Princess is wholly tragic. She was her father's

[1] Monypenny and Buckle, ii. 979 (16.xii.76), Disraeli to Lady Bradford.
[2] Ibid. 1017 (14.vi.77), Disraeli to Salisbury.
[3] Ibid. 1020 (27.vi.77), Queen to Beaconsfield.
[4] Ibid. 1089 (10.i.77), Queen to Beaconsfield.
[5] Ibid. 1117 (9.ii.78), Queen to Beaconsfield.

favourite child and most apt pupil. Her unhappiness in being torn away from him and from England on account of her marriage in 1858 was increased by her sorrow at his death three years later. It is true that hers was a love match, but the marriage was from the first unpopular in Prussia. The explanation of her unpopularity is no doubt partly contained in Colonel Swaine's charge: 'She wearies and disgusts Germans by her laudation of England and everything English.'[1] Be that as it may, the Crown Princess was throughout these difficult years able to find a proper consolation in looking forward to a point in the future when her husband as the German Emperor and herself as Empress would be able, with the example of English constitutionalism always before their eyes, to liberalize the Reich. It has already been said that it was one of the most profound tragedies of the nineteenth century and a great disaster for Europe that these hopes were not realized. The Emperor William I lived to be ninety-one. The Emperor Frederick succeeded in March, 1888, and died in June of a cancer of the throat, and it was freely alleged that his death might have been avoided if an English specialist, Sir Morell Mackenzie, had not in the early stages of the illness advised against an operation of tracheotomy.

[1] Esher, i. 115 (23.vi.85), Journal. Colonel Swaine was Military Attaché at Berlin. For another solution of the problem of the Crown Princess's unpopularity cf. C. Grant Robertson's *Bismarck* (Constable, 1918), 236: 'The complete failure of Great Britain to understand the character of the struggle waged in Germany from 1850 onwards . . . killed the enthusiasm for England in the great Liberal camp. . . . The old feeling and ideas continued to be concentrated in the court and circle of the Crown Prince and Princess, but Germany steadily moved away from them.' Cf. also 396–7: 'Bismarck's devotion to his sovereign was limited to the King Emperor.' The author in reviewing Bismarck's conduct to the Crown Prince and Princess employs the adjectives jealous, vulgar, mean, petty, insincere, and unscrupulous to describe the Chancellor's character. But Princess Catherine Radziwill in her extremely sympathetic account of *The Empress Frederick* sees not Bismarck, but the Empress Augusta, as the villain of the piece.

Queen Victoria had already cause to be embittered against Germany for the treatment her daughter had received while the old Emperor had been alive. She had a more definite and more justifiable grievance in the treatment her daughter received from her grandson, Emperor William II, after 1888, not that he seems to have treated his mother well before his accession to the throne. The Queen remained very fond of her grandson as a grandson, but within two months of the Emperor Frederick's death, we find evidence of a distrust of the new German Emperor: '. . . Trust that we shall be *very cool*, though civil, in our communications with my grandson and Prince Bismarck, who are bent on a return to the oldest times of government.'[1] Stringent criticism shortly follows: 'How sickening it is to see Willy, not two months after his beloved and noble father's death, going to banquets and reviews! It is very indecent and very unfeeling!'[2] Before the end of the year the Emperor had quarrelled with his uncle, the Prince of Wales. The Queen wrote to her son: 'William must *not* come [to England] *this* year, *you* could not meet him, and I could *not* after all he has said and done.'[3] To Lord Salisbury she had written: 'As regards the political relations of the two Governments, the Queen quite agrees that that should not be affected (if possible) by these miserable personal quarrels; but the Queen much *fears* that, with such a hot-headed, conceited, and wrongheaded young man, devoid of all feeling, this may at ANY moment become *impossible*.'[4] This was precisely the point. It was not desirable that the political relations of the English and German Governments should be affected by personal quarrels between an uncle and a

[1] *L.* vii. 429 (7.vii.88), C. T. to Salisbury.
[2] Ibid. 433 (24.vii.88), Queen to Prince of Wales.
[3] Ibid. 467 (7.ii.89), Queen to Prince of Wales.
[4] Ibid. 441 (15.x.88), Queen to Salisbury.

nephew. But when the uncle and the nephew were the Prince of Wales and the German Emperor this could not always be avoided.

The number of instances of strained relations could easily be multiplied. In 1892 Sir E. Malet, British Ambassador at Berlin, was asked, if possible, to hint that the Emperor's regular annual visits to Cowes were not quite desirable;[1] they finally came to an end three years later. In 1894 a suggestion that the Emperor, who had already been made an Admiral, should be given an equivalent British military rank, was emphatically rejected.[2] Two years later the dispatch of the famous telegram of encouragement to President Kruger gave further offence to the Emperor's Uncle Edward: 'The Prince of Wales desires me to write to you and say that he feels sure the Queen looks upon the German Emperor's message to President Kruger as a most gratuitous act of unfriendliness,'[3] and a hope is expressed that the Emperor will not come to Cowes that year. In 1897 the Queen herself, offended at the attitude of hostility to Greece taken up by Germany in the Crete crisis, wired to Lord Salisbury: 'I wish you would desire Sir F. Lascelles[4] to tell the German Emperor from me, that I was astonished and shocked at his violent language against the country where his sister lives.'[5] In 1899 a disagreement over Samoa led the Emperor to show animosity towards Lord Salisbury, who uttered a mild protest: 'He entirely concurs with your Majesty in thinking that it is quite new for a Sovereign to attack in a

[1] *L.* viii. 125 (24.vi.92), Ponsonby, C. T. to Sir E. Malet.

[2] Ibid. 347 (15.i.94), Queen to Ponsonby, and 348 (17.i.94), Queen to Ponsonby: 'This fishing for uniforms on both sides is regrettable.'

[3] *L.* ix. 7–8 (4.i.96), Sir F. Knollys to Sir A. Bigge.

[4] British Ambassador in Berlin, 1896–1908.

[5] Ibid. 138 (21.ii.97), C. T. to Salisbury. The reference is to the Empress Frederick's seventh child, Sophia. She married Constantine, who became King of the Hellenes in 1913.

private letter the Minister of another Sovereign: especially one to whom he is so closely related.'[1]

These incidents are all so many straws showing which way the wind was blowing, and indeed that the wind was changing. With extraordinary acumen the Queen grasped the great difference between the Europe of her old age and the Europe of her youth, and informed Lord Salisbury: 'Affairs now are so different from what they used to be, that the Queen cannot help feeling that our *isolation* is dangerous.'[2] With these words the Triple Entente is foreshadowed, twelve years before its structure was actually completed. But her distrust of republicanism meant that the idea of an entente with France could not as yet be considered. However, at one moment estrangement from Germany induces her almost definitely to propound the idea of a Russian alliance: '. . . Think it is most desirable to try to be on best terms with Russia, it is the only way to keep Germany in check. . . . Think a good understanding with Russia will also keep France quiet. . . . Germany behaves very badly.'[3]

But at the same time the Queen was doing her best to calm English public opinion and to moderate criticism of Germany. In this connexion a letter from Sir Theodore Martin, the biographer of the Prince Consort, throws a little light on a topic which is mysteriously dark, the influence of the Crown on the Press: 'Sir Theodore Martin. . . is now able to assure her Majesty that all the leading Journals will adopt a quite altered tone towards the Emperor of Germany and the German people.'[4] Obviously, Sir Theodore had been quietly employed to exercise pressure on the editors of the foremost newspapers.

[1] *L.* ix. 379 (3.vi.99), Salisbury to Queen.

[2] Ibid. 22 (14.i.96), Queen to Salisbury.

[3] Ibid. 226 (25.i.98), C. T. to Salisbury. Cf. also Lord Askwith's *Lord James of Hereford*, 249.

[4] *L.* ix. 224 (13.i.98), Sir T. Martin to Queen.

The main story of the part played by Queen Victoria in the conduct of British foreign policy between 1861 and 1901 has now been told, but before summarizing or generalizing, one or two of its less important aspects must be reviewed. The Queen's attitude to the United States, like her attitude to France, was coloured by her dislike of republicanism. She gained great popularity in America by her message to Mrs. Lincoln after the assassination of her husband, but she was told,[1] and no doubt believed, that the United States was only waiting for a suitable opportunity to attack England, and in 1898 her judgement on the Spanish-American War (she was personally acquainted with the Queen Regent of Spain) was simply: 'It is monstrous of America.'[2]

Queen Victoria's antipathy to France, because France was republican, found more open and direct expression. Possibly her intimacy with Napoleon III may have in some small part been due to the Second Empire seeming to her in welcome contrast to the preceding Second Republic. While the Franco-Prussian war was raging she was so pro-German as to speak of the French as '. . . that nation wh, with but few exceptions seems to be entirely devoid of *truth*, & to live upon vanity, deception, amusement, and self-glorification'[3]. In 1880 the Queen is anxious to draw Gladstone's attention 'to the frightful tyranny & *want* of religious liberty now existing in the French Republic. . . . Is monarchical constitutional Great Britain to look on & be on the most intimate terms with a Republic, which in fact approaches the Commune? There is no oppression & tyranny so great as that of a

[1] e.g., by Lord Clarendon, to Queen, *L.* iv. 594 (1.v.69): 'There is not the smallest doubt that if we were engaged in a continental quarrel we should immediately find ourselves at war with the United States.'

[2] *L.* ix. 244 (21.iv.98), Journal.

[3] Guedalla, i. 258 (10.x.70), Queen to Gladstone.

Republic.'[1] In 1882 in connexion with the Egyptian crisis she writes: 'Do not approve single action with France, especially *Republican* France;'[2] and at the time of the Panama scandals her entry in her Journal was '. . . were there but a good candidate, this would be the moment for a restoration of the Monarchy, but I fear there is no really good one. Oh! if only the dear Prince Imperial were alive, he would be on the throne now, I am convinced.'[3] But in spite of this antipathy she was a frequent visitor to Cimiez.

Taking the Queen's influence on foreign policy as a whole, one of the most important questions demanding an answer is whether that influence tended to promote peace or to promote war. Possessing, as she did, a vast experience of diplomacy, she was so far as international relations were concerned no theoretical idealist. Her head was not in the air and her feet were firmly planted on the solid earth. We have no right to expect her to have been in advance of her own times. She did not concern herself with the possibilities of disarmament or permanent peace, nor was she an out and out militarist, believing in war for the sake of war, though she did once say '. . . there is nothing I admire more than great military exploits and daring.'[4] Her object was to avoid war wherever and whenever war was avoidable, but in common with the great mass of her contemporaries she believed that there were occasions on which the only honourable course was to take up arms.[5] It seems unfortunate, from her

[1] Guedalla, ii. 120 (11.xi.80), Queen to Gladstone.

[2] *L.* vi. 301 (30.v.82), Queen to Ponsonby.

[3] *L.* viii. 192 (21.xii.92), Journal.

[4] *L.* ii. 219 (10.iv.49), Queen to King of Belgians.

[5] Cf., for example, *L.* vi. 451 (30.x.83), Queen to Gladstone (also quoted above, p. 78): 'What she fears is a growing tendency to swallow insults and affronts and not taking them up in that high tone which they used formerly to be. . . .'

point of view, that her reign did not end on a note of 'dignity and greatness and peace', and that she was not spared the alarums and excursions of the Boer War. The last chapter of the last volume of the *Letters*, most remarkable reading, shows the Queen in her extreme old age taking as close an interest in all its details as she had taken in the details of the Crimean War or of the Tel-el-Kebir campaign, and she never had a moment's doubt as to the morality of these undertakings. But it is impossible to deny a certain grandeur in the Queen at the moment of 'Black Week' saying: 'Please understand that there is no one depressed in this house; we are not interested in the possibilities of defeat; they do not exist.'[1]

The cynic might suggest that the Queen was enthusiastic for peace only on those occasions when no English interest would be served by war, and that it was for that reason, for example, that she was so bellicose at the time of the Eastern Crisis and so pacific at the time of the Franco-Prussian War. That is not quite the truth, and what element of truth it contains is not a condemnation of Queen Victoria but a condemnation of the standard of international morality of her times. The Queen was never in advance of her age; she was herself the great Victorian. But the evidence does tend to show, especially in her later years, a genuine, humanitarian desire for peace, and there are in these years four conspicuous instances of attempts on the part of the Queen to avert the catastrophe of war.

To take them in chronological order. The first is the famous incident of 1875, when Germany was contemplating a 'preventive' war against France. On May 6 the Queen 'saw Mr. Disraeli and talked about the very alarm-

[1] Cecil, III, 191.

ing rumours from Germany, as to war. This began by dictatorial and offensive language to Belgium, then by reports of the Germans saying they must attack the French, as these threatened to attack them, and a war of revenge was imminent, which the increase in their armaments proved. I said this was *intolerable*.'[1] On the 10th she 'wrote to the Emperor of Russia to Berlin, appealing to him to use his influence to maintain peace and prevent an attack on France'[2]. 'It was mainly owing to the Tzar's opposition to Bismarck's policy [writes one commentator] that the Prussian statesman's plan of 1875 was foiled, but the postponement of the evil day may be assigned, in part at least, to the resolute stand taken by the Queen and her sons.'[3] She herself pointed the moral to her daughter: 'You know that the Prussians are not popular unfortunately, and *no one* will tolerate any Power wishing to dictate to all Europe. This country, with the greatest wish to go hand in hand with Germany, cannot and WILL *not stand it*.'[4] Here once again is the old distinction between Prussia and Germany, and for this reason it is going slightly too far to say that this letter shows 'how little the great Queen's attitude was affected by the family ties that bound her to the German Royal Family'[5]. It is true that on this and on many other occasions her attitude was not affected by the fact of her eldest daughter's Prussian marriage, but on many more occasions her attitude was affected by all the other family ties which bound her to Germany.

In 1887, when the histrionic antics of General Boulanger seemed likely to provoke another war between France and Germany, she wires to Lord Salisbury: 'Think you

[1] *L.* v. 391 (6.v.75), Journal.
[2] *Quarterly Review*, July, 1919 (10.v.75).
[3] Lee's *Edward VII*, i. 350, n. 2.
[4] *L.* v. 406 (8.vi.75), Queen to German Crown Princess.
[5] R. S. Rait in the *Quarterly Review*, July, 1919.

should urge Germany and France to declare to us or Great Powers that they do not intend to attack each other. We must try and prevent a general conflagration.'[1] Again, in 1896: 'Pray try and get the Powers, Germany, Russia, Austria, and if possible France, [to] interfere with us to put a stop to this awful war between China and Japan.' But the effect of pure pacifism is immediately marred by the addition of the realist argument: 'It is not for our interest to see China weakened.'[2] Finally in 1898 the Queen took up a remarkably liberal attitude towards the Fashoda crisis, caused in Lord Salisbury's language by the presence of 'a distinguished French explorer in a difficult position' on the Upper Nile: 'I feel very anxious about the state of affairs, and think a war for so miserable and small an object is what I could hardly bring myself to consent to.'[3] Once again it is instructive, though not in any way surprising, to see that the objection is perhaps partly to war as such, but more to war for an immaterial object. But the fact remains that the Queen did her best to avert war, and war was averted, and in spite of her professional antipathy to Republican France, she urged that everything possible should be done to enable the French to retreat honourably from Fashoda itself, and, more generally, from the false diplomatic position which they had taken up: 'It will be important I think to help the French as much as is proper and dignified out of the foolish and horrible *impasse* they had got into.'[4]

Before finally taking leave of these questions of foreign affairs, there are two noteworthy instances of a way in which the influence of the Crown made itself felt in a very definite manner, namely, by securing the removal of

[1] *L.* vii. 262 (24.i.87), C. T. to Salisbury.
[2] *L.* viii. 418 (31.vii.94), C. T. to Rosebery.
[3] *L.* ix. 305 (30.x.98), C. T. to Salisbury.
[4] Ibid. 309 (5.xi.98), C. T. to Salisbury.

Ambassadors. In May, 1864, the Crown Princess of Prussia wrote to her mother suggesting that Sir A. Buchanan, the British Minister at Berlin, was not fit for the post he held and should be removed.[1] The Queen replied that she would do what she could without compromising any one,[2] and we find that in October Sir A. Buchanan did, in fact, cease to be Minister at Berlin.[3] Possibly emboldened by recollection of this earlier success the Crown Princess wrote in 1870 similarly suggesting the removal of Lord A. Loftus.[4] Lord Granville expressed himself as being convinced that the Crown Princess was right about Lord A. Loftus,[5] and Mr. Odo Russell was substituted for him. It is not for a moment suggested that the Crown Princess's estimate of Sir A. Buchanan or Lord A. Loftus was at fault. Indeed, she showed her power of discrimination in these matters by demanding very early that Sir Robert Morier, whose sheer knowledge of German politics was so great, and on whose hostility to Bismarck she could count, should be made Secretary of Embassy at Berlin.[6] Her judgement of Loftus is subsequently confirmed by Beaconsfield's: 'It is quite useless to communicate with Loftus. He was absurd in quiet times, but now that there is real business, he is not only absurd, he is mischievous. . . . He is a mere mouthpiece of Gortchakoff: imitates all his *tournure* of phrase and benign advice.'[7] But the technique by which the Crown Princess of one country secures the removal of the accredited representative to it of another is interesting.

[1] *L.* iv. 204 (26.v.64), Crown Princess of Prussia to Queen.
[2] Ibid. 206 (31.v.64), Queen to Crown Princess of Prussia.
[3] Ibid. 243 (8.viii.64), Queen to Russell.
[4] *L.* v. 80 (7.xi.70), Crown Princess of Prussia to Queen.
[5] Ibid. 85 (14.xi.70), Granville to Queen.
[6] *L.* iv. 461 ff.
[7] *L.* v. 477 (10.ix.76), Beaconsfield to Queen.

On imperial questions the Queen exercised no very special influence. On this subject, as on most, she shared the common opinions of her time. It was only in her old age that she succeeded, to use Chamberlain's phrase, in thinking imperially,[1] and her thought was then the stock thought of the day. She accepted what might be called the doctrine of territorial compensation, that imperialist annexations by one Power justified similar annexations by other Powers. For example, she laid down this doctrine on the occasion of the occupation of Wei-hai-wei: 'It is I think important that the world at large should not have the impression that we will not let any one but ourselves have anything. . . .'[2] Her sentiments towards the native races of our imperial possessions were those of genuine benevolence, and she had no doubt that their interests were best served by their being placed under British rule. She showed that she accepted this doctrine of 'the white man's burden' on the occasion of our annexation of New Guinea: 'It is no doubt a serious step, but she rejoices at it as it will enable us to protect the poor natives and to advance civilization, which she considers the mission of Great Britain.'[3]

The gorgeous East held Queen Victoria in fee. At an age far in advance of that when most people think it possible to master a new language she took lessons in Hindustani, and John Brown's place was to a certain extent filled by various Indian servants. A letter from Sir Henry Ponsonby to Lord Granville shows that the Queen had conceived the idea of styling herself Empress of India as early as 1873,[4] and as far back as May, 1859,

[1] Strachey, 262.

[2] *L.* ix. 238 (27.iii.98), C. T. to Balfour.

[3] *L.* vi. 525 (8.viii.84), Queen to Lord Derby.

[4] *L.* v. 238 (26.i.73), Sir H. Ponsonby to Lord Granville: 'Would it not be desirable that the Queen should at once adopt the style of Empress of India

there is a hint of the title in a letter from Disraeli to the Queen on the India Bill of that year:

'It is, the Chancellor of the Exchequer really thinks, a wise and well-digested measure . . . but it is only the ante-chamber of an imperial palace, and your Majesty would do well to deign to consider the steps which are now necessary to influence the opinions, and affect the imaginations of the Indian populations. The name of your Majesty ought to be impressed upon their native life.'[1]

Probably the actual moment chosen was suggested by the success of the Prince of Wales's Indian tour. The legislation of 1876 which conferred on her this additional title was piloted through the House by Disraeli, but was, in fact, initiated by the Queen herself: 'The Empress-Queen demands her Imperial Crown,'—he had written to Lord Cairns.[2]

It is not easy now to understand the parliamentary opposition[3] which this Royal Titles Bill aroused. Lord James of Hereford candidly confesses: 'Looking back upon our proceedings, I cannot very clearly account for the course we took.'[4] The march of events has shown that even if the assumption of the title of Emperor of India has

in addition and subordinate to the title her Majesty now proudly bears as Queen of Great Britain and Ireland?'

In 1876 Lowe claimed that the Queen had urged two previous Ministers to make her Empress of India. This gave great offence to the Queen (cf. above, p. 67, n. 2), and was officially denied, but the denial thus appears to have been not altogether justified.

[1] Martin, iv. 233.

[2] Monypenny and Buckle, ii. 797 (7.i.76).

[3] The Bill does not seem to have aroused any very strong feeling of hostility in the country. But a Mr. Edward Jenkins, seated at his breakfast on March 25, 1876, 'feeling a deep repugnance to the Royal Titles Bill, and seeing how rapidly it was being forced through Parliament' conceived the idea of a pamphlet which 'with the energetic assistance of his publishers [was] wholly written and printed in eleven hours. . . .' This pleasing trifle was entitled: *The blot on the Queen's head, or how little Ben, the Head Waiter, changed the sign of the Queen's Inn to the Empress Hotel Ltd.*

[4] Askwith, 94.

not done very much to increase the Sovereign's popularity in his Indian Dominions, it has certainly not in any way decreased his popularity in Great Britain. The opposition to the Bill was really based on opposition to 'new-fangledness'. It was led in the House of Commons by Lord Hartington. A minority of 46 peers voted against a majority of 228. John Bright on several occasions noted in his Diary that the Commons were voting for a Bill of which they did not really approve.[1] On January 1, 1878, Queen Victoria was proclaimed Empress of India at Delhi. That night at Windsor she came to dinner 'a mass of Oriental jewellery . . . though effective as a blaze of colour, they did not suit her Majesty, as they required a big and a dark woman to carry them effectively'[2]. It is more common to meet the first half of this quotation than the second.

The real significance of the episode of the Royal Titles Bill is that in it we can now see 'the movement begun by Disraeli, to identify the symbolism of monarchy with the symbolism of Empire'[3]. The progress of this movement can be studied in Lord Esher's record of some table-talk of Arthur Balfour's:

> 'He sees no danger in the position of the King, whatever course he may adopt. "You forget", he said, "the changed circumstances since 1832. During the latter half of Queen Victoria's reign, and more than ever now, Great Britain means the British Empire. Our people oversea do not care a rush for Asquith or me. They hardly know our names. For them the symbol of the Empire is the King." '[4]

Thus it is in a sense true that the growth of royal popularity

[1] e.g. *The Diaries of John Bright*, 377 (9.iii.77): 'House: debate on Titles Bill. House insincere and voting what it is secretly against.'

[2] Lord George Hamilton's *Parliamentary Reminiscences and Reflections*, 120–1.

[3] Kingsley Martin in the *Edinburgh Review*, April, 1926, 384.

[4] Esher, ii. 421 (17.xi.09), Journal.

which (as we shall see) occurred between, say, 1875 and 1901, was a part of the general growth of imperialism which was one of the principal movements in the history of these years. For Disraeli, however, the Empire meant India rather than the Colonies, and it is only since the Great War that there has come a full realization of the fact that the Crown is almost the only institutional link, and certainly of these the most effective, between Great Britain and the Dominions. There is much wisdom in the words of a living writer on the British Constitution: '. . . one of the chief difficulties of contemporary British government is the necessity of remembering other parts of the Empire besides the metropolis, and it may be that in the immediate future the keeping of this necessity in the minds of British Ministers may become the essential political function of the Crown.'[1]

It has been said that Queen Victoria lost Ireland for England. This, of course, is an over-statement, and by some at any rate the loss might be thought to be a gain. But it is true that the Queen neglected to do what she could have done to ensure a measure of popularity for the Union, for undoubtedly her own occasional presence in Ireland would have enormously increased her popularity with the Irish, and with it that of the English connexion generally. As it was she steadfastly set her face against all projects for a Royal Residence in Ireland, and in the sixty-three years of her reign she spent there less than five weeks compared to seven years in Scotland.[2] Certainly it was a heroic sense of devotion to duty which took her to Dublin in the spring of 1900, and so almost directly to her death, but a keener sense of her duty to Ireland would have taken her there on many previous occasions. In March,

[1] Kenneth Pickthorn, *Some Historical Principles of the Constitution*, 105.
[2] Lee's *Queen Victoria*, 565.

1868, however, Prince Alfred was shot in the back by a Fenian in Australia, and in May, 1871, Fenians tried to blow up a statue of the Prince Consort on the Leinster Lawn in Dublin. Possibly it is a correct view to say that 'these viciously personal insults closed the Queen's heart against Ireland for ever'[1]. Dereliction of duty to Ireland was as characteristic of the Prince of Wales as of the Queen, for his biographer says: 'Some blame, when all is said, may attach to his refusal, before he became King, to return . . . after the visit of 1885.'[2]

The Queen took a close interest in the affairs of her Navy and Army, and displayed a constant anxiety for their efficiency as fighting forces. She was more interested in the latter than in the former, telling Rosebery that '. . . not caring about being on the sea I have always had a special feeling for the Army'.[3] In 1900 Lord Esher, discussing the problems facing a newly appointed Secretary for War, wrote that Brodrick's

'main trouble will be with the older generation of soldiers and with the Crown. The Navy is a constitutional force.[4] Every commission is signed by the Board. The Army is a royal force and, while the Queen never interferes with the Navy, she interferes very much with the Army. As she listens to soldiers rather than to Ministers, the task of the Secretary of State for War is never easy.'[5]

[1] Bolitho, 73–4.

[2] Lee's *Edward VII*, i. 245.

[3] Crewe's *Rosebery*, 437.

[4] Cf. *Constitutional Law* by E. C. S. Wade and G. Godfrey Phillips (London, 1931), 324–5: '. . . the Navy had never been used by the King to coerce Parliament and so was not included in the prohibition against a standing armed force in the Bill of Rights. It has remained a prerogative force maintained on a permanent footing. So much is this so that the recruitment of the Navy by impressment has never been declared illegal, though the press-gang has, of course, long fallen into disuse. Enlistment is governed by the Naval Enlistment Acts, 1853 to 1884, discipline by the Naval Discipline Acts, 1866 and 1884. Both types of enactment are permanent and do not come under review annually by Parliament for renewal'—in contrast to the Army and Air Force (Annual) Act.

[5] Esher, i. 269 (15.xi.00), Journal.

This special interest of the Queen's in the Army did, indeed, prove a great hindrance to many army reformers. Her natural conservatism, in this case increased by the influence of her cousin, the Duke of Cambridge, the Commander-in-Chief, who could hardly have been more conservative than he was, meant that any army reformer was bound to meet with opposition from the Court. She expressed hostility to Cardwell's proposals, and showed as great an anxiety for his removal from his work as she was later to show for the removal of Gladstone:

'The Queen hears that the Speaker [Denison] is to resign. Would not that be an excellent opening for Mr. Cardwell? It is all very well saying that the Duke [of Cambridge] is satisfied. It *never* will work well, and Mr. C. is much disliked by the Army. . . . Personally the Queen has the greatest regard for Mr. C., but she has never thought him fit for his present post. Lord Hartington is fittest for this office.'[1]

In April, 1873, the Queen pressed for a Royal Commission to inquire into the grievances of officers about the abolition of purchase.[2] To this proposal Cardwell demurred, but in July a commission was appointed. In 1880 the Queen noted that she had told Mr. Gladstone 'how Lord Cardwell's plan had broken down, which he seemed *not* to be *aware of*!'[3] A little later Lord Wolseley was bold enough to remind her that: 'Those who have read through the pages of Sir Theodore Martin's work are now aware, most people for the first time, that the Army owes more to the late Prince Consort than to any other General officer since the death of the Duke of Wellington. Surely

[1] *L.* v. 162 (1.xi.71), Queen to Lord Halifax. Cf. *L.* vi. 76 (8.iv.80), Queen to Ponsonby: 'The Secretary of State for War must be chosen *most carefully*. No mere theorist, but some one who will act cordially and well with the Commander-in-Chief.'

[2] *L.* v. 252 (1.iv.73), Queen to Cardwell.

[3] *L.* vi. 85 (23.iv.80), Memorandum.

therefore it may be said of the great Prince that he was in the highest sense a great army reformer.'[1]

But this reminder does not seem to have made the Queen any more of an army reformer when the question arose again with the appointment of the Hartington Commission in 1888. The Queen expressed herself as being deeply interested in the work it was to undertake,[2] and asked for regular reports of its proceedings. But its final report made her furious. She disclosed her feelings to Sir Henry Ponsonby referring to '. . . this really abominable report, which she beyond measure is shocked should have emanated from a Conservative Government'[3]. The item to which she took strongest exception was the proposal for the abolition of the office of Commander-in-Chief. She felt that this proposal struck at the Throne itself. When Ponsonby first told her: 'He is alarmed by Lord Hartington's Committee's report, which proposes to abolish the office of Commander-in-Chief,' the Queen's marginal note was: 'This cannot be allowed for one moment, and Sir Henry should take steps to prevent this being even discussed.'[4] What steps are not indicated. To Lord Salisbury '. . . the Queen observed that the abolition of the office of Commander-in-Chief did very distinctly alter her position'[5]. She also argued that 'one of the greatest prerogatives of the Sovereign is the *direct communication* with an immovable and non-political officer of

[1] *L.* vi. 389 (27.xii.82), Wolseley to Queen.

[2] *L.* vii. 413 (8.vi.88), Queen to Salisbury.

[3] Ibid. 582 (20.iii.90), Queen to Ponsonby. The naïve astonishment at the report emanating from a Conservative Government is interesting, as another indication not only of the Queen's marked preference for a Conservative Government, but also of her ignorance of the workings of the Constitution. A Government, of course, cannot be held in any way responsible for the report of a Royal Commission, except in so far as the character of that report has been predetermined by the character of the Commission's personnel.

[4] P. H. Emden, 186.

[5] *L.* vii. 589 (25.iii.90), Ponsonby to Duke of Cambridge.

high rank, *about the Army*. . . .'[1] Perhaps she remembered, or in her archives consulted, a letter in which the Prince was urged by the Duke of Wellington to become Commander-in-Chief because in his view 'with the daily growth of the democratic power the Executive got weaker and weaker, and it was of the utmost importance to the stability of the Throne and the Constitution that the Command of the Army should remain in the hands of the Sovereign, and not fall into those of the House of Commons'[2].

The other side of the question was best put in letters from Lord Wolseley to Ponsonby. No doubt he intended those letters to be read by the Queen, or possibly to be summarized at Ponsonby's discretion. He stood high in her favour, but even so, he was greatly daring. He explained the objections to the Duke of Connaught being made Adjutant-General by saying that 'Hartington and all the Secretaries of State here in my time have suffered so much at his [the Duke of Cambridge's] hands, have had all needful reforms in the Army so blocked by him that one and all were determined never to have another Prince here. . . .'[3] He further explained that even if the office were to be retained he was well aware that 'to secure to any future Commander-in-Chief the powers which the Duke of Cambridge inherited from the Duke of Wellington . . . the Duke of Cambridge has himself rendered impossible.'[4] Nevertheless, it was not until 1895 that the Queen's opposition was overcome and the Duke induced to resign. But in August of that year she wished it to be 'made clear that the Duke of Connaught must not be kept out of the Command-in-Chief for long'[5]. However, the

[1] *L.* vii. 600 (30.iv.90), Queen to Ponsonby.
[2] Martin, ii. 287 (April, 1850).
[3] *L.* vii. 625 (2.viii.90), Wolseley to Ponsonby.
[4] Ibid. 627 (7.viii.90), Wolseley to Ponsonby.
[5] Newton's *Lansdowne*, 133, Queen to Lord Lansdowne.

only two subsequent holders of that office, the tenure of which was now limited to five years, were Lord Wolseley and Lord Roberts successively.

The Queen was always a firm believer in the doctrine of 'trust the man on the spot', and to her commanders in the field of action she constantly offered the same kind of encouragement as had Queen Anne to Marlborough when she wrote: 'Whatever misfortune may attend you, at least I shall, being very sure nothing will be wanting on your part.'[1]

[1] Hopkinson, 236.

## VI

## THE HEIR TO THE THRONE

THE reasons for treating with comparative brevity the subject of the relations between the Queen and the Prince of Wales, and of his political influence before his accession, have already been stated in the Preface. The story of the misery of his education has often been told and re-told. But an Oxford man must be allowed a protest against the Prince Consort's principle that: 'The only use of Oxford is that it is a place for *study*. . . .'[1] He would have done better to take Melbourne's advice: 'Be not over-solicitous about education. It may be able to do much, but it does not do so much as is expected from it. It may mould and direct the character, but it rarely alters it.'[2] In the case of the Prince of Wales this proved all too true, with the consequence that a régime which would have admirably suited John Stuart Mill or even the Princess Royal made so little impression on him that at the end of it all Dean Stanley wrote: 'It is hardly possible to over-estimate the difficulty of producing any impression on a mind with no previous knowledge or interest to be awakened.'[3] The Prince Consort at the end of his life seems to have begun to understand his son's character better: 'He has a strange nature . . . he has no interest in things, but all the more for persons. This trait in his character, which is often found in the Royal Family, has made the family so popular. But it also arouses the dangerous inclination for what the people here call "small talk".'[4]

[1] Lee's *Edward VII*, i. 76 (27.x.59).
[2] *L.* i. 365 (1.xii.41), Lord Melbourne to Queen.
[3] Bolitho, *The Widow and Her Son*, 11.
[4] Bolitho's *Albert the Good*, 264 (27.iv.60), Prince Consort to his brother.

When the Prince Consort died a year later it might have been expected that his eldest son, then twenty years old, would to some extent have taken his place in the Queen's confidence. This assumption appears all the more reasonable in the light of the fact that she was then expecting an early death with such complete conviction that General Bruce 'was ordered to sober his charge's thoughts'[1] by keeping before his mind an immediate prospect of his accession. But this did not induce the Queen to make any attempt to train him for the Throne:

> 'An earlier resolve to prevent any encroachment of her son's hereditary status on her husband's dignity would have seemed to colour her present sentiment and action. Before the Prince Consort's death she had nursed an uneasy fear that the Prince [of Wales] might in time fill in affairs of state the first place after herself—a place to which she regarded her husband [as] alone entitled.'[2]

Indeed in 1857 she had appealed to Palmerston to introduce a Bill giving her husband legal precedence over her eldest son. Fortunately she was dissuaded from this project. In 1862 Lord Clarendon remarked that the Prince Consort himself would have found for his son at full age some kind of regular work whether as 'Regent of Scotland, or a clerk in the Audit Office, or Bailiff of the Home Farm'[3]. *The Times* was then suggesting that at any rate the Prince of Wales should always play the host to visiting foreign royalties.[4] The Prince himself was always 'anxious for employment'; indeed at one time he desired to be 'successively attached to each of the great public offices where he would learn the habits of business in general and the work of the Department in particular. . . .'[5] Both Disraeli and Gladstone pressed on the Queen proposals for the

[1] Lee, i. 131. [2] Ibid. 127.
[3] Maxwell's *Clarendon*, ii. 284. [4] Lee. i. 140.
[5] Guedalla, i. 341 (8.iii.72), Ponsonby to Gladstone.

Prince's employment as her representative in Ireland. There is no need here to consider the details of these many and various proposals. It is sufficient to notice that in her attitude to them the Queen seemed to resemble the traditional 'inverted Mr. Micawber—always waiting for something to turn down'. But it is important to observe that Gladstone with his keen sense of duty towards the Monarchy 'was more anxious than Lord Beaconsfield to counteract the effect of the Queen's resolve to exclude her son from regular public employment'[1].

To all these appeals the Queen was deaf. In her Journal she wrote: '. . . as years go on I strongly feel that to lift up my son and heir and keep him in his place near me, is only what is right,'[2] but the thought was not father to the deed. It was only in 1880 that: 'For the first time the Prince played behind the scenes an important part in the formation of a government.'[3] In 1886 Rosebery, as Foreign Secretary in the third Gladstone Ministry,

> 'without the Queen's specific authority, caused the foreign despatches to be forwarded from the Foreign Office direct to the Prince in the red leather boxes which habitually circulated among ministers. The boxes were of two kinds, graded according to the confidential nature of their contents. The most secret documents were enclosed with others in boxes, keys to which were alone in the hands of the sovereign, the Prime Minister, and the heads of the Foreign Office. The second class of box had another kind of key, known as "the Cabinet key", which was in [the] possession of all ministers and their private secretaries. Lord Rosebery accorded the Prince the most exclusive right by making over to him the special gold key (of the first class) which had belonged to the Prince Consort and was now discovered to be lying forgotten in the Foreign Office. Lord Rosebery also handed to the Prince a "Cabinet Key".'[4]

[1] Lee, i. 546.
[2] *L.* v. 140 (3.vii.71), Journal.
[3] Lee, i. 512.
[4] Ibid. 216–17.

Even as late as this the Queen protested against the concession of the Prince Consort's key, and we find that 'Lord Salisbury, when he became Foreign Secretary, qualified the situation by sending boxes of the second class only. . . .'[1]

In 1892 the Queen learnt that 'for several years past' it had been the practice to keep the Prince of Wales informed of Cabinet decisions. At once she wrote to Ponsonby: 'Would Sir Henry ask Lord Salisbury and ask Mr. Gladstone to pause before pursuing this course regularly? She thinks it can only have been on very particular occasions.' The Prince's private secretary reported to the Queen's private secretary: 'Monty Corry in Lord Beaconsfield's time, and McDonnell under Lord Salisbury, were always employed to forward the Cabinet decisions to the Prince of Wales.' Ponsonby also made discreet inquiries of Gladstone's private secretary, Sir Algernon West, who replied:

> 'In answer to your whisper, I had better say that I hope you will trust to my discretion in what I say to the Prince of Wales. My idea was to let him know generally what was going on rather than anything else. If there were anything personal to H.M., or unhappily any difference of opinion in the Cabinet, I should not mention it. I certainly do not mean to send a copy of Mr. Gladstone's letter to H.M.'[2]

In the end the Queen seems to have given her consent to this practice on condition that Sir Algernon West's 'transcripts should be punctually returned to him as soon as the Prince had read them'[3]. 'Only during the last eight years of his career of heir to the Crown did he come into authorized touch with the full range of the confidential deliberations and decisions of the ministry on both home and foreign affairs.'[4]

[1] Lee, i. 216–17.
[2] For this incident see P. H. Emden, 173–4.
[3] Lee, i. 217.
[4] Ibid. 218.

It does the Prince credit that in spite of receiving this kind of treatment from his Mother his affection for her was unwavering. But if the future Queen Alexandra had possessed the same force of intellect and of character as her elder sister-in-law, there might well have been as fierce conflicts between the Prince and Princess of Wales and Queen Victoria as there were between the Crown Prince and Princess of Prussia and the Emperor William I.[1]

Queen Victoria always accused her son of talking too much. It was a just charge. Indeed it is possible to detect a certain symbolism in the story of how '. . . it was his eldest son's heedless exclamation, "Papa is going to France", at a children's party given by his great-aunt, the Duchess of Gloucester, that made public property of his parents' changed attitude to Napoleon III.'[2] And after all, the Queen was at first every whit as reluctant to entrust any political secret to her husband as later to her son. But while the former gradually won her confidence by repeated proofs of conspicuous capacity in politics, the latter could not similarly prove his worth because he was not in fact as able. It is, surely, clear enough that he was the intellectual inferior not only of his father but also of his mother, and of this she was perfectly well aware. The

'spurious reputation as a successful diplomatist which the Prince won in his short reign as King was founded on nothing more than charm of manner and superficial tact. . . . There was no real knowledge or judgement behind it. . . . Good-humoured geniality is no substitute for statesmanship. Therefore as the years have passed the Queen's verdict would seem to have been justified, namely, that he was not capable of any profound thought and was not equipped to reach the standard of sagacity and wide vision which she had been accustomed to in her husband.'[3]

[1] Cf. Bolitho, 29. [2] Lee, i. 36.
[3] Lord Ponsonby in *The Observer* (1.vii.34), 7.

It has already been argued that the Queen's political opinions were not purely expressions of her own personality, in as much as they were shared by the Heir to the Throne.

'The Prince is, of course, in fact, a strong Conservative [wrote Dilke in 1882] and a still stronger Jingo, really agreeing in the Queen's politics, and wanting to take everything everywhere in the world and to keep everything if possible, but a good deal under the influence of the last person who talks to him, so that he would sometimes reflect the Queen and sometimes reflect me or Chamberlain. . . . He has more sense and more usage of the modern world than his mother, whose long retirement has cut her off from that world, but less real brain power. He is very sharp in a way, the Queen not sharp at all. . . .'[1]

In Sir Sidney Lee's opinion to call the Prince 'a strong Conservative' is a crude characterization.[2] But Sir Sidney himself strikes the same note in a lower key when he says that 'The main political opinions to which the Prince was faithful through life reflected Lord Palmerston's creed. . . . His Palmerstonian faith never completely reconciled him to the full claims of political democracy.'[3] 'We have always been an Aristocratic Country [wrote the Prince himself to his Mother] and I hope we shall always remain so, . . . unless we become so Americanized that they are swept away, and then the state of things will be quite according to Mr. Bright's views, who wishes only for the Sovereign and the People, and no class between.'[4] He fully shared her view of the Eastern Crisis, deeply deploring the agitation 'over the so-called Bulgarian atrocities. . . .'[5] It was his view that 'Sooner or later we must come to blows with our Northern friends [Russia] and I am

[1] *Life of the Rt. Hon. Sir Charles W. Dilke.* Begun by Stephen Gwynn. Completed and edited by Gertrude M. Tuckwell (London, 1917), i. 500.
[2] Lee, i. 518. [3] Ibid. 199, 201. [4] Ibid. 170 (1867).
[5] Ibid. 420 (14.ix.76), Prince of Wales to Disraeli.

inclined to think the sooner the better'[1]. 'If I had my way [he wrote] I should not be content until we had taken the whole of Afghanistan, and kept it. . . .'[2] He fully shared also the Queen's point of view about Egyptian policy.[3] He was completely opposed to Irish Home Rule: 'If Lord Spencer is talked over [he said, at the time of the formation of the third Gladstone Ministry] I lose for ever all the high opinion I have ever held of him as a politician and a man of honour.'[4] In the Prince's 'intimate social circle . . . the *right wing* [the *italic* is mine] of the [Liberal] party was always amply represented'[5].

The Prince of Wales was almost as much at home in Paris as in London, and the conservatism of his politics can be as clearly seen in his attitude to the affairs of the Third Republic. We are told, when the period between 1886 and 1900 is under discussion, that 'The French monarchist aristocracy continued to figure largely among his hosts and guests on the Riviera, and at times he impetuously flattered such society by disparaging the bourgeois manners of the leaders of the Republic whom he held responsible for the hostility to England'[6], and previously that 'While the Prince overcame his mistrust of republicanism of the sane and moderate type, which men like M. Gambetta or General Galliffet espoused, the Prince never failed to reprobate revolutionary aims which he imputed to M. Clemenceau and other leaders of the extreme left wing of the republican party'[7]. Later, however, he and Clemenceau were to become friends.

It is true, of course, that as with Gambetta, so with

[1] Lee, i. 421 (14.x.76), Prince of Wales to Sir Bartle Frere.

[2] Ibid. 406 (17.i.79), Prince of Wales to Sir Bartle Frere. Cf. also *L.* v. 559 (1.viii.77), Prince of Wales to Queen.

[3] *L.* vi. 650 (21.v.85), Prince of Wales to Queen.

[4] Lee, i. 526 (31.i.86), Prince of Wales to Ponsonby.

[5] Ibid. 516. [6] Ibid. 701. [7] Ibid. 352–3.

Dilke, with Chamberlain, with Gladstone, with every one in short except the Kaiser, the Prince found good personal relations easy to secure with men to whom he was politically opposed. In this respect the contrast between him and his mother is most striking in the case of Gladstone. For example, there is the incident of a royal dinner-party at which the Queen 'was very cold and distant to [Gladstone]. The Prince of Wales was kindly and gracious. The Princess was so charming and her treatment of Mr. G. was in such marked contrast to that of the Queen, that Ponsonby said to her, "I believe, Ma'am, you are a Home Ruler"; and she replied, "Well, I believe I am".'[1] Four years later Gladstone said: 'No royalty I have ever met had such charm and tact as the Prince of Wales,'[2] and well might he say that after the letter which he had received from the Prince on his final retirement from office in 1894:

> 'After your long and valuable services to the Crown and Country, I can well understand that you need the repose to which you are so fully entitled, but to those of your many friends and admirers amongst which I hope I may be counted, we shall naturally deeply regret the step you are about to take. Let me also assure you how greatly we value your advice on all occasions as no one in this Realm has greater knowledge and experience in public affairs than yourself, and we should never hesitate to ask it.'[3]

The corresponding letter from the Queen Gladstone handed to his secretary, saying with a sigh: 'And this is the only record that will remain of 51 years as Privy Councillor.'[4]

The Prince of Wales was markedly pro-French and anti-German. It seems going a little too far back to say

[1] Esher, i. 161 (4.ix.92), Journal. [2] Lee, i. 537.
[3] Ibid. 538 (1.iii.94), Prince of Wales to Gladstone.
[4] Sir Algernon West's *Diaries*, 289 (4.iii.94).

that '. . . it was the Crimean War which first stirred into life his French proclivities'.[1] At any rate during the Schleswig-Holstein crisis in 1864 'He flung himself with impulsive warmth on his father-in-law's side into the controversy . . .'[2] and 'The experience impaired for life his faith in the honesty of Prussia, and stimulated his leanings towards Prussia's rival, France'[3]. It was his opinion that 'This horrible war will be a stain for ever on Prussian history, and I think it is *very* wrong of our government not to have interfered before now. As to Lord Russell's everlasting Notes nobody cares twopence about them on the continent, and the Foreign Ministers to whom they are addressed probably only light their cigars with them.'[4] Also: 'I always say that if we had sent our fleet to the Baltic at the beginning, all this bloodshed might possibly have been avoided, and we should cut a much better figure in Europe than we do at present.'[5] On June 6, 1866, ten days before the outbreak of the Austro-Prussian War, he said to the French Ambassador in London: 'Complications could best be avoided and the general interests of Europe could best be served by an *entente* between England and France.'[6] Three months earlier the Queen had said almost exactly the same thing.[7] For a fleeting moment in 1870 the Crown Princess of Prussia expressed a fear that France might win the war. Her brother's thought was that this would make her realize 'what the feelings of little Denmark must have been when they heard that the armies of Prussia and Austria were against them'[8].

When in December, 1863, the Prince and Princess of

[1] Lee, i. 36. [2] Ibid. 248. [3] Ibid. 246.
[4] Ibid. 250 (17.ii.64), Prince of Wales to Mrs. Bruce.
[5] Ibid. 251 (5.v.64), Prince of Wales to Lord Spencer.
[6] Ibid. 259. [7] Cf. above, p. 153.
[8] Lee, i. 303 (20.vii.70), Prince of Wales to Queen.

Wales and the Crown Prince and Princess of Prussia were all four staying at Windsor the Queen had forbidden the subject of Schleswig-Holstein to be mentioned.[1] But in more normal times the Prince of Wales got on well with his brother-in-law, and if the Emperor Frederick had lived to be the colleague of King Edward VII, they might together have done much not only to directly promote Anglo-German but also indirectly to promote Franco-German friendship. But we have already seen some of the evidence of the bad relations between the Prince of Wales and his nephew, the Emperor William II.

The only other of the Queen's sons of any political importance was Prince Leopold. She thought him 'the cleverest & most studious of our 4 sons. . . .'[2] Even Mr. Bolitho describes him as an 'unfortunate influence near to the Queen'.[3] The Prince of Wales said that he deliberately delighted in persuading the Queen that Gladstone was the enemy of the Queen and the Royal Family instead of their friend.[4] A Lord Steward condemned him for indiscretion: 'I had a letter from Victor Montagu last evening which said he had "been put behind the scenes" of what they call "the Memorable Day". It is very wrong in Prince Leo telling such matters to indifferent people, especially to a Tory sailor—not famous for discretion. . . .'[5] 'The Memorable Day' was January 5, 1881, and we have already seen how on that occasion Prince Leopold (in advance even of Beaconsfield) laid down the false constitutional doctrine that the Speech from the Throne was that of the Queen and not of her Ministers.[6] At the time of the Franco-Prussian War he was as Francophile as the Prince

[1] Lee, i. 250.
[2] Guedalla, i. 168 (9.iv.69), Queen to Gladstone.
[3] Bolitho, 196. [4] Lee, i. 514.
[5] Ponsonby's *Sidelights*, 153 (9.i.81), Lord Sydney to Ponsonby.
[6] Cf. above, p. 76.

of Wales: 'We are all of us for the French', Prince Leopold said at dinner.[1] Sir Almeric Fitzroy has spoken of

'the persistent and unremitting interference of Prince Leopold in State matters. Not content with influencing the Queen's action in its relation to individuals, he appears to have aimed at being her political guide, and, where the range of her political information was not extensive, his intervention was often the cause of acute difficulty, and always of friction.'[2]

[1] *Quarterly Review*, July, 1919.
[2] From Sir Almeric Fitzroy's *Memoirs* (1925); quoted P. H. Emden, 274.

## VII

## THE PRESTIGE OF THE QUEEN

WE have considered the Queen's attitude to her people; we must now make the easy transition to her people's attitude to the Queen, for the question of her popularity is of great political importance.

Perhaps a large part of the explanation of loyalty to a Monarchy is the phenomenon known to the psychologists as 'projection'. Thus it is immensely illuminating to read in H. G. Wells's autobiography:

'A favourite book of my mother's [Sarah Wells] was Mrs. Strickland's *Queens of England* and she followed the life of Victoria, her acts and utterances, her goings forth and her lyings in, her great sorrow and her other bereavements, with a passionate loyalty. The Queen, also a small woman, was in fact my mother's compensating personality, her imaginative consolation for all the restrictions and hardships that her sex, her diminutive size, her motherhood and all the endless difficulties of life, imposed upon her. The dear Queen could command her husband as a subject and wilt the tremendous Mr. Gladstone with awe. How would it feel to be in that position? One would say this. One would do that. I have no doubt about my mother's reveries. In her latter years in a black bonnet and a black silk dress she became curiously suggestive of the supreme widow. . . .'

Mr. Wells himself did not indulge in this kind of day-dreaming:

'For my part, such is the obduracy of the young male, I heard too much of the dear Queen altogether: I conceived a jealous hatred for the abundant clothing, the magnificent housing, and all the freedoms of her children and still more intensely of my contemporaries, her grandchildren. Why was my mother so concerned about them? Was not my handicap heavy enough without my having to worship them at my own mother's behest? This was a fixation that has lasted all through my life.'[1]

That may have been the right reaction, but it was the abnormal reaction of a super-normal man.

But although Mrs. Wells and countless others like her were so deeply loyal, the Victorian Monarchy was not popular with 'all the people all the time'. Men like Leopold I of Belgium and the Prince Consort made Monarchy respectable. They showed the middle classes that a sovereign could behave like a middle-class gentleman. And yet this new respectability of Monarchy did not ensure that it was everywhere respected. The aristocratic order usually feels itself to be on a level with the Monarchy. Indeed the aristocratic order of the Victorian period perhaps felt just a little inclined to look down on a Monarchy which had so many of the bourgeois characteristics of the Monarchy of Louis Philippe. Bagehot emphasized the fact that the Court stood aloof from the rest of the London world and had 'but slender relations with the more amusing part of it'[2]. There was, in fact, very little connexion between the Royal Family and London Society, until the days when the Prince and Princess of Wales became leaders of fashion at Marlborough House. The middle and lower middle classes look up to the Monarchy, have a deeper loyalty than the classes above them, and delight in the realization of the fact that the Monarch is, after all, just like one of themselves. But the Court was criticized for not being splendid enough, and was unfavourably contrasted with that of Napoleon III and the Empress Eugénie, for the Victorian middle classes were not content merely that the Royal Family should resemble a Victorian middle-class family. They also required from the Monarchy colour and ceremonial,

[1] *Experiment in Autobiography*, i. 46. [2] Bagehot, 45.

pomp and pageantry; above all, they required that it should be seen.

But it was not seen. The Queen was hardly ever in London. Her year was divided into approximately three parts, spent at Osborne, Windsor, and Balmoral.[1] This arrangement had grave political disadvantages, as it seriously incommoded the work of the Ministers. In 1886 Mr. Goschen 'begged Sir Henry Ponsonby not to lose a moment, but to see Mr. Gladstone at once, and if possible to have [his appointment as Prime Minister] announced in the newspapers. There was a disagreeable cry getting up that the delay was caused by the Queen being at Osborne. . . .'[2] The Prince of Wales went even farther than Mr. Goschen. He sent a telegram to Sir Henry Ponsonby saying: '. . . I hope you will be able to induce the Queen to come up soon to Windsor. The inconvenience to ingoing and outgoing Ministers while she is at Osborne is obvious. People are much astonished that she has not come up at once, and most unfavourable criticisms are made on the subject.'[3] Sir Henry Ponsonby did his best, doubtless with all his wonderful tact and persuasiveness, but the only answer he could send to the Prince was: 'I suggested H.M. going up, but was told by Jenner I had made H.M. quite ill with such a proposal. . . .'[3] A month or two later Lord Salisbury gave as one reason for a dissolution being inadvisable the difficulty of a new ministry being formed while the Queen was at Balmoral, and the detriment to her health of her not going to the Highlands at the usual time.[4] She herself had many years earlier produced what was for her a decisive argument on this kind of question, apropos of her being at Osborne at a

[1] *L.* iv. xi–xii.

[2] *L.* vii. 27 (30.i.86), Ponsonby to Queen.

[3] Ibid. 39, n. 1 (Jan.–Feb. 86), T, Prince of Wales to Ponsonby.

[4] Ibid. 129 (15.v.86), Memorandum by Lord Salisbury.

moment when, on account of the Irish Church Bill, Gladstone anticipated 'if differences were to arise between the Houses . . . a crisis, for a parallel to which we must revert to the year 1832'[1]. But she had pointed out that 'the Queen has had repeated Crisises [*sic*] *there*, in the PRINCE's *time*'[2]. 'There is no doubt [wrote Gladstone at that same time] that Osborne during the Session is the great enemy: absence there is almost the same thing for the world as absence at Balmoral, and there is absolutely no compensation in the belief that the Queen derives a benefit from it. This is the mischief I should like to see abated.'[3]

Since Sir William Jenner has just been mentioned, it is at this point worth saying a few words about the influence of the man who had been Physician-in-Ordinary since 1862. Its character is clearly shown by two quotations. Gladstone wrote that 'fanciful ideas of a woman about her own health, encouraged by a feeble-minded doctor, become realities to [the] effect of producing in a considerable degree the incapacity which but for them would not exist'[4]. Lord Granville was more suave: '. . . unfortunately there is an almost universal opinion that Sir William Jenner, notwithstanding his great professional reputation, is somewhat swayed by a natural desire to avoid saying anything which might run counter to the Queen's wishes.'[5]

But in this matter Gladstone showed not only the kindness which was always customary with him but also a certain perspicacity of insight which was rarer:[6]

'Like you I am far from satisfied with the view which Sir W. Jenner takes of his position and duties, but I should be disposed,

[1] *L.* iv. 613 (4.vii.69), Gladstone to Queen.
[2] Guedalla, i. 54 (3.vii.69), Queen to Dean Wellesley.
[3] Ibid. 180 (7.vi.69), Gladstone to Grey.
[4] Ibid. 184 (10.vi.69), Gladstone to Grey.
[5] Fitzmaurice, ii. 19 (3.viii.71), Granville to Mr. Helps.
[6] But cf. above, p. 60.

though with much inferior means of observation, to allow rather more than you do for reality in the Queen's ailments or risks of them. I have a strong sense of the weariness and shrinking of mind which the want of interruption in her work must produce, especially after she has stood for years and may look to stand for many more without any one to fall back upon. Also the political circumstances of the present session have had for her a degree of difficulty which I trust is not likely to recur.'[1]

But Lady Augusta Stanley, whose means of observation were undoubtedly superior to Gladstone's, spoke of the Queen's 'best self . . . taken out of herself—taken out of doctors and maladies (I mean her own) and nerves . . .'[2]; and General Grey, who also knew her well, quite annoyed her by insisting that she was well when she was insisting that she was ill:

'. . . *How* good Grey *could* give you a good account of me is indeed marvellous, for I have been very unwell the whole time I have been home, and have hardly been a day free from headache and nervous pains, but this gentleman sees me *only* on business, and when I talk I get excited and flushed and very feverish, and *that* THEY call being well.'[3]

The Queen's seclusion was not only politically inconvenient, it also led to a recrudescence of royal unpopularity. The nation was sympathetic to the natural desire of a widow for a period of mourning. But as year after year passed, and the Queen remained in seclusion and took no part in public ceremonies, criticism began to grow. The Queen justified her seclusion, not primarily on account of her sorrow, but on account of

'her *overwhelming work* and her health, which is greatly shaken by her sorrow, and the totally overwhelming amount of work and responsibility—work which she feels really wears her out. Alice Helps was wonder-struck at the Queen's rooms; and if Mrs.

[1] Guedalla, i. 178 (3.vi.69), Gladstone to Grey.
[2] *Later Letters of Lady Augusta Stanley*, 149.
[3] *L.* iv. 62 (21.i.63), Queen to the King of the Belgians.

Martin will look at it, she can tell Mr. Martin what surrounds her. From the hour she gets out of bed till she gets into it again there is work, work, work—letters, boxes, questions, &c., which are dreadfully exhausting—and if she had not comparative rest and quiet in the evening she would most likely not be *alive*. Her brain is constantly overtaxed.'[1]

That the Queen worked hard was true enough: that her health was bad was not so true. Her constitution was really exceptionally strong. It is almost impossible not to believe that the real reason for her reluctance to appear in public was that which we have just heard spoken of by Lady Augusta Stanley, sheer 'nerves'. And yet she was still in a way avid of popularity, and slightly and naïvely jealous of its being enjoyed by others: 'Everyone said that the difference shown, when *I* appeared, and [when] Bertie and Alix drive, was *not* to be described. Naturally for *them* no one stops, or *runs*, as they always did, and *do* doubly now, for *me*.'[2]

Queen Victoria's distaste for grand public functions, before the event, had been shared by Queen Anne, who before a Lord Mayor's Banquet at the Guildhall had written to 'Mrs. Freeman': 'Since you have stayed as long at Windsor I wish now for your own sake that you would stay till after my Lord Mayor's day, for if you are in town, you can't avoid going to the show, and being in the country is a just excuse; and, I think one would be glad of any to avoid so troublesome a business. . . .'[3] 'Before the event' is important; it might take months of protracted correspondence to induce the Queen to consent, say, to open Blackfriars Bridge, but once she had screwed her courage to the sticking point she seems usually to have thoroughly

[1] Martin, *Queen Victoria*, 28, Queen to Sir Theodore Martin (1863).
[2] *L.* iv. 233 (30.vi.64), Queen to King of the Belgians.
[3] Hopkinson, 196.

enjoyed herself. Lytton Strachey suggests that Queen Victoria 'bore a grudge against her people for their refusal, in spite of all her efforts, to rate her husband at his true worth'[1]. It seems true to say that only recently has his greatness come to be fully appreciated. More probably the Queen was anxious enough to be popular with her subjects, but attached far more importance to a conscious sense of duty done, and duty for her was mainly bureaucratic duty: 'There is not the slightest indication that her advisers . . . ever made any serious attempt to warn the Queen that her lack of understanding for popular feeling was bound to lead to a decrease in her popularity.'[2] If the strict performance of her duties was rewarded with the popularity which she felt she deserved, well and good; if not it seems to have been a case of 'I care for nobody, no not I, for nobody cares for me.' Probably also the Queen never understood the immense importance of popularity for the monarch as a means of preserving the strength of the monarchy.

But Gladstone did attach enormous importance to making the monarchy popular, and Gladstone did utter such warnings. He worked far harder than the Queen to win for her the good opinion of the masses. For this cause again and again he risked her good opinion of himself by strenuously pressing upon her the necessity of making public appearances.[3] Constantly he kept his finger on the pulse of the people in order to be fully informed as to the state of public opinion about the Crown. To his wife he wrote of 'fresh evidence on the painful subject of the feeling as to the Monarchy'[4]. To the Queen he wrote, when in the summer of 1871 he was explaining some criticism

[1] Strachey, 203. [2] P. H. Emden, 146.
[3] Most spectacularly in 1871, cf. above, pp. 60–2.
[4] Guedalla, i. 69 (18.iv.71), Gladstone to Mrs. Gladstone.

by the Commons of the Queen's departure for Balmoral before the Prorogation:

'Your Majesty may view with surprise the difference between the humour (so to call it) now existing, and that which has prevailed on other occasions. . . . [Many] members take credit to themselves for their ready and zealous support of the Annuity to Prince Arthur; as the votes of many of them in its favour are stated to have been given with a full knowledge or belief that they would be unacceptable to, and perhaps resented by, considerable bodies of their constituents.'[1]

In fact, as we have seen, Gladstone's attempt at this time to persuade the Queen to postpone her departure led to the first serious breach between them.

The Queen's seclusion has been described as causing a recrudescence of royal unpopularity. Few monarchs can have been more popular at the moment of their accession than was Queen Victoria. In this respect she derived an enormous advantage from the contrast between her character and those of her uncles. The Royal Dukes, according to Wellington, had 'insulted, personally insulted, two-thirds of the gentlemen of England'[2]. The House of Commons which had voted £230,000 for the Coronation of George IV was only willing to vote £70,000 for that of Victoria.[3] Of him *The Times* obituary was: 'The truth is—and it speaks volumes about the man—that there never was an individual less regretted by his fellow-creatures than this deceased King. . . . If George the Fourth ever had a friend—a devoted friend—in any rank of life, we protest that the name of him or her has not yet reached us.'[4] Victoria's immediate predecessor, William IV, 'was

[1] Guedalla, i. 297 (9.viii.71) Gladstone to Queen.

[2] Creevey, i. 277 (17.vii.18).

[3] Farrer, 177.

[4] Quoted by Sir Sidney Low, *Governance of England* (1915 edition), 279. Cf. H. J. Laski's *Democracy in Crisis*, 115: 'Anyone who compares the comment of *The Times* upon the death of George IV with the national sympathy

a man who, coming to the throne at the mature age of sixty-five, was so excited by the exaltation that he nearly went mad, and distinguished himself by a thousand extravagances of language and conduct, to the alarm or amusement of all who witnessed these strange freaks; and though he was shortly afterwards sobered down into more becoming habits, he always continued to be something of a blackguard and something more of a buffoon.'[1] 'He was such an ass [elsewhere says Greville] that nobody does anything but laugh at what he says . . .', and again, he is described as 'one of the silliest old gentlemen in his dominions, but I really believe he is mad'. The Duke of Wellington complained of the necessity of having to write long answers to letters from his sovereign 'respectfully telling him what an old fool he was'. The Duke also found it 'difficult to imagine anything more irksome for a Government beset with difficulties like this than to have to discuss the various details of their measures with a silly, bustling old fellow, who can by no possibility comprehend the scope and meaning of anything'[2].

But of William IV at least Greville could also say: 'It is but fair to his memory . . . to say that he was a good-natured, kind-hearted, and well-meaning man, and he always acted an honourable and straightforward, if not always a sound and discreet, part.'[3] Similarly a modern writer speaking of his correspondence with Lord Grey during the years of the Reform Ministry (1831–2) says: 'Although his letters were, in the main, the composition of his secretary, Sir Herbert Taylor, the spirit revealed in them of constant tact and courtesy is that of the King,

in the illness of George V can hardly regard the change in temper as other than a political miracle.'

[1] Greville, iii. 418. [2] Ibid. 208–9. [3] Ibid. 418.

for whom it is clear that his Ministers felt much real affection.'[1]

Nothing of this kind could possibly have been said of the Duke of Cumberland, who until the birth of the Princess Royal was heir to the throne: 'With the exception of the Duke of Sussex [advised Uncle Leopold], there is no *one* in the family that offers them anything like what they can reasonably hope from you, and your immediate successor, with the mustaches, is enough to frighten them into the most violent attachment for you.'[2] If Cumberland had ever become King of England he might have wrecked the English Constitution as he wrecked that of Hanover. If Queen Victoria had died without issue, and he had succeeded, quite probably that would have meant the end of monarchy in England, so low had its prestige then sunk.

The moral of all this is that Queen Victoria beginning her reign with all the immense sentimental and moral appeal of fresh maidenhood and upright character had only herself to thank if later she lost her popularity. For a moment in the summer of the year of revolutions she seems, not unnaturally, to have thought her throne in danger:

> 'When one thinks of one's children, their education, their future—and prays for them—I always think and say to myself, "Let them grow up fit for *whatever station* they may be placed in —*high or low*." This one never thought of before, but I *do* always now. Altogether one's whole disposition is so changed—*bores* and trifles which one would have complained of bitterly a few months ago, one looks upon now as good things and quite a blessing—provided one can *keep one's position in quiet*.'[3]

Certainly to keep her position was one of the ruling passions of her life.

[1] Farrer, 134.
[2] *L.* i. 72 (17.vi.37), King of the Belgians to the Princess Victoria.
[3] *L.* ii. 184 (11.vii.48), Queen to King of the Belgians.

Then in 1854 there was a sudden and quite irrational explosion of popular animosity against the *Lovely Albert* of the ballad: 'My being committed to the Tower was believed all over the country, nay, even that the Queen had been arrested. People surrounded the Tower in thousands to see us brought to it.'[1] This single quotation is sufficient to show that this was a sudden outburst of long hidden hatred and suspicion of the Prince, rather than of the Queen. It has been suggested that the newspaper attacks on the Prince were stimulated by Palmerston.[2] Foremost among those who at this time hastened to the defence of the monarchy was Gladstone:

'Lord Aberdeen hopes he may venture to congratulate your Majesty on the commencement of a change with respect to the newspaper attacks upon the Prince. He observed the article, to which your Majesty refers, in the *Morning Chronicle* of yesterday; and he believes he may certainly say that it was written by Mr. Gladstone, although he would not wish it to be known.'[3]

In May, 1864, there was a Parliamentary criticism of the Queen. In a debate in the House of Lords on the Schleswig-Holstein crisis Lord Ellenborough said:

'I cannot but think there is a strong impression on the Continent, and especially in Germany—an impression which it would be contrary to constitutional principle to admit to have any real foundation . . . that in all public questions relating to Germany Her Majesty's Ministers have as much difficulty in carrying out a purely English policy as was experienced in . . . the reign of the two first sovereigns of the House of Hanover. . . . I do trust that in this question of Denmark, Her Majesty's Ministers will so act as to show to Germany and to the whole world that the policy and feeling of George III—those truly

[1] Martin, ii. 562.
[2] See Bolitho's *Albert the Good*, 214.
[3] *L.* iii. 7–8 (17.i.54), the Earl of Aberdeen to Queen.

English feelings—which regarded only English objects—still animate the Government of this country. . . .'[1]

Couched as this criticism was in the cautious language of historical allusion, it at once drew from Lord Russell a most spirited defence of the Queen. She, of course, was furious, and countered—this was comparatively rare with her—with an attack on Lord Ellenborough for his lack of chivalry in criticizing a woman:

'. . . she must own that she thought her terrible misfortunes, her unprotected position without a husband . . . , her known character for fearless straightforwardness . . . ought to have prevented *such* an attack—which *to a lady* she can only characterize as ungentlemanlike. . . . The Queen hopes everyone *will* know *how* she resents Lord Ellenborough's conduct and how she despises him! But with a good *conscience* one must bear calumny with patience!'[2]

She also wrote to Lord Derby to express 'her regret that, when Lord Ellenborough made his malignant and unmanly insinuations against her, Lord Derby, as head of the party to which Lord Ellenborough belongs, and as one who, having been twice her Prime Minister, must well know how *utterly* unfounded such accusations are, should not have marked his condemnation by a few words of contradiction or reproof[3].'

Meanwhile the Queen's seclusion had for the first time been attacked in the Press. Delane, in *The Times* of April 1, 1864, had played the well-known journalistic trick of announcing as a fact what he was hoping to accomplish by giving out that the Queen's protracted seclusion was

[1] *Parl. Debs.* 3rd Series, vol. clxxv, p. 609. House of Lords (26.v.64).
[2] *L.* iv. 197 (27.v.64), Queen to Russell.
[3] Ibid. 199 (28.v.64), Queen to Derby.

about to come to an end. In the result he achieved the distinction of drawing from the Queen what is perhaps the only letter the reigning sovereign has ever written to *The Times* (April 6). The statement was, of course, unsigned, but to those already acquainted with it the style must have been quite unmistakable. But Delane returned to the charge in December. *Punch* in September of the next year published a full-page cartoon in which Paulina (Britannia) unveiled a statue of Queen Hermione (Victoria), with a quotation from the *Winter's Tale*: 'Tis time! descend; be stone no more!'

The Queen, however, found a defender in the man who had been suggested as the first President of the second English Republic, John Bright. At a Reform meeting in 1866 he said:

'Mr. —— referred further to a supposed absorption of the sympathies of the Queen with her late husband to the exclusion of sympathy for and with the people. I am not accustomed to stand up in defence of those who are possessors of crowns. But I could not sit and hear that observation without a sensation of wonder and pain. I think there has been, by many persons, a great injustice done to the Queen in reference to her desolate and widowed position. And I venture to say this, that a woman —be she the Queen of a great realm, or the wife of one of your labouring men—who can keep alive in her heart a great sorrow for the lost object of her life and affection is not at all likely to be wanting in a great and generous sympathy with you.'[1]

This impromptu oratory proved so moving that it brought the whole meeting to its feet to sing *God Save the Queen*. In 1867, after a meeting with the Queen, Bright's entry in his diary was: 'I am not a "courtier", but I can respect an Ancient Monarchy, and can admire and even reverence a Monarch whom monarchy has not spoiled; and I have

[1] G. M. Trevelyan's *Bright*, 398–9.

always felt a true sympathy with the Queen in her deep sorrow.'[1]

But her seclusion was not only unpopular with those sentimentally minded souls who derived a simple pleasure from seeing the Queen. It was also unpopular with powerful economic interests, to whose advantage it was that there should be a splendid Court. Queen Victoria was accused of being extravagant, but the charge of extravagance came to the same as a charge of meanness. The point was that she was receiving large sums of money, but not laying money out. A lavish expenditure would have been a stimulus to trade, and would have enormously increased her popularity. As it was, popular discontent at her seclusion, which had long been latent, suddenly came to a head in the year 1871.

In that year Gladstone informed the Queen that he foresaw opposition to a grant of £30,000 to form the Princess Louise's dowry on her marriage with the Marquis of Lorne,[2] though in this particular instance the minority turned out to consist of only three persons, with two tellers. There was further opposition to the proposal for an annual allowance of £15,000 to Prince Arthur, now Duke of Connaught, on the occasion of his coming of age. Fifty-three M.P.s voted to reduce the grant by £5,000, and eleven against any grant at all. It is by contrast worth noting that in 1857 Parliament had not been the least niggardly or reluctant in granting a dowry to the Princess Royal. In April, 1871, there was a republican demonstration in Hyde Park to express sympathy with the Paris Commune. But the Home Secretary was able to report to the Queen that the numbers present had never exceeded six hundred, and to add the generalization that the over-

[1] *The Diaries of John Bright*, 337.
[2] *L.* v. 120 (8.ii.71), Journal.

throw of the Second Empire had produced far less revolutionary fervour in England than corresponding events in 1789, 1830, and 1848.[1]

The Home Secretary was almost certainly right in minimizing the extent of republicanism in England in 1871. But even if positive republicanism was only the creed of a few, there was plenty of negative dissatisfaction with the Monarchy, and this dissatisfaction found its expression in a sudden burst of newspaper criticism.

> 'A few weeks ago, [said *The Pall Mall Gazette*] a deep and universal feeling of discontent at the Queen's seclusion (or rather at its consequences) found voice in the journals of the country. No public print of any importance failed to take part in the chorus which was equally remarkable for its suddenness, fulness, and harmony. Indeed, the suddenness of the cry was surprising—till we remembered that what was then said had lain unexpressed in the minds of the whole community for years with annual increment . . .'[2]

1871 is also the year of the publication of the famous pamphlet: *What Does She Do With It?*[3] The anonymous author takes as his text the Annuity Bill for Prince Arthur, and claims that: 'There is not a lady in Christendom better able, out of her own resources, to provide for every one of her family than our Queen', and simultaneously that '. . . all the spirit of the English constitution is opposed to the possession of a great private fortune by the holder of the throne'. The argument runs that the annual sum of £385,000 provided for the Queen by the Civil List Act 'has not been applied to the purposes for which it was expressly given, that of maintaining for the Queen a Royal Court, and a Royal Establishment, on the same

[1] *L.* v. 130 (17.iv.71), Mr. Bruce to the Queen.

[2] *Pall Mall Gazette* (29.ix.71), quoted by Morley, ii. 325.

[3] Tracts for the Times, No. I, *What Does She Do With It?* By Solomon Temple, Builder.

scale as that of William IV'. Plainly Queen Victoria's expenditure was not so lavish as that of her immediate predecessor. It is further argued that, quite contrary to the spirit, if not to the letter, of the Civil List Act, money saved on certain classes of expenditure has been transferred to the Privy Purse, and that by this means the Queen has accumulated a private fortune of at least £2,500,000, to which must be added a legacy of £1,500,000 left by an eccentric millionaire, Mr. Nield, and £1,000,000 left by the Prince Consort. The tone throughout is respectful and reasonable.

This was a question to which Lord Brougham had already called attention as far back as 1850, when in the House of Lords he moved: 'That an humble Address be presented to Her Majesty, for a return of how much of the 38,000 *l.* and upwards, Savings on the Civil List for the Year ending 5th April, 1850, arises from the Salaries, Pensions, and Allowances'[1] (i.e. one particular class of expenditure). He also laid it down as a principle that 'It was not in conformity with the genius of the constitution that the Sovereign of this country should have the means of acquiring wealth, but that he should be dependent on Parliament'. But Brougham was stiffly answered by Lord Monteagle with the words: 'A precedent of greater danger to the constitution of this country, and one more foreign to previous precedents in the history of England, could never take place, than the opening of this question. He did not mean that Parliament had not ever been called on to review the Civil List, but that was when there were exceedings and debts . . . this was the first time it had ever been proposed to inquire into the expenditure of the Civil List when the Crown was not in debt. . . .'

Radicals long continued to criticize the cost of the

[1] *Parl. Debs.*, 3rd Series, vol. cxiii, pp. 685–97. House of Lords (2.viii.50).

Crown. As Labouchere put it in an article in the *Fortnightly Review* for February, 1884:[1]

> 'Radicals are essentially practical . . . they do not approve of the fuss and feathers of a court, and they regard its ceremonies with scant respect, for they are inclined to think that they conduce to a servile spirit, which is degrading to humanity. They admit, however, that the scheme of a monarch who reigns but does not rule has its advantages in an empire such as ours, where a connecting link between the mother country and the colonies is desirable.[2] Their objection to the present state of things is mainly based upon financial grounds. Admitting that there is to be a hereditary figure-head, they cannot understand why it should cost so much. . . .'

Of the grant to Prince Arthur Labouchere asks why this young gentleman should have received 'so very ample a pension for condescending to be the son of his parents. Nothing has conduced more to shake that decent respect for the living symbol of the State, which goes by the name of royalty, than the ever-recurring rattle of the money-box.' But he adds that Radicals 'have a sincere respect for the Queen, not only as the constitutional head of the State, but also on account of her excellent personal qualities'.

We have looked back to 1850 and forward to 1884. We must now return to our point of departure, the year 1871. On November 6 of that year Sir Charles Dilke made a famous speech of a Republican tendency at Newcastle. His own account of it is as follows: 'I visited Newcastle, and there spoke chiefly upon the Dowry question, which had led to a division in the House of Commons.[3] . . . But in the course of the recess I had gone into the question of the Civil List expenditure upon the Court, and at New-

[1] Quoted in *The Life of Henry Labouchere* by A. L. Thorold (London, 1913), 212–13.

[2] Cf. above, p. 177.

[3] Princess Louise's dowry, cf. above, p. 207.

castle I made references to this subject which were accurate, though possibly unwise.'[1] This speech drew from Chamberlain the comment: 'The Republic must come, and at the rate at which we are moving it will come in our generation. The greater is the necessity for discussing its conditions beforehand, and for a clear recognition of what we may lose as well as what we shall gain.'[2]

Gladstone, with his great loyalty to the Crown, was seriously perturbed by Dilke's Republicanism, which he rightly thought to be evidence of a new phenomenon: 'Mr. Gladstone thought . . . that a severe denunciation by him of Sir Charles Dilke's declaration . . . would have tended to exasperate and harden such persons as composed the Newcastle meeting. They are a small minority, as he hopes, in the country. But a few years ago that minority (so far as he knows) did not exist.'[3] A little later he made a note of certain remarks of his to the Queen on the same topic: '. . . What we should look to I thought was not merely meeting that movement by a more powerful display of opposite opinion, but to getting rid of it altogether, for it never could be satisfactory that there should exist even a fraction of the nation republican in its views.'[4]

Early the next year Dilke returned to the attack with a motion in the House of Commons for inquiry into the Civil List, which was, however, defeated by 276 votes to 2, amid somewhat disorderly scenes.[5] The two were Dilke and Auberon Herbert; the tellers of this small and select minority were George Anderson and Sir Wilfred Lawson.

1 Gwynn and Tuckwell, i. 139.
2 Ibid. 140.
3 *L.* v. 167 (22.xi.71), Gladstone to Queen.
4 Viscount Gladstone, 335. Memorandum by Gladstone (21.xii.71).
5 *L.* v. 202 (19–20.iii.72), Gladstone to Queen.

On March 13, 1880, Dilke was publicly asked whether he was a Republican:

> 'I replied to the effect that while as a matter of speculative opinion I thought that a country starting afresh—as France after Sedan—would in these days generally do better to adopt a republican form of government than a limited monarchy, yet that in a country possessing a constitutional monarchy it would be mere folly to attempt to upturn it, and consequently folly even to try to disturb it.'[1]

This answer was quoted to the Queen when she demanded an explanation of his supposed Republican views on the occasion of the formation of the second Gladstone Ministry.[2] She insisted on a further letter explaining his views on the Civil List,[3] and in the end he received, not Cabinet rank, but the Under-Secretaryship of the Foreign Office.

But the Queen, whose memory in this kind of matter was tenaciously long, remained on the alert, and in March, 1882, she writes to Gladstone: 'Is it true that Sir C. Dilke & Mr. Fawcett did not vote for p$^{ce}$ Leop$^{d}$'s annuity? If so—the Queen must say she thinks it vy unfortunate that such people sh$^{ld}$ be in the Gov$^{t}$ & it must put an effectual bar to their ever being Cabinet Ministers.'[4] Gladstone explains that Dilke's reason was that he thought that the practice as to the assessments of such grants should be the same as the practice with regard to the Civil List, namely that the amount should be fixed by a Committee of the House and not by the Cabinet.[5]

At the end of that year it was proposed that Dilke should enter the Cabinet as President of the Local

[1] Gwynn and Tuckwell, i. 308 (24.iv.80), Dilke to Chamberlain.
[2] *L.* vi. 95 (2.v.80), Dilke to Granville.
[3] Ibid. 95 (3.v.80), Queen to Granville.
[4] Guedalla, ii. 183 (26.iii.82), Queen to Gladstone.
[5] *L.* vi. 291 (8.v.82), Memorandum by Gladstone.

Government Board. Apparently the Queen was still unappeased:

'The Queen must again refer to the Speeches of Sir C. Dilke w$^{h}$ though spoken ten years ago, contain statements w$^{h}$ have never been withdrawn. . . . Does he still maintain these views? If so, he *cannot* be a *Minister* in the Gov$^{t}$ of a *Monarchy*. Has he changed his principles? If so, there *can* be *no difficulty* in *avowing* it *publicly*.'[1]

From Gladstone he received encouragement:

'Notwithstanding the rubs of the past, I am sanguine as to your future relations with the Queen. There are undoubtedly many difficulties in that quarter, but they are in the main confined to three or four departments. Your office will not touch them, while you will have in common with all your colleagues the benefit of two great modifying circumstances which never fail—the first her high good manners, and the second her love of truth. . . .'[2]

What were the causes of this wave of Republican feeling in 1871? To a minor extent the ground had been prepared by the course of lectures on the four Georges which Thackeray had given in different parts of the country in 1856. It has also been suggested[3] that as the result of the crushing victory of Germany in the Franco-Prussian war English public opinion had veered simultaneously towards France out of sympathy for her defeat, and against the Queen because she was known to be pro-German. But undoubtedly the prime cause was the example of the declaration of a Republic in France. The French Revolution of 1830 had as one of its principal results the English Reform Bill of 1832. Similarly, the French Revolution of 1870 had as one of its consequences the English Republican agitation of 1871. But this, as the Home Secretary

[1] Guedalla, ii. 220 (12.xii.82), Queen to Gladstone.

[2] Gwynn and Tuckwell, i. 497 (23.xii.82), Gladstone to Dilke.

[3] E. F. Benson's *Edward VII*, 96.

had already implied,[1] was of infinitely less importance than the agitation which had led to Reform.

At the end of November, 1871, the Prince of Wales fell dangerously ill with typhoid fever, and this proved in itself enough to prick the bubble of Republicanism. For example, Lord Spencer, the Viceroy, was able to write from Dublin:

'It was remarkable to notice how the tone of the most Fenian and extreme papers, the *Irishman* and the *Flag of Ireland*, was changed. When the Prince first became seriously ill these papers had articles stating that whatever the English and Scotch felt, the Irish were indifferent as to the recovery of the Prince; but this evidently did not accord with the sentiments of the people who like these low papers, for the following week they . . . expressed sympathy for your Majesty and the Princess of Wales. The Home Rule Association adjourned on account of the illness. . . .'[2]

More sober was the attitude of John Richard Green:

'I am sorry when any young fellow dies at thirty, and am far more sorry when any mother suffers; but the sentiment of newspapers and town councils over "telegrams from the sick-bed" is simply ludicrous. However, one remembers that all France went mad with anxiety when Lewis the Well-beloved fell sick in his earlier days, and yet somehow or other '89 came never the later.'[3]

But the fact that the Thanksgiving Service for the Prince's recovery held on February 27, 1872, was followed within two days by an attempt at the assassination of the Queen set the seal on the revival of royal popularity.

We have already seen what a damp squib in consequence was Dilke's motion on the Civil List. In 1872 Bradlaugh published his *Impeachment of the House of Brunswick*. His charge against Queen Victoria was that 'in real

[1] Cf. above, pp. 207–8. [2] Lee, i. 322 (27.xii.71), Spencer to Queen.
[3] Ibid., 329, n. 3.

State policy her interference has been most mischievous, and this especially where it affected her Prusso-German relations. In the case of Denmark attacked by Prussia, and in the case of the Franco-Prussian war, English Court influences have most indecently affected our foreign relations.' But he makes a special exception of Queen Victoria in contrast to the majority of the members of the Brunswick family as not being 'hostile to the welfare of the mass of the people', and says: 'I do not pretend here to have pleaded for Republicanism—I have only pleaded against the White House of Hanover [and submitted] reasons for the repeal of the acts of Settlement and Union, so far as the succession to the throne is concerned, after the abdication or demise of the present monarch.' In May, 1873, the last Republican conference was held at Birmingham. Fifty-four accredited delegates were present. Chamberlain did not come, and Bright specifically dissociated himself from the movement. The leading figures were Bradlaugh and George Odger. It seems true to say that what was begun by the example of France was finally ended by the example of Spain.

Early the next year, when the question arose of how to provide for the cost of the entertainment of the Shah of Persia at Buckingham Palace, and a proposal was made for a parliamentary grant, Gladstone was able to approve of the grant on the ground that the state of public sentiment had changed materially since the time when the Sultan of Turkey had last paid a visit to England.[1] In other words, Gladstone thought that there was not likely to be any objection to the expense not being met out of the Civil List. Disraeli's influence was responsible for the Queen making more frequent public appearances than formerly. If ever there was a touch of Gloriana about

[1] *L.* v. 251 (29.iii.74), Gladstone to Queen.

her homely figure, it was his doing. There was much popular sympathy with the Queen in a series of personal losses which occurred at this time: in 1878, the death of Princess Alice, the Grand Duchess of Hesse, amid peculiarly tragic circumstances; in 1879, the loss of the Prince Imperial in the Zulu War; in 1881, the death of Lord Beaconsfield; in 1883, the death of John Brown, the Queen's Highland servant; and, in 1884, the death of her youngest son, Prince Leopold, Duke of Albany. In 1874 the Prince and Princess of Wales paid a successful visit to the supposed stronghold of Republicanism, Birmingham, and were loyally received by Chamberlain as Mayor, the man who three years earlier had written to Dilke: 'The Republic must come. . . .'

In the remaining years of the reign there were one or two more attacks on the Crown, direct and indirect. In 1879 the Queen recorded in her Journal: 'In both Houses of Parliament most impertinent remarks were made about my message of condolence and encouragement to Lord Chelmsford and Sir Bartle Frere, but they were stiffly and decidedly answered, especially by Lord Beaconsfield.'[1] In 1883 there was a sudden final flare of Republican sentiment from Joseph Chamberlain. At a meeting of 20,000 people in celebration of John Bright's jubilee as a Member for Birmingham, Chamberlain went out of his way flauntingly to mark the contrast between that jubilee ceremony and the recent coronation of the Tsar, concluding with the words: 'Your demonstrations on Monday lacked nearly all the elements which constituted the great pageant of the Russian coronation . . . the representatives of royalty . . . were absent and nobody missed them.'[2] The Queen wrote to Gladstone to draw attention to this

[1] *L.* vi. 13 (19.iii.79), Journal.
[2] J. L. Garvin's *Life of Joseph Chamberlain*, i. 395.

'dangerous and improper language': 'The Queen had from the first greatly deprecated Mr. Chamberlain's being in the Cabinet, and she must say she thinks her fears have been fully realized.'[1] He apologized to Gladstone by saying that he had 'never consciously failed in respect to the Sovereign or the Royal Family'[2]. Perhaps his more considered view on Republicanism was contained in a speech which he made as Mayor of Birmingham in 1874, just before the city was to be visited by the Prince and Princess of Wales:

'If to be a Republican is to hold, as a matter of theory at all events, that that is the best government for a free and intelligent people in which merit is preferred to birth, then I hold it to be an honour to be associated with nearly all the greatest thinkers of the country and to be a Republican. But if a Republican is one who would violently uproot existing order, who would thrust aside the opinion and affront the sentiment of a huge majority of the nation, merely to carry to a logical conclusion an abstract theory, then I am as far from being a Republican as any man can be. I have never, in private or in public, advocated Republicanism for this country. We may be tending in that direction, but I hold that the time has not arrived yet—even if it ever arrives—and I hold also that Radicals and Liberals have quite enough to occupy their best energies without wasting their time in what seems to me a very remote speculation. At the same time, gentlemen, there may be an exaggerated loyalty as well as an exaggerated Republicanism. . . .'[3]

In 1888 and 1889 there is evidence of a certain recalcitrance on the part of the House of Commons to make further financial grants to members of the Royal Family. Salisbury advocated the replacement of separate grants by the setting up of a 'Dotation Fund'. His ground was

[1] *L.* vi. 431 (27.vi.83), Queen to Gladstone.
[2] Ibid. 435 (2.vii.83), Chamberlain to Gladstone.
[3] *Mr. Chamberlain's Speeches*, i. 46 (17.x.74).

that 'for many years past the character of the House of Commons has been deteriorating; and the arrangement by which it was necessary at each marriage of a Prince or Princess to recur to the House of Commons for money has been becoming less and less desirable'[1]. Bradlaugh's motion for including the Civil List within the terms of reference of a proposed committee on Royal Grants was defeated by only 313 votes to 125.[2] Sir George Otto Trevelyan voted for Bradlaugh's motion. Gladstone and John Morley voted against it. Sir William Harcourt abstained. The Queen, foreseeing opposition, abandoned the idea of pressing for grants to the children of the Dukes of Connaught and Albany.[3] A Bill to provide for the Prince of Wales's children passed against minorities averaging about forty.[4] The opposition to this Bill was led by Labouchere, who argued that the Queen had enough money of her own to provide for her family. In 1894 when the present Prince of Wales was born, when President Carnot was assassinated, and 251 Welsh miners were killed in a colliery disaster, the House of Commons passed addresses of congratulation to the Queen and of condolence with the French people, but there was no resolution of sympathy with the widows and children of the miners. This brought about an outburst of Republican sentiment from Keir Hardie:

'For the lick-spittals of the Press who have no care for the cry of the poor widow and orphan, and who attempt to see in the birth of a child to the Duke and Duchess of York an event of Divine significance to the nation, there can be nothing but contempt. The life of one Welsh miner is of greater commercial and moral value to the British nation than the whole Royal

[1] *L.* vii. 384 (15.ii.88), Salisbury to Queen.
[2] Ibid. 509 (4.vii.89), W. H. Smith to Queen.
[3] Ibid. 514 (18.vii.89), C. T. to Salisbury.
[4] Ibid. 520 (2.viii.89), W. H. Smith to Queen.

crowd put together, from the Royal Great Grand-mama down to the puling Royal Great-Grandchild.'[1]

But these are isolated incidents. The point is that the Republican wave of the '70's had spent itself, and that the Queen's popularity had never stood higher than it did towards the end of her reign. Her death was felt by her subjects as a personal loss.[2] During the last years of her reign she could with Elizabeth have made it her highest boast that she ruled with her people's love. Perhaps the height of her popularity was marked not so much by the two spectacular Jubilees as by her more informal drives through London during the Boer War. Who was it who said, and when, that 'Republicanism has ceased to be a heresy, but it has also ceased to be a faith'? In 1901 it had not only ceased to be a faith, but had once again become a heresy. The process seems not unlikely to end with some Englishmen adopting an attitude to their King almost similar to the reverence of the Japanese for their semi-divine Mikado. Thus had it come about that Queen Victoria 'was regarded by the vast mass of her subjects as a divine institution, without flaw . . . at the very moment when she was behaving more unconstitutionally than ever before. . . .'[3]

It is now fairly easy to see why this Republican movement came to nothing. At that time the first French Revolution still spread alarm among conservatively minded people in the same way as the Russian Revolu-

[1] Godfrey Elton's *England Arise*, 243.

[2] This historical fact has been given vivid dramatic expression in Mr. Noel Coward's *Cavalcade*, and it seems worthy of remark even in a study of this kind that by general consent it was this incident out of the many incidents of public affairs portrayed in that play which seemed most to touch the chords of memory of older members of the audiences.

[3] Laurence Housman's *Victoria Regina* (Cape, 1934), 13. It is pleasant to be able to refer the reader to this *Dramatic Biography*, comprised of the plays which have previously appeared in *Angels and Ministers* (1921), *Palace Plays* (1930), *The Queen's Progress* (1932), and *Victoria and Albert* (1933), together with one, *Aims and Objects*, now published for the first time.

tion to-day. Republicanism then appeared to be the final stage of political and social advance. Apparently it was not realized that: 'A republic differs from a constitutional monarchy only in form: a constitutional monarchy differs from an absolute monarchy in substance;' not realized, in spite of Tennyson's saying so, that England was a 'crown'd republic'. We see now that the dominant issue of politics is the issue between Capitalism and Socialism; that the difference between a monarchical capitalist democracy and a republican capitalist democracy is normally immaterial, so that, for example, it becomes possible for a distinguished journalist to say: 'It would be easier to overthrow the monarchy, than to depose the inner governing class from the authority which it has usurped over the external policy of the Empire.'[1] The English Republican movement of 1871 was in no way identified with Socialism Its model was the United States of America. It was, in short, a political house built on social sand, and for that reason did not stand.

[1] H. N. Brailsford's *War of Steel and Gold* (London, 1914), 203.

## VIII

# CONCLUSION

It is now necessary to attempt a summing-up on the political influence of Queen Victoria from the year 1861 to the year 1901.

The first point to be emphasized is the Queen's extraordinary industry and her extraordinary command over detail. Mr. Buckle rightly says of the volumes of the *Letters* which he has edited: 'Nothing will strike the reader of these pages more than the diligent care with which her Majesty applied herself without remission, day after day, to her duties as a Constitutional Monarch.'[1] Mr. A. C. Benson and Lord Esher, the Editors of the First Series of the *Letters*, point the moral:

> 'Nothing comes out more strongly in these documents than the laborious patience with which the Queen kept herself informed of the minutest details of political and social movements both in her own and other countries. It is a deeply inspiring spectacle to see one surrounded by every temptation which worldly greatness can present, living from day to day so simple, vivid, and laborious a life; and it is impossible to conceive a more fruitful example of duty and affection and energy, displayed on so august a scale, and in the midst of such magnificent surroundings.'[2]

In 1854 Napoleon III 'seemed astonished' when the Prince Consort told him 'that every Despatch went through the Queen's hands, and was read by her. . . .'[3] The Emperor would have been even more astonished if he had known that 'Lord Palmerston alleges that'—in the admittedly rather exceptional year of 1848—'28,000

[1] *L.* iv. xiii. [2] *L.* i. v. [3] Martin, iii. 110.

despatches were received and sent. . . .'[1] At the time of the Eastern Crisis the Faery may have written every day and telegraphed every hour to her Prime Minister, but at the time of the Egyptian campaign in 1882 '. . . one day alone brought seventeen letters from Her Majesty, or her private secretary . . .'[2] to her Secretary of State for War. She was indeed a great worker, but primarily a desk worker. Her method was not the method of personal contact employed by her son:

'. . . I suppose that few sovereigns have been less in personal contact with her ministers with the single exception of Lord Beaconsfield, than Queen Victoria was after the defeat of Lord Melbourne. . . . Of the permanent officials she personally made no use. She never sent for them or consulted them, and I much doubt whether she knew the heads even of the Foreign Office or Treasury by sight.'[3]

Further to illustrate this point. In the midst of domestic worry and anxiety, caused by the premature birth of the Prince of Wales's eldest son, later the Duke of Clarence, the Queen succeeded, after a tussle with Palmerston, in securing an alteration to an important dispatch, which really involved the issue of peace or war.[4] Two years previously the Queen had said that the things of this world had ceased to interest her, but within four days of this announcement she insisted that Russell should take care 'that the *rule* should not be departed from, viz. that no drafts should be sent without the Queen's having first seen them'[5]. In 1867 Lord Stanley explained that in order to save time dispatches had sometimes been sent out without the royal approval, because they could always be recalled

[1] *L.* ii. 221 (19.vi.49), Lord John Russell to the Prince Albert.
[2] S. Childers's *Life and Correspondence of H. C. E. Childers*, ii. 104.
[3] Lord Redesdale's *Memories* (London, 1915), i. 183.
[4] *L.* iv. 143–50 (8–12.i.64).
[5] Ibid. 10 (14.i.62), Queen to Russell.

or modified by telegraph.[1] The Queen insisted on a reversion to the earlier practice. Lord Palmerston as Prime Minister may have secured the removal of iron hurdles from the Park,[2] but Queen Victoria took an interest in the question of whether sailors should grow beards,[3] insisted that no important orders should be given to the Channel Squadron without her previous knowledge,[4] and protested strongly against the Admiralty having made additions to the Queen's Regulations without her consent.[5] She showed 'much indignation at learning that the Guards had been seen wearing brown gaiters when in marching order, and that a D.A.A.G. had been appointed before her assent had been asked for'[6]. When she read in a newspaper that the troops in Egypt were complaining that they could not get any tobacco she wrote the next day to the Secretary of State with the hope 'that something can be done for the purpose of supplying them with this almost necessary of life out there. Her Majesty wished to help in sending out tobacco. . . .'[7] In her days 'no promotion to the rank of Major-General, nor reward nor appointment of any kind of an officer over the rank of Colonel, was made without a large written explanation to the Sovereign, a considerable time before there was any question of a Gazette, and always in the handwriting of the Minister, asking the Sovereign's approval or advice'[8].

Lord Chancellor Westbury was forced to postpone the first reading of a Bill respecting Crown Livings, about which the Queen had not been consulted.[9] She laid

[1] *L.* iv. 473 (12.xii.67), Lord Stanley to Queen.
[2] Guedalla's *Palmerston*, 397.
[3] Strachey, 213.
[4] *L.* iv. 160 (22.ii.64), Phipps to the Duke of Somerset.
[5] Ibid. 30 (30.iv.62), Queen to Palmerston.
[6] Newton's *Lansdowne*, 153.
[7] *Life of Childers*, ii. 123 (6.9.82), Ponsonby to Childers.
[8] Esher, ii. 104 (28.viii.05), Lord Esher to Lord Knollys.
[9] *L.* iv. 77 (13.iii.63), Granville to Queen.

emphasis on the rule against the disclosure of Cabinet proceedings without her consent:[1]

'. . . her Majesty expects that, whenever a Privy Councillor makes any statement in Parliament respecting proceedings in her Majesty's Councils, the Queen's permission to do so should be first solicited, and the object of the statement made clear; and that the permission thus given should only serve for the particular instance, and not be considered as an open licence.'[2]

When Gladstone disclaimed a general jurisdiction over the speeches of his colleagues, and any right to prescribe their tone and colour, he was met with the assertion that: 'the Queen thinks, and maintains that the Prime Minister *has* and *ought to have* that power, and that former Prime Ministers did exercise it'[3]. She refused to allow questions of honours to be discussed by the Cabinet:

'Mr. Gladstone implies that the question was brought before the Cabinet, but the Queen, as the fountain of honour, does not think that such matters are ever discussed by her Ministers. . . . The Queen thinks the Prime Minister may privately consult the Secretaries for Foreign and Colonial Affairs, &c., but the distribution of honours is not a question for the Cabinet.'[4]

It is perfectly clear, then, that Queen Victoria was an extremely industrious ruler, with a really remarkable

[1] This rule was recently reaffirmed when Mr. Lloyd George's request for the publication of Cabinet Minutes relating to the American Debt Settlement of 1922 was refused. On this occasion the Lord President of the Council (Mr. Baldwin) said: 'I learn from the proper constitutional authorities that the publication of Cabinet Minutes would require the approval of the King. The approach to the King should be made through the Prime Minister of the day, as the custodian of Cabinet archives, and it would be the duty of the Prime Minister of the day to advise His Majesty whether permission should be given for publication or not',(Hansard, 273, *H. C. Deb.*, 5 series, p. 526) (15.xii.32).

[2] *L.* v. 634 (25.vii.78), Ponsonby to Lord Derby.

[3] *L.* vi. 526–7 (10.viii.84), Queen to Gladstone.

[4] *L.* viii. 347 (14.i.94), Queen to Gladstone.

power of attention to detail. But that is not to say that she was a strictly constitutional ruler:

'It was for long the custom for courtly historians and polite politicians to compliment the Queen upon the correctness of her attitude towards the Constitution. But such praises seem hardly to be justified by the facts. . . . The complex and delicate principles of the Constitution cannot be said to have come within the compass of her mental faculties. . . .'[1]

This is borne out in several instances. We have seen, for example, that she was ignorant of her own constitutional position in the Church,[2] that she was ignorant of the nature and powers of a Royal Commission,[3] and of a Select Committee,[4] and that she completely mistook the main trend of the constitutional developments of her reign.[5] She considered that the Attorney-General ought to be 'set at' speakers at anti-Turkish meetings during the Eastern Crisis,[6] and not only did she instruct Disraeli to stop the theft of ladies' jewels,[7] but she also wrote to Delane, the Editor of *The Times*, asking him 'frequently [to] *write* articles pointing out the *immense* danger and evil of the wretched frivolity and levity of the views and lives of the Higher Classes'[8].

But when we condemn Queen Victoria's attitude to the Constitution as incorrect we must remember as an extenuating factor that the Queen was splendidly isolated. To say that 'all her mistakes grew out of her social isolation'[9] is an over-statement. But it is true to say that in

[1] Strachey, 261. [2] Cf. above, p. 132. [3] Cf. above, p. 180.
[4] Cf. above, p. 129. [5] Cf. above, p. 79.
[6] Moneypenny and Buckle, ii. 979 (16.xii.76) Disraeli to Lady Bradford: 'I found the Faery most indignant about the St. James's Hall 'Conference'. She thinks the Attorney-General ought to be set at these men; it can't be constitutional. . . .' Among 'these men' were Ruskin, Froude, Carlyle, Burne-Jones, the Duke of Argyll, and Canon Liddon (Guedalla, ii. 11).
[7] Cf. above, p. 34. [8] Strachey, 235.
[9] Bolitho's *The Widow and Her Son*, viii.

1862 'there was not one man in England whom the Queen both loved and respected'[1]. It was Granville's opinion that, so dominant had been the influence of the Prince Consort, that for twenty years the Queen had given up, 'every year more, the habit of ever deciding anything either great or small, on her own judgement . . .'[2]; and she herself admitted as much to Dean Stanley:

'Lord Melbourne was very useful to me, but I can never be sufficiently thankful that I passed safely through those two years to my marriage. Then I was in a safe haven, and there I remained for twenty years. Now that is over, and I am again at sea, always wishing to consult one who is not here, groping by myself, with a constant sense of desolation.'[3]

Yet even at the moment of greatest tragedy she positively refused, when there was a suggestion of it, as she had similarly refused at the beginning of her reign, to accept the help of her uncle:

'I am also anxious to repeat *one* thing, and *that one* is *my firm* resolve, my *irrevocable decision*, viz. that *his* wishes—*his* plans—about everything, *his* views about *every* thing are to be *my law*! And *no human power* will make me swerve from *what he* decided and wished—and I look to *you* to *support* and *help* me in this. I apply this particularly as regards our children—Bertie, etc.—for whose future he had traced everything *so* carefully. I am *also determined* that *no one* person, may *he* be ever so good, ever so devoted among my servants—is to lead or guide or dictate *to me*. . . . Though miserably weak and utterly shattered, my spirit rises when I think *any* wish or plan of his is to be touched or changed, or I am to be *made to do* anything. . . . What a Xmas! I won't think of it!'[4]

It is a strange commentary on this letter that the one

[1] Bolitho's *The Widow and Her Son*, 7. [2] Fitzmaurice, i. 404.

[3] *A Victorian Dean*, A Memoir of Arthur Stanley, edited by the Dean of Windsor and Hector Bolitho (Chatto & Windus, 1930), 219.

[4] *L.* iii. 476 (24.xii.61), Queen to King of the Belgians.

person among her servants who was in the end to lead and guide the Queen should have been Disraeli.

It has been said that queens are superior to kings, because when a woman is on the throne it is men who govern, whereas with a man, it is women.[1] Certainly while Queen Victoria was on the throne it was men who governed, not women. No one played in her reign the part of Sarah Jennings or Abigail Hill. But for the Queen's marriage, it is conceivable that Baroness Lehzen might have risen to that role. 'The influence of the Duchess of Atholl upon the Queen was unique. No one, perhaps, ever charmed her Royal Mistress so completely.'[2] But no jot or tittle of published material shows that the Duchess had any political influence over the Queen.

We must also keep constantly in mind, as another extenuating factor, a wise saying of Bagehot's: 'If we look at history, we shall find that it is only during the period of the present reign that in England the duties of a constitutional sovereign have ever been well performed.'[3] The Monarchy is as subject to the process of evolution as any other institution, and it is possible to argue that Victoria began, and Edward VII and George V have continued, to develop a new type of Monarchy. That is to say that Queen Victoria was carrying out an experiment in the art of government for which there was no precedent. Therefore, even when we are inclined to disagree with Bagehot in thinking that her duties as a constitutional Sovereign were well performed, we must remember that

[1] Cf. Maurois's *Edward VII*, 12.

[2] *Quarterly Review*, April, 1901. In this connexion a passage is worth recording from Lady Ponsonby's diary (*Mary Ponsonby*, 63; 8.ii.68): 'Had a long talk with the Duchess of Atholl; she understands everything, and nothing can be truer than all her views about things. The complete folly of opposition if started at once, without any care, and the ease with which advice may be given and well received, if you don't begin in antagonism.'

[3] Bagehot, 74.

they were, at any rate, far better performed than they had ever been performed in the past. In short, Queen Victoria may not have been a strictly constitutional ruler according to the notions of the constitutional theorists of her time or according to the standards of impartiality accepted today. But they, though important, are not the only standards; it is the duty of the historian also to appraise the period from 1861 to 1901 by the standards of 1861. People in the reign of George V, and the Victorians themselves, may have been mistaken in thinking of Victoria as a model constitutional monarch. But it must be remembered as a point in her favour that she was at any rate a great improvement on her predecessors. 'All trades must be learned, and nowadays the trade of a *constitutional Sovereign, to do it well, is a very difficult one.*'[1]

Sir William Harcourt once described a message from the Queen as 'most George-the-Thirdian'[2]. The remark is inaccurate. She cannot be compared with her grandfather. George III came to the Throne determined 'to be a King'. In this he was really defeated along with Cornwallis at Yorktown. The loss of the American War meant that the government of England was to be a constitutional Monarchy. But that this was the consequence of the English defeat was not immediately apparent: 'When in 1812 the Prince Regent was accused of bad faith in not dismissing his Tory ministers and bringing in his old allies the Whigs into office, it was not even suggested that he would have had any difficulty in securing for them a majority in the House of Commons.'[3] But by contrast when in November, 1830, 'Wellington resigned on being

[1] *L.* i. 105 (16.i.38), King of the Belgians to Queen.
[2] Gardiner, i. 353.
[3] Erskine May's *Constitutional History*, iii. 17.

defeated in the House of Commons, the King had no alternative but to appoint Grey as Prime Minister. On this historic occasion his freedom of choice was non-existent; and in this respect, as in others, it was evident that a new era had set in.'[1] The explanation of this new development was that '. . . the "group system", into which party government had degenerated in the early nineteenth century, afforded peculiar facilities for the retention of rights which were in fact obsolescent. If there had been two clearly divided parties under George IV, it is doubtful whether he would have been able to sustain his view of the prerogative.'[2]

But greatly as the two-party system would by itself have limited the power of the Crown, the final step in the process of limitation was taken when the two parties began to base themselves on a popular electorate. For that reason though 1830 may be a significant date, 1832 is the decisive date. On Queen Victoria's accession the old question of whether the power of the State was to be the possession of the Crown or of Parliament had been definitely and finally settled in favour of Parliament, because its power had by then become broad based on the will of the people, or, more accurately, of the upper middle classes. In other words the passage of the Reform Bill completed the work which had been begun by the loss of the American War. Lowes Dickinson indeed traced a direct connexion between these two events. For speaking of the motives of the Whigs in introducing the Reform Bill, he said:

'The evil as it was analysed by the Whig reformers centred about one point, the influence of the crown and the ministry. It was during the latter years of the American war that this abuse began to make itself felt. The war, in its later development, was

[1] C. S. Emden's *The People and the Constitution*, 146.
[2] Ibid. 143.

at once unpopular and calamitous; it was continued, against the clear sense of the nation, by the personal influence of the king, exercised through the minister and his bought majority; and it ended in the loss of the American colonies. These were the facts that gave rise to the reform agitation.'[1]

It was this new factor of a popular electorate which decided the question whether the Crown was to continue to retain political power.[2] 'How could the King hereafter change a Ministry? [asked Peel during a debate on the Reform Bill] How could he make a partial change in the administration, in times of public excitement, with any prospect that the Ministers of his choice, unpopular perhaps from the strict performance of necessary duties, would be returned to Parliament?'[3] Echo answers, how indeed? Similarly the Duke of Wellington grasped the historical significance of a fleeting moment, when he wrote that he did not believe the King of England 'had taken a step so fatal to his monarchy since the day that Charles I passed the Act to deprive himself of the powers of proroguing and dissolving Parliament, as King William IV did on the 22nd April last' [1831], when he dissolved Parliament.[4] Lord Brougham, since he is generally supposed to have been the Friend of the People, whose *Letter to the Queen on the State of the Monarchy* appeared in 1837, says in this connexion:[5]

'This great and bloodless change, the most important alteration by far that our form of government ever suffered, the largest indeed that any country ever underwent without violence, was effected while you, Madam, were yet in the nursery; and it was

[1] G. Lowes Dickinson's *The Development of Parliament during the Nineteenth Century* (Longmans, 1895), 17. This stimulating little book deserves to be more widely known. [2] Cf. above, pp. 122–5.

[3] 11 *Parl. Debs.*, 3rd series, 757 (quoted C. S. Emden, 147).

[4] Duke of Buckingham's *Court and Cabinets of William IV and Queen Victoria*, i. 296 (21.v.31), Duke of Wellington to Duke of Buckingham (quoted Farrer, 140). [5] p. 16.

the fashion of the courtiers at Kensington to congratulate your royal mother upon all the storm being well blown over, long before it became your lot to fill the throne; a feeling much more natural than sagacious. For, assuredly the most turbulent and difficult times through which your predecessors ever passed, while the ancient parliamentary constitution remained, were calm weather and smooth water compared with those that await your Majesty under the new dispensation.'

It was true that it was 1832 that posed the problems which were most pressing for the monarchy between 1837 and 1901. Uncle Leopold was wise after the event: 'When one looks to the changes, brought about in England in consequence of the [French] Revolution of July [1830], one is quite astounded.[1] Here [he was writing from France] they changed nothing but the dynasty, in England *the very* spirit of the old monarchy has been abolished . . . .'[2]

Stockmar too perceived, a little dimly perhaps, the significance of this great event. In 1845 he wrote to the Prince:

'Previous to the Reform Bill, the theory of this balance was perhaps much more defective than it has been since; but the system worked better in practice than it does now. . . . In reference to the Crown the secret is simply this. Since 1830 the executive power has been entirely in the hands of the Ministry, and these being more the servants of Parliament—particularly of the House of Commons—than of the Crown, it is practically in the hands of that House. This is a distortion of the fundamental idea of the English Constitution, which could not fail to grow by degrees out of the incapacity of her Sovereigns rightly to understand and to deal with their position, and out of the encroachments on their privileges by the House of Commons.

'This perversion of the fundamental idea of the English Constitution is fraught with this great mischief for the State, that the head of the Ministry for a time can only be the head of

[1] Cf. above, pp. 207–8 and 213.

[2] *L.* ii. 118 (15.i.47), King of the Belgians to Queen.

a party, and consequently must only too often succumb to the temptation of advancing the imagined interests of his party to the prejudice of the public weal. . . . Still, the right of the Crown to assert itself as permanent head of the Council over the temporary leader of the Ministry, and to act as such, is not likely to be gainsaid even by those who regard it through the spectacles of party.'[1]

It was mistaken, of course, to see a development as a distortion, and equally mistaken to explain as the result of personal incapacity what was due to the rise of democracy; it is as well always to be on guard against the vagueness of those two words 'deal with'. It was in vain to kick against the pricks of the party system. Certainly Queen Victoria could not with any good grace have claimed a position as 'permanent head of the Council over the temporary leader of the Ministry', on the ground that as between parties she was impartial.

But age did not weary nor the years condemn the peculiar constitutional opinions of the Baron. In 1854 he argued that 'Constitutional Monarchy has been constantly in danger of becoming a pure Ministerial Government', and that the definite interpretation of the law of the Royal prerogative is to be placed no higher '*than a right on the part of the King to be the permanent head of his Ministerial* Council', since the Prime Minister

'can be nothing else but the *Chief of the Party then in power*. . . . The Sovereign may even take a part in the initiation and the maturing of the Government measures; for it would be unreasonable to expect, that a King, himself as able, as accomplished, as patriotic as the best of his Ministers, should be prevented from making use of these qualities at the deliberations of his Council. . . . Thus, then, do I vindicate for the Sovereign the position of a permanent Premier, who takes rank above the temporary head of the Cabinet, and in matters of discipline

[1] Martin, i. 313–15.

exercises supreme authority . . . as matters now stand, the necessary equilibrium of the Constitution, can only be established and maintained by throwing a well-merited and deeply-seated popularity on the part of the Sovereign into the scale against the weight and pressure of that democratic element, which has become so powerful in the House of Commons.'[1]

It is difficult to see what precisely Stockmar had in mind when he speaks in this way of the Council. It is scarcely credible that he was asserting for the Sovereign the right, which not even George III had dared to revive, of actual attendance at meetings of the Cabinet, though the words 'making use of these qualities at the deliberations of his Council' can be made to bear that interpretation without undue strain. Stockmar accused those who differed from his view of seeing the Constitution 'through the spectacles of party'; the counter-accusation is that he saw the English Constitution of 1833 through the spectacles of 1831, and thereafter continued to judge constitutional questions in pre-Reform Bill terms.

One of the principal effects of that Bill and of the two-party system, taken together, was that Queen Victoria in appointing a Prime Minister could sometimes pick and choose between various leaders of the same party, but could not, like Queen Anne, appoint either a Whig or Tory ministry at her pleasure. Thus in 1859 Victoria had complete freedom of choice between Palmerston and Russell, and actually sent first for Granville; so in 1868 she could have sent for the Duke of Richmond or Lord Stanley in preference to Disraeli,[2] for Russell in preference to Gladstone;[3] in 1880 it was entirely her personal preference which led her at first to send for Hartington and not for Granville, though in the end she found herself unable to avoid taking Gladstone; in 1894 it was on her

[1] Martin, i. 545 (5.i.54), Stockmar to Prince.

[2] Cf. above, p. 36.

[3] Cf. Fitzmaurice, i. 536.

own initiative and without even asking for the advice of the retiring Prime Minister that she sent for Rosebery. Similarly, to take a final example, when Mr. Bonar Law resigned in 1923, George V had it in his power to choose between Lord Curzon and Mr. Baldwin. But this power to discriminate between politicians of the same party is very different from the power to remove a Ministry, when in possession of a majority in Parliament.

This was done in 1834, but only at the cost of proving that it could never be done again. It was for this reason that Queen Victoria, despite Gladstone's forebodings (for it was this incident surely that he had in mind), could not have turned out the Ministry of 1880 after the manner of her uncle in 1834. Melbourne was then by no means unready to be dismissed. Peel was ready to assume the responsibility for Melbourne's dismissal. William IV would have been right in thinking that according to the precedents his action in dismissing him was perfectly constitutional. Indeed his action was partly justified by the results of the general election which followed the Dissolution of December, 1834, when the 'Reform party' lost approximately a hundred seats. Partly, but not wholly, for the fact remained that it had been proved that the Crown could no longer rely on a parliamentary majority being returned in its favour. What had been constitutional in the past was proved to be impracticable for the future.

It has been said that Peel accepted responsibility for the dismissal of the Whig Ministry. In the House of Commons his words were:

'I have been asked whether I would impose on the King in his personal capacity the responsibility of the dismissal of that Government. In answer to this question I will at once declare that I claim all the responsibility which properly belongs to me as a public man; I am responsible for the assumption of the duty which I have undertaken, and, if you please, I am, by my acceptance of office, responsible for the removal of the late Government.'[1]

One wishes one could have the great advantage which through the medium of the gramophone record and the talking film will sometimes be open to the future historian of hearing the tone in which he pronounced these three words 'if you please'. Were they spoken merely as a polite formality, or was the emphasis on 'you' in order deliberately to imply that this acceptance of responsibility was subject to the right of the House to compel his own resignation by a hostile vote?

If the latter, that would have been in accordance with the doctrine laid down by Lord Grey in 1807. In that year George III dismissed the Ministry of all the Talents and replaced it by the Duke of Portland's Tory Ministry. Motion was made: 'That this House, considering a firm and efficient Ministry is indispensably necessary, in the present crisis of affairs, had seen with the deepest regret the late change of his Majesty's Councils.' In the debate: 'Lord Howick (afterwards Lord Grey) expressed the views of many who voted in favour of the motion when he said that, while the King's right by his prerogative was acknowledged, the House of Commons had the privilege of giving its opinion on the fitness of a newly appointed Ministry to fill the situation in which it was placed.'[2] In other words the King has a right of appointment, but the House of Commons has a right of veto. Thus we can see that the position which was finally confirmed in 1834, was in theory being anticipated in 1807.

It is now necessary to estimate the consequences of the Reform Bill in relation to a much broader context. Lytton Strachey failed to appreciate its effects when he

[1] Quoted, C. S. Emden, 149.

[2] C. S. Emden, 144.

wrote that Queen Victoria played a passive part in the developments which the Constitution underwent during her reign:

> 'From 1840 to 1861 the power of the Crown steadily increased in England; from 1861 to 1901 it steadily declined. The first process was due to the influence of the Prince Consort, the second to that of a series of great Ministers. During the first Victoria was in effect a mere accessory; during the second [also a mere accessory]. . . . Paradoxically enough, Victoria received the highest eulogiums for assenting to a political evolution which, had she completely realized its import, would have filled her with supreme displeasure.'[1]

Lytton Strachey sees an increase of power between 1840 and 1861, followed by a decrease of power between 1861 and 1901. The former he attributes to the influence of the Prince Consort, whose main constitutional work had been that of establishing his own position, and whose influence had consequently not really begun to be felt when he died prematurely in 1861. The latter he attributes to 'a series of great Ministers', presumably Gladstone, Rosebery, Beaconsfield, and Salisbury. Whether the implication that they were greater than Melbourne, Peel, Wellington, Palmerston, and Russell is justified, is an open question. But it is at any rate clear that the Queen had much less reason to be agreeable to the wishes of the statesmen of the second half of her reign than to those of the statesmen of the first half of her reign, and was in fact decreasingly malleable with the passage of the years.

Strachey was a first-class literary craftsman and writer of 'psychological' biography, but he was not a constitutional historian. The significance of the Reform Bill has escaped him. The power of the Crown did not decline between 1861 and 1901, nor indeed between 1837 and

[1] Strachey, 261.

1901, but between 1782, which is the year of the resignation of Lord North, and 1835, which is the year when the full effects of the Reform Bill were made apparent by the return of a Whig majority in direct opposition to the wishes of the King. At the end of the reign of Queen Victoria, says Strachey, 'the Crown was weaker than at any other time in English history'[1]. But why the end, and not the beginning? The truth is that the Crown was weaker than at any other time in English history, not at the death, but at the accession, of Queen Victoria.

This is the fact which invalidates Lytton Strachey's arguments. The question of the power of the Crown had been settled by 1837. The question which had not been settled was the question of its influence: 'The history of the monarchy since 1837 has been one of a constant growth in social prestige. What may be called the Hanoverian experiment has been abandoned, and the Crown has, little by little, exchanged power for influence.'[2] This is an echo of Gladstone speaking of a 'beneficial substitution of influence for power'.[3]

But this raises two further questions. First, did that influence increase or decrease between 1861 and 1901? Second, how great and how effective was it?

[1] Strachey, 261. Sir John Marriott (*Queen Victoria and Her Ministers*, 227) describes as 'shallow critics' those who say that at the end of Queen Victoria's reign 'the Crown was weaker than at any other time in English history'. The reference is no doubt to Strachey, but applies as well to Mona Wilson's *Queen Victoria*, 157: 'Between 1861 and 1901 the weight of the Crown in the constitutional balance declined almost to nothing. . . .'

[2] H. J. Laski's *Democracy in Crisis*, 112.

[3] Gladstone, *Gleanings*, i. 38. The distinction was also grasped by so acute an observer of our national life as Walter H. Page: 'Just how much power—perhaps "influence" is a better word—the King has, depends on his personality. The influence of the throne . . . is very great—greatest of all in keeping the vested interests of the aristocratic social structure secure.' Burton J. Hendrick's *Life and Letters of Walter H. Page*, Crown Library edition, ii. 237.

The first question can be quickly answered. According to the Queen's official biographer, her 'personal influence was far greater at the end of her life than at her accession'[1]. It was far greater also, it is claimed, at the end of her life than at her husband's death. Mr. Farrer, speaking of the whole period, from 1760 to 1901, covered by his book, says that 'the whole course of events, whilst reducing the appearance of monarchical power, has tended to its increase in reality. For, although the actual Veto has passed into disuse, the Veto precedent has become a more serious barrier against any legislation distasteful to the Crown.'[2] Thus, for example, when the Reform Bill was still only in draft, Grey cut out proposals for reducing the life of Parliaments to terms of five years in deference to the King's wishes, and also cut out a proposal for Vote by Ballot in advance of actually knowing, though in correct anticipation of, the King's wishes on that point.[3] It is an absurd exaggeration to say: 'It may, indeed, be doubted whether any of the nominal "autocrats" of Europe ever had as much personal effect upon national policy as, for instance, King Edward VII, strictly constitutional monarch though he was, had upon the policy of his country.'[4] None the less all the accumulated evidence goes to show that between 1861 and 1901 Queen Victoria ruled as well as reigned. That being so, it is worth looking ahead to Lord Esher's comparison of the authority of Edward VII with that of Victoria: 'If anything the King's is greater and more openly acknowledged.'[5]

But we must bear in mind the factor of prestige as well

[1] Sidney Lee's *Life of Queen Victoria*, 544.

[2] Farrer, 330. My claim, of course, is that 'its increase in reality' has been an increase of influence as opposed to power—but this is only another way of putting Mr. Farrer's point. His meaning is clear enough.

[3] Farrer, 137.

[4] R. H. Gretton's *The King's Majesty*, 18.

[5] Esher, ii. 107 (2.ix.05), Lord Esher to Lord Knollys.

as the factor of influence. We have already seen how enormously the prestige of the Crown increased between 1837 and 1901. It is, in fact, almost impossible to exaggerate this increase. We have drawn a distinction between the power and the influence of the Monarchy. A further distinction can be drawn between the influence and the importance of the Monarchy. The equation is that influence plus prestige equals importance. The influence of the Crown increased between 1861 and 1901. The prestige of the Crown increased between 1861 and 1901. There was therefore a great increase in its importance.

The second question as to the extent and actual effects of the royal influence is by far the most difficult to answer. Unfortunately it is not a question which can be answered with any precision. It has already been shown that Bagehot's view of the Queen as 'a retired widow' was false. He was less well informed than those courtiers, of whom he spoke, who were 'agreed as to the magnitude of the royal influence', and held, and rightly, the 'doctrine that the Crown does more than it seems'. Lord Esher, a courtier in excelsis, when engaged in the task of editing the Queen's correspondence, wrote: '. . . I have been finishing off the years 1853–1856 of the Queen's letters . . . Certainly her influence over events was most remarkable. *They* [the Queen and Prince Consort] were the real Ministers of the Crown, and even Palmerston, now and then, had to take a back seat.'[1] Neither was Queen Victoria from 1861 to 1901 a mere passive agent in the workings of the Constitution. Of that period it would be by no means true to say with H. G. Wells: 'A constitutional monarchy substitutes a figure-head for a head.'[2]

[1] Esher ii. 97 (9.viii.05), Lord Esher to M. V. B.

[2] *Experiment in Autobiography*, ii. 793.

In foreign affairs the Queen repeatedly laid it down that no step was to be taken without her previous sanction, and exercised a close control over the form of telegrams and dispatches. She took a special interest in the Foreign Office, and strove to secure that so far as possible questions of foreign policy should be settled by the Foreign Secretary and herself without being canvassed in the Cabinet.[1] On numerous occasions her knowledge of, and contacts with, foreign rulers proved to be of immense value, and she had a great influence in questions of diplomatic patronage. Her policy towards Schleswig-Holstein was in fact the policy which was carried out. On the other hand, her advocacy of a more positive British foreign policy between 1866 and 1870 did not prove acceptable to her Ministers, and the Eastern question was peacefully settled in 1879 without our having 'fought and beaten the Russians'.

To turn to domestic affairs. She obstructed the work of Army Reform. She carried out her duties as to ecclesiastical appointments with great conscientiousness. In two instances, those of the Public Worship Regulation Act and the Royal Titles Act, she in fact promoted legislation. She performed from time to time a most useful political function, involving work of great delicacy, in bridging the 'great gulf fixed' between Her Majesty's Government and Her Majesty's Opposition. She seemed to claim a right to select the Leader of a Party, in cases where it was not quite clear who the Leader was.[2] She claimed a right to know what were the individual opinions on questions of policy of Cabinet Ministers. She acted entirely on her own discretion in selecting her Prime Minister, in cases where no choice was so obvious as to be inevitable. On the other hand, due emphasis must be laid on the fact that in 1880

[1] Cf. above, p. 105.

[2] Cf. above, p. 69.

the Queen was forced against her will to choose Gladstone as her Prime Minister, because he was 'the chosen of the people'. But that is only another illustration of the process by which the power of the Crown had been gradually whittled away. Moreover it is clear that Lowell's view that the Queen exercised no influence over Cabinet appointments is without historical foundation. Melbourne himself had advised her that: 'Your Majesty will do well to be from the beginning very vigilant that all measures and all appointments are stated to your Majesty in the first instance. . . .'[1] It was advice which she never for a moment neglected; here her vigilance was perpetual.

In short, the three great rights of the Crown—to be consulted, to encourage, and to warn—were, between the death of the Prince Consort and the death of the Queen, being daily exercised. Clearly it would be immensely difficult to assign limits to the political influence permitted on those conditions to a monarch with the industry, experience, accuracy of memory, strength of mind and force of character of Queen Victoria. We have seen that she was directly responsible for troops being dispatched to Egypt,[2] and for the Fleet not being dispatched to the Baltic.[3] We have also seen why it is difficult to point to many other definite instances of her influence being directly responsible for decisions of the Cabinet.[4]

But the most striking fact which emerges from a review of the Queen's multifarious activities during the period under consideration is the extent of her hostility to Liberal

[1] *L.* i. 156 (7.v.39), Melbourne to Queen.
[2] Cf. above, p. 98.
[3] Cf. above, p. 149.
[4] Cf. above, p. 124.

Governments.[1] On two occasions, first, after the death of Gordon, and, second, as a consequence of Rosebery's proposals for the reform of the House of Lords, there are distinct suggestions of the likelihood of the resignation of Liberal Governments, because they lacked the confidence of the Crown.[2] Moreover, it was in her dealings with Liberal Governments that the Queen went furthest beyond the bounds of her constitutional duties. It would be hard to find any justification for the famous letters to Lady Wolseley,[3] to the Duchess of Roxburghe,[4] and to Lord Hartington.[4] In each case the Queen's object was to embarrass her own Ministers. Further, from the point of view of strict constitutional etiquette, there is something a little indecent in the Queen's letter to the Duke of Argyll pressing for the formation of a third party of 'Constitutionalists' under his leadership,[5] in her letters to Goschen and Forster pressing for the formation of what would, in fact, have been a Liberal-Unionist party,[6] and in her approaches to Salisbury,[7] making clear her anxiety that he should again become Prime Minister.

In short, Bagehot erred in asserting that the Crown was of no party, even though it was non-partisan in appearance, and Palmerston was the last statesman to dare to rebuke the Queen for partisanship.[8]

[1] The Queen's opposition to Liberal Governments during this period corresponds to the similar and simultaneous cyclical opposition of the House of Lords to Liberal Governments: cf. A. L. Rowse's *The Question of the House of Lords* (Hogarth Press, 1934), 17: '. . . from Gladstone's first government of 1868–74 there starts the regular rhythm of the Lords' activity in the modern period: a vigilant and destructive opposition to the programmes of all Liberal Governments, alternating with complete acquiescence and submission whenever the Conservative Party was in power.'

[2] Cf. above, p. 84 and p. 109; also p. 113.

[3] Cf. above, p. 85.

[4] Cf. above, p. 94.

[5] Cf. above, p. 91.

[6] Cf. above, pp. 92–4.

[7] Cf. above, p. 100 and p. 108.

[8] Cf. above, p. 151.

'The Queen does interfere constantly [wrote Dilke, with great perspicacity]; more, however, when Liberal Ministers are in power than when she has a Conservative Cabinet, because on the whole the Conservatives do what she likes, as she is a Conservative; whereas the Liberals are continually doing, and indeed exist for the purpose of doing, the things she does not like. But it is very doubtful how far her interference is unconstitutional, and it would be quite impossible to prove it, unless Mr. Gladstone, for example, were to publish her letters—a not very likely supposition. The Queen is a woman of great ability. . . . She writes to the Prime Minister about everything she does not like, which, when he is a Liberal, means almost everything that he says or does. She complains of his colleagues' speeches. She complains, with less violence, of his own. She protests against Bills. She insists that administrative acts should not be done without delay, for the purpose of consulting with regard to them persons whose opinions she knows will be unfavourable. . . .[1]

It is only fair, first, to complete the quotation:

'. . . her action, to my mind, is strictly speaking, constitutional . . . it would be difficult to maintain that with her immense experience the Queen is not justified in asking for time in order that men of distinction should be consulted upon various acts . . .';

and, second, at the same time to point out that Dilke wrote these words as early as 1879, that his 'not very likely supposition' of the publication of the correspondence between the Queen and Gladstone has now (at any rate for the bulk of it) become an accomplished fact, and has shown that in that year 'the worst was yet to come'.

There is still a widespread notion that the Sovereign is a mere mandarin figure compelled to nod or shake its head in assent or denial as his Ministers please. Shaw's *Apple Cart* ought by now to have disabused popular imagination of that fallacy. Few men placed in the position of

[1] Gwynn and Tuckwell, i. 286.

being king, even without Magnus' brains, would be content to allow themselves to be used as a mere rubber stamp, unless indeed for the purpose of signing Army Commissions.

When Charles I was confronted with the Nineteen Propositions he expressed his reluctance to become what was known in the language of that day as a Duke of Venice, or what we should now call a limited monarch, with the words:

> 'These being passed we may be waited on bare-headed, we may have our hands kissed, the style of Majesty continued to us, and the King's authority declared by both Houses of Parliament may still be the style of your commands; we may have swords and maces carried before us, and please ourselves with the sight of a crown and sceptre . . . but as to true and real power, we should remain but the outside, but the picture, but the sign of a King.'[1]

Neither was Victoria willing to be but the outside, but the picture, but the sign of a Queen. Unlike Lear she was desirous not only of 'the name and all the additions to a king', but also of 'the sway, revenue, execution of the rest'. For this we cannot blame her. It is asking far too much to have expected her to have been a complete figure-head. An impartial monarch would not only have to restrain the expression of any strong views in public, but also in private. Now to be absolutely impartial in that way would require either an exceptionally clever man, genuinely able to see that most questions are many-sided, or an exceptionally stupid man, a kind of magnified

[1] Quoted in J. R. Tanner's *English Constitutional Conflicts of the Seventeenth Century*, 117. Cf. also Charles II (Ibid., 233): 'he did not wish to be like a Grand Signior, with some mutes about him and bags of bowstrings to strangle men as he had a mind to it; but he did not think he was a king as long as a company of fellows were looking into all his actions, and examining his ministers as well as his accounts.'

William IV, naturally unable to acquire the least interest in public affairs. Any normal Sovereign is pretty well bound to succumb to the normal human failing of having opinions and expressing them. This point had been grasped by Disraeli:

'I know it will be said that, however beautiful the theory, the personal influence of the Sovereign is now merged in the responsibility of the minister. I think you will find there is a great fallacy in this view. The principles of the English Constitution do not contemplate the absence of personal influence on the part of the Sovereign; and if they did, the principles of human nature would prevent the fulfilment of such a theory.'[1]

Nevertheless it is worth while pointing out how very much less impartial in fact was Queen Victoria than her contemporaries thought. It is right, too, to emphasize to what depths of unconstitutionality she sank. Every allowance made, it may be difficult for a monarch to be completely impartial, but it would be easy for a monarch to be much less partisan than Victoria. The Speaker of the House of Commons is scarcely ever accused of partiality; Sir Henry Ponsonby won the praises of both Disraeli and Gladstone alike for his absolute fairness. But the Queen lamentably failed to achieve the same high standard of impartiality as her own private secretary.

'If . . . it is the duty of the English monarch to be passive and impartial, the Queen was the least constitutional of sovereigns. That she retained the reputation of a model monarch was due to the fact that, though she strained the constitution almost to breaking point, her prejudices and her convictions were so exactly those dominant in her age that she seemed to embody its very nature within herself. Her influence . . . was almost always in the direction which middle-class sentiment would have approved.'[2]

[1] *Selected Speeches of Lord Beaconsfield*, ii. 493 (3.iv.72).
[2] Kingsley Martin in the *Edinburgh Review*, April, 1926, 383.

This last point had been made, less consciously perhaps, by Lord Salisbury when he spoke of the Queen in the House of Lords just after her death:

'She had an extraordinary knowledge of what her people would think—extraordinary, because it could not come from any personal intercourse. I have said for years that I have always felt that when I knew what the Queen thought, I knew pretty certainly what view her subjects would take, and especially the middle class of her subjects.'[1]

In short, Queen Victoria, in a historical period marked by the rise and dominance of the middle classes, was the middle-class monarch *par excellence.*

One great, final question inevitably suggests itself. No doubt it was the influence of the Prince Consort which was responsible for the measure of impartiality shown by the Queen's remark that '. . . it would be very desirable that there should be a strong Conservative Party'[2]. That remark, then, may be made the text for putting this last question in this form. Was the Prince Consort, who really does appear to have been in party politics completely impartial, the ideal constitutional sovereign? Were the Queen's political shortcomings, therefore, purely the result of personal shortcomings? Or, alternatively, if he had lived as long as she, would he too have become as furiously partisan?

The question is whether these repeated clashes between the Crown and Liberal Governments from 1880 onwards were in reality nothing more than a clash between two personalities, Queen Victoria and Mr. Gladstone, or whether they were not the outcome of fundamental antagonisms between the Crown and 'progressive' forces. For it is possible to argue that between 1832 and 1867 there was no fundamental point of difference between Con-

[1] Cecil, iii. 186 (25.i.01).

[2] Cf. above, p. 115.

servatives and Liberals, except that at any given moment the one were in and the other out, and that therefore it was then perfectly easy for the Crown to be non-party. Those were the years of the quiet middle period of Victorian politics, which followed the settlement of the great question of Reform. But Russell was called 'Finality Jack' all in vain. In 1867 the question of further advances to democracy is reopened, the storm rises, issues become more real, feelings more bitter, there begins to be talk of a new social order, until, not to come too near the present day, we reach the state of acute political tension of the immediately pre-war years. Is it this which explains the alliance of the Crown with Conservatism, and its conflicts with Liberalism? If so, are such conflicts bound to arise in the future? Have they occurred in the recent past? For, if they have, the ordinary political student is bound to be as ignorant of the real facts as was the contemporary student between 1861 and 1901.

These are questions which we cannot hope to answer until we have the same knowledge of the inner history of the reigns of King Edward VII[1] and King George V as we now have of that of Queen Victoria. But they are inevitably raised by a consideration of her political influence in the second half of her reign.

[1] We have one most striking admission from Lord Esher, who wrote in 1910: 'About Feb. 10th the Prime Minister will be asking the King for a promise to create Peers. That is *certain*. If the King says yes, he mortally offends the whole Tory party to which he is naturally bound. If he says no, he lets loose all the Radical gutter press at his position as Sovereign and his person as a man. A charming dilemma, full of revolutionary possibilities.' Esher, ii. 433 (4.i.10), Lord Esher to M. V. B.

# APPENDIX

In the years between 1861 and 1901 the Queen's readiness to open Parliament in person was a kind of barometer of the state of her feelings towards the Ministry of the day. It is therefore worth noting that the following seven were the only occasions during the period when she did sufficiently favour her Ministry to perform this ceremony in person:

1. February 6th, 1866. (Russell.)
2. February 5th, 1867. (Derby.)
3. February 9th, 1871. (Gladstone.)
4. February 8th, 1876. (Disraeli.)
5. February 8th, 1877. (Disraeli.)
6. February 8th, 1880. (Disraeli.)
7. January 21st, 1886. (Salisbury.)

On none of these occasions did she read her own Speech. This was usually done by the Lord Chancellor.

# INDEX